Sometimes
Music is My Only Friend.

Harry Buckle.

Sometimes Music is My Only Friend. By Harry Buckle.
Published by --- MarosaJokato Media.
www.MarosaJokato.com
Email: MarosaJokatoMail@Yahoo.com
Paperback ISBN: 978-0-9935576-0-6
Kindle cbook ISBN: 978-0-9935576-1-3
©MarosaJokato.2016

Four lines of lyrics from 'It's Good News Week.' By K. King are reproduced with permission from JonJo Music ltd.
Parts of two lines of lyrics from 'Johnnie B Good 'by Chuck Berry are referred to in the description of music development and are quoted by permission of the publishers: Arc Music Inc.
Song and recording titles are reported on and referred extensively herein. Such titles, words and phrases being in the public domain. But readers should be aware that the actual songs and recordings are the copyright of various rights holders and any further or more extensive use of such songs or lyrics needs permission from the aforesaid rights owners in each case.
While every effort has been made to trace the owners of any other copyright material referred to herein, the publishers would like to apologise for any omissions and will be pleased to incorporate missing acknowledgements in any further editions of the book.
Whilst the events reported on in this book are described as they happened, inevitably I have recreated some of the detailed conversations from my notes made at the time, from articles and stories I wrote and / or published then or later, and from my memories of them. For instance some conversations may have taken place over a number of days or meetings, and in order to save space herein and keep some continuity in the reporting I have, with no attempt or intention of changing the emphasis or meanings of such conversations amalgamated some such conversations.
The cover illustration is by Bob Wagner. Wagner Design Unit.
The book cover design is by Sam Buckle of DesignAndFilmCornwall.co.uk.
Photographs of the author by B.Pern.
Edited by Wayne Deakin at Far East Editorial.
Wayne@FarEastEditorial.com

Call me old fashioned, but I'd prefer you pay for music you listen to. Radio costs just pennies a day or less, properly licensed downloads are usually competitively priced.

Pirating, copying, or just stealing with free downloads mainly hurts the writers, composers .. musicians...and...singers.
Most of us on the business side of things can turn our hand to many jobs—even writing books.
But someone with music in their hearts and minds, who has learned to master the many million combinations of musical notes and bring us melody and joy is probably doing what they do best.
So play fair --- and pay --- and give the new generation of musicians a chance.

At 70 years of age I have a T shirt- which says:
"I may be old but at least I heard the best bands."

We need to ensure there's a business structure that will enable the artistic freedom for your children and grandchildren to produce future generations of 'best bands'.

This book is dedicated to all the following;

My children; Sam, Joe, Katy and Tom Buckle.
So now you know a little more of what your Dad did.

My wives: Mandy, then Anne and now Mali.
Without their care, support and still on-going friendship over all the years none of this would have been possible.
****

Gordon Small and Allen McDougall of DC Thomson's
who in 1962 opened the door and
Leslie Paul, music publisher, who then in 1967 opened another door of opportunity for me.
****

Dag Haeggqvist of Sonet. Gazell. Stockholm Sweden.
Dag's quiet, modest creativity, taste, style and business integrity in the world of music and more, added a quality to the lives of several generations of Swedes and touched millions worldwide.
His vision and then forty years of total support with Gunnar Bergstrom and Sven Lindholm also enabled me to start our joint company in London.
They enabled Sonet to be the best and get the best from that.
****

The team at Sonet UK. Alan Whaley, Susie Todd and Diana Melbourne without whom ....
The full Sonet list follows on the next page.
****

Daniel Miller at Mute, and Seymour Stein of Sire
for their creative inspiration and trust.
Vince Clarke not only for his songs for Depeche Mode, Yazoo, Assembly, Erasure but for his quiet loyalty..
****

Joanna Sheen for inspiring a new start.
****

Much of the best of what we created came thanks to the skills of:
Recording Engineer / Producer Kenny Denton.
Graphic designer Bob Wagner and the talented, but undeservedly unrecognised songwriter Geoff Griffith.

Dedications continued.

'Sometimes Music is My Only Friend', is both a title and statement.

The great team at Sonet and Habana UK delivered many and varied styles of music and made many friends.
Our music made people smile, sometimes dance, sometimes think, even fall in love. Most of that music is still out there for all to hear, when you want-or sometimes-when you need it.

So thank you from me- and I am sure from the millions who enjoyed so much of what we all did...
Over the years the team included:
Alice Bryson, Barry Brown, Ben Matthews, Bob Cunningham, Brian Harris, Claire Faller, David Sandison, Dee Sparrow, Dhiran Bhat, Dominic Woosey, Emma Gordon, Heather Allen, Henrik Larsen, Jenny Bennett, Leon Samuels, Lisa Anderson, Mark Diamond, Mike Box, Mike Puplett, Mike Watts, Nicki Denaro, Philippa Feltham, Richard Wootton, Ronnie Remnant, Ruth Walters, Sandy Sneddon, Sonnie Rae, Sue Wiseman, Tony Rees, Tony Macintyre and Veronica Cross.

'All supported by' understates the vital roles of:
Andy Keeling, Caroline Slade, Carlos Jorge, Anna Kari Armandt, Douglas Callerstrand, Henry Denander, Jacques Attali, Bruno Rosignol, Helene Larson, Stefan Grahl, Jonas Holst, Sam Charters and John Coon.

Terry Connolly and David Reilly helped me weather some terrible storms. As did Alan Geller and Jenny Fairman.

It all began for Sonet UK in 1967 with a record from Ola Hakkanson's top Swedish band, Ola and the Janglers... and Nordic navigation lessons from Rune Ofwerman, Lars Olof Helen and Olle Nordstrom.

Dedications... in the world that is 2016.

With much respect to Nina Myskow and the many dedicated and talented journalists, illustrators, designers and editors who kept Jackie top of the pops all the way through to 1993... Jackie was always your friend when you needed a friend like Jackie.

Wayne Deakin of Far East Editorial made sense of and then edited my jumbly input.
Of course any and all remaining errors are my responsibility, as with any new typo's that have snuck in after Wayne's work as I fidgeted with the manuscript on its way to the printers.

I fear, despite that extensive list, that over the forty or so years I may have forgotten a name or two. Age does that to you! If so then apologies of course and let me know.

Harry Rodney Buckle. Cornwall and the Spicelands. May 1st 2016.

Contents

Welcome.

Welcome all. You will, I hope, enjoy this book, particularly if you, your mum or even your gran read any or all of the following at any time from the 1960's on: Jackie, (of course), Valentine, Roxy, Rave, Romeo, Boyfriend, Mirabelle, Cherie, Fabulous, or Fab 208, Marilyn, Honey, Patches, Oh Boy, My Guy, Blue Jeans, Petticoat, and others I have surely forgotten. Around 85% of all UK teenage girls read one or more of those magazines- with Jackie being by far the most successful and widely read.

So welcome all. Also welcome to your brothers and dads. There's stuff in here for all . Welcome now also to your children, and, dare I say it grand children.

It seems they all want to know a little more about how on earth you survived in the primitive world, that in the sixties at least, had no music radio, no colour TV, very few phones- certainly no mobiles- or online social networks.

Never fear, this is no stuffy history book, or deep social study of the powerful importance and influences of Jackie in particular, on several generations of teenagers.

True and as important as that influence and effect was.

This is, as it says on the cover: A fascinating look behind the scenes, the shows, the music, the business and the stars, bringing you...All the Hits and More... An easy reading, but factual , roller coaster ride through a world of Pop and a Passion for music.

When I joined Jackie as a journalist, writing and being featured complete with weekly photo's of yours truly, as Pete Lennon, just a few weeks after the launch in January 1964- the main attraction for our readers was the music and the pop stars. Bringing them the best of that was an adventure in it's self.

Then, from the early seventies, with more pop radio across the UK , more music on TV (in colour) and more pop and gossip in the national press , *fashion* indeed became one of the main likes for our readers. From day one, Jackie's advice columns were a vital read for all.

9

Over time, new and talented generations of caring journalists, artists, and other creative folk, updated and nursed our, by now well established, national treasure into a bright and ongoing future. Jackie girls remained in good hands.

But, who'd have thought, almost fifty years on, following the flag flown by the excellent Nina Myskow, that our loyal fan base would have hatched a series of big selling cd releases. Acres of ongoing press coverage. A fashion collection. Many learned, and some fun books, and now the ultimate in party party party, but still meaningful musicals.

I hear that the fans are already eagerly wanting a follow up to the current hit show. Jackie the Musical, Part Two, sounds good to me.

I suggest a prequel, as is so fashionable in the movie business.
I think that blokey from One Direction can play Pete Lennon as the young (true) and hip (surprisingly also true) chap that he was, and maybe George Clooney as the older version. Not!!!

For me, after all the years, abandoning my assigned Pete Lennon pen name, and under the name my mates and my mum called me, Rod Buckle, or as it says on my passport, Harry Rodney Buckle, I moved on from apparently being the 1960's most read pop man, to a series of adventures and some surprising successes with my own music companies.

The story of those years is presented here.

As both John Peel and Terry Wogan said to me at a charity fundraising lunch in 1990: "It's all a bit worrying that you're still bringing us some of the soundtrack to our lives."

Having spent much of the sixties attending Top of the Pops as a journalist and then through the next thirty years I was also there almost monthly, then as a music company owner, publisher or manager, I suspect I am more qualified than many to comment on recent reports that have dominated the media.

But detailed reporting on them is more suited to newspapers, than a book, so this is NOT about those events. You will find the focus in here is more on recalling the overall scene and style of those various decades.

I was indeed, 'Happy indeed to be part of the industry of human happiness'.

It's a collection of memories, some from notes made at the time, others more recent. Here and there there's a little repetition, as I decided to leave certain explanations in place as it makes-dipping in and dipping out of the various sections somewhat easier.

In this collection of memories, in the best traditions of all those pop magazines of the era: We Focus on the Facts...and the Fun.

Mind you having said that, when I signed up to work in this world of music, I didn't expect the Americans to drop an H bomb on my head...

Read on.

Harry Buckle . Cornwall and the Spicelands. March 2016.

Contact: MarosaJokatoMail@Yahoo.com

2. How, for me, it all began. May 1962.
(Pop Music will resume shortly.)

Opener : Ian Fleming is looking a bit p***ed off. Author and creator of James Bond, he was by then by far the biggest selling popular author in the western world. Many millions of books sold, the first Bond film 'Dr. No, 'with Sean Connery as Bond, just about to be premiered. Even soon to be assassinated, US President, JFK was an 007 fan.

I am sitting, nervously, opposite Fleming at the lunch table , it is apparent that I'm the only one of the people there who had read the books, presumably excepting Fleming of course.

Fleming was having his portrait painted just a few doors away from my aunts home. She, who had set up the lunch, had been an SOE (Secret Operations Executive) operative, had known Fleming, also in the secret service, during the war, and she could see that he was somewhat irked by this lack of literary appreciation. For that brief moment I think OOP's joined joined JFK, SOE and 007 in the abbreviation business.

It's May '62. I have recently left school in Devon. I was able to leave early that last term to start my summers' employment as I had completed my O' level exams, (retakes) the previous term. The need for retakes created by my achieving terrible results first time around the year before. University did not beckon.

The original terrible results, were mainly due to me having discovered girls, or more accurately, a local girl, named Patricia, in that hot summer of 1961. That discovery, by the way, no mean feat in a boys only boarding school. But sneaking out at night, during evening study periods and supposed afternoon 'Cricket Nets or Athletics Practice', thanks to my trusty bike and a girl who seemed as keen on nervous exploration and certain (very limited) discovery up by the Tiverton Canal as I was. Played havoc with my Hay Fever though.

My summer job, for the third season with the same company, really was one of the best. Working on the Salters River Steamers that, filled with day trippers and tourists, twice daily plied the River

Thames between Kingston, Surrey up to Royal Windsor, or from Marlow, Bucks, down to Her Maj's. Windsor Castle. And then back in the afternoon.

"Please leave the boat here to visit the Castle and the town. Please take all your belongings. Please note the boat will depart for the return trip (upstream to Marlow, or downstream to Kingston) on time at 2.30."

The fact that the four crew, having scoffed their free lunch on board, given the boat a quick sweep, had then retired to the Donkey House pub , just steps away from the boat mooring, for a few pints, on occasions meant that a downstream boat would depart in the wrong direction.

Fortunately we had a well rehearsed response to panicked passengers who were invariably (and luckily for us) quick to notice. Quick as a flash, Billy Macready the Captain, or I would say, "Indeed we know, we just want to be sure that all passengers on both sides of the boat get equal chances to get some good photo's of the Castle from the river."

The fact that, as we passed the Salter's offices for the second time, this time in the correct downstream direction, the area manager, a Mr. Simms (who had once reached down from the boat and saved my life when I fell in between the heavy, still moving ship and the high concrete sides of Penton Hook lock) could be seen shaking his fists and mouthing: "Macready, Buckle it's the last time you do that." At least I think that's what he was saying, ' Buckle', could have been worse.

My Aunt, told me when she asked me to come along, "Ian's terribly busy, but he always was, so it's just a quick bite." She had always taken me to lunch around my May birthday, but I was just amazed at the James Bond connection.

On the day, it turned out that she had a plan to ask for some timely and sensible career advice for me, from her old wartime acquaintance. I don't think that, Aunty, realised quite how busy Mr. Fleming was.

As I have already referred to, he is somewhat exasperated as no one else except me has read his books. Also my Aunt is expecting him to order me, 'Get a proper job, lad.' But no, he is very keen to discuss the joys of River Steamers...Result. A very exasperated Aunty.

Of course Eton College grounds run down to the River on the other bank of the Thames from Windsor, and Fleming as an old Etonian knew the attractions of the river well. Not to mention, as a student, him having had a few clandestine drinks in the Donkey House Pub. Not only that, but quite a few of the boats were still steam powered, as he had seen regularly in his pre war school days.

Salters Steamers of Folly Bridge Oxford, founded in 1858, and still operating today, were even then a venerable company. So some detailed discussions about *Steam* and *Diesel* were underway, seemingly of great interest to the three men and one boy around the table.

Looking back, at Bonds fascination with gadgets and cars, 'Thank you Q,' and later understanding that Fleming also went on to write Chitty Chitty Bang Bang, his apparent interest in my very tentative, nervous engineering input was flattering.

Also looking back, I am wondering now about the exasperation factor of the others at the table. They were, my Uncle Sir Duncan Anderson, then a Director of various companies including BOAC (now British Airways). He was a civil engineer from Aberdeen, but had worked his way through University checking steam train safety at night.

The others were, Sir Edward Lewis and his wife Masie. He was the owner of Decca, originally an electronics company, and even then one of the worlds largest record companies. Decca was home, from January 1963, to the Rolling Stones amongst many others.(Oh that I had known that would happen)

Decca's other key business was with their Decca Navigator equipment for ships. This, was an early form of 'radar or GPS' that enabled ships to safely make their way into and out of difficult harbours. Ian Fleming was instantly very keen to discuss Decca Radar. Obviously such secret navigation systems could have James Bond like implications.

I was all ears to learn about that.

But no. Exasperating Aunty, very sweet but remarkably single mindedly brings back the conversation to yours truly, and the need for practical careers advice. Sir Edward mutters about, 'Electrical apprenticeships and junior sales training positions.' At the end of the meal he gives me a business card and says, "Call his secretary and she'll arrange an interview", with someone, "who deals with those matters."

Aunty beams, and with a smile re- commences her interrogation of Fleming. After his wartime Secret Service activities, he had eventually become a renowned journalist, working mainly on the Sunday Times , before embarking on his career as a novelist.

In fact the Sunday Times had, just a few months before in Feb. '62 become the first British newspaper to launch a Colour Supplement, and I can remember Fleming questioning all of us about our views on it.

Talking, 'over my head', both literally and figuratively, Aunty pressures him on, 'possible careers with 'The Service.'

That perks me up a bit.

But they decide instantly that, with my abysmal showing at all types of languages that I won't even get to be interviewed. (Huh, little did they know, had they known then, what I found out later...)

Given that my only skill seemed to be some degree of excellence at English, both Language and Literature they decide quickly that indeed writing and journalism was the way forward.

Quite understandably, no business cards or introductory suggestions were forthcoming from Fleming, but I was, despite my love of the river boat life (in summer) ,rather taken with the idea of becoming a news hound.

Fleming, as had we all, enjoyed a little red wine, with his Sausage Stroganoff and after, with some figs (a first for me) and cheese. The Stroganoff, in this case with a mix of German and English sausages, and of course originally a Russian recipe, caused much joking between the adults.

That joking I only fully appreciate now, with my aunt referring to it as, her, 'Berlin Special'. After the Germans had lost the war, there had been a race to control their city of Berlin. It had ended up a divided city run by the English, Americans and the Russians. In 1962, with parts of London still showing signs of German bombs dropped during the blitz, wartime memories were still very fresh.

Apparently my Aunt and Fleming, and indeed my Uncle had some associations with the 'Control Commission' which was set up to liaise between the various occupying parties wishing to get Berlin back on it's feet.

The familiarity of all those around the table, except of course for me, with Berlin, also lead to a conversation about the recent, February that year, release in Berlin by the Soviets, of Francis Gary Powers the American U2 spy plane pilot who had been shot down over Russia some time before. Powers was swapped, for a Rudolf Abel, a Soviet spy held by the US.

The swap, made in an exchange over the Glinecke Bridge, linking the Russian sector with the American sector of that city. Now of course the story of a Tom Hanks movie: Bridge of Spies. But then very much a reality. Particularly to ex Secret Service operatives such as Fleming and my Aunt.

Little did I know then, as I listened completely amazed to those who had been involved, in more ways than one, in the real James Bond world, that in slightly less than two years, in April '64 that bridge would again be headline news.

This time it was British spy. Greville Wynne, sentenced to 10 or more years by a court in Moscow for his work in collecting secrets from a Russian, Oleg Penkovsky. Wynne was exchanged for a Gordon Lonsdale, (real name Konon Melody) who had been caught spying for the Russians in the UK.

Greville Wynne arrived back 22 April. 1964. "Looking forward," he said, "To an English breakfast."

Across the nation, over their breakfasts that very day in '64, a million or so school girls and older readers were studying the question of Mini Skirts: Very well documented in that weeks Jackie Magazine issue. No 16 with a two page, ' Jackie Fashion spread: Make the Scene with Mary Quant'.

As Fleming stood to leave he invited us to walk around to nearby Holland Street and see the part completed portrait. Aunty regretfully declined. "I'm sure the artist would prefer we wait until it's finished and anyway Duncan has a meeting, and Rodney has a train to catch back to those blessed boats."

True at the time. But I learned, just some weeks later, what a lost and very unique opportunity that was. What I hadn't appreciated at the lunch was that Fleming's portrait was being painted by Charles Amherst Villiers. A legend to schoolboys even then.

Before the war he had been the inventor of various turbo charging systems that turned already awesome Bentley cars into extra powerful and fearsome machines. (They were described in some detail on some early Bond books.)

Villiers, had also designed Malcom Campbell's land speed record car. Bluebird. (Land speed record 1927 was 174 mph.) Not only that, but he, Villiers, had then spent 20 years or so in America, on engineering for the space rockets that would soon (in 1969) take men to the moon.

As if that wasn't enough, Flemings friend Graham Hill, Grand Prix Motor Racing Champion, and father of F1 Champion Damon, was also having his portrait worked on at the same time.

Of course as we departed from the lunch, none of that was known to me.

Some I have learned whilst writing this book. But a few weeks after our lunch, walking along Kensington Church Street with my aunt, she introduced me to the portraitist, Charles Amherst Villiers.

What I did learn then, was a bit of a shock to my system, so much so that I remember it very well, as it was my first understanding of my Aunt's SOE work, about which then we knew very little.

Villiers said to me , "Of course, without Sally's war time smuggling work with the team in Scandinavia, we wouldn't have had any engines to drive our ships and tanks or fly our planes. Let alone for me to tinker with."

In a nutshell, Sweden had remained neutral and un-invaded whilst the German enemy had invaded the countries all around. The Swedish SKF company were just about the only remaining (unbombed) producers of ball bearings.

Without ball bearings, no engine of any kind can run.

Lets repeat that, without ball bearings no engine of any kind can run, and England's main ball bearing factories had been bombed into the ground.

My mothers sister, christened Alcyone, but always called Sally, sweet innocent seeming, but obviously with a steely side was a key member of the SOE team that obtained those vital parts from the (sometimes unwilling) Swedes.

As their neutral status required, they were also supplying the Germans with ball bearings.

So obtaining the actual supplies against the German competition in Sweden was difficult enough, but then those many tons of steel parts had to be smuggled past the enemy ships, submarines, sentries, stuka's and other aircraft across to an England, so desperately in need of them.

At first SOE tried with flotillas of big ships, sadly the losses were horrendous. Only two from ten got through. They tried with small planes but they could only carry a few kilo's each ,not the tons needed.

In the end, with smallish, fast motor gun boats they succeeded.

As I write this in 2016 , in my home office, on my wall, I have a painting, sketched out on old packing paper, done at the time, on the harbour side, of the last two boats, loaded with those vital engine parts, leaving Lysekil on the West coast of Sweden.

Their departure, as shown in the painting, was in the darkening of an evening snow storm. Such stormy conditions all the better to hide them from the enemy. On the back , the artist, the Press attaché at the British Legation In Stockholm, Peter, later, Sir Peter, Tennant has written: *To Sally. 1/4/1944.*

Amazing. She always remained modest and never revealed much about those days. "Oh, but I was only part of team." It is only now with the recent opening of secret files from the period, and the publishing of several books that I learn more. Sir Peter refers to himself doing that very painting in his autobiography.

She was a fun Aunt as well, and eventually as my music companies started to have some success, she was very supportive of me having a go at building a company in a new and growing industry. My lucky choice of Swedish partners was a bonus. She liked Swedes and Sweden.

But back again then to May '62.

After what I now realise was a very privileged lunch I returned, indeed by train, back to my job on the River Steamers. Majestically the largest boats on the Upper Thames. Definitely not fast, and also very definitely, no guns.

 But what a great summer. For me, not much live music but a journey of discovery on some well programmed jukeboxes, in riverside pubs and coffee bars along the whole length of the River Thames.

After a fun and almost endless summer, the cold mists of Autumn crept across the river most mornings, as we waited , huddled in our ex army coats (There was a Millets, ex forces clothing store in every town) for our passengers. But daily, there were fewer and fewer of them to enjoy the likelihood of freezing on our four hour trips to Windsor and then back again.

So, by early September I was a landlubber again. Somewhat over ambitiously I set off on my trusty Vespa Scooter for the most outrageous adventure yet. 1000 miles or more right across France, over the Pyrenees near Perpignan riding an increasingly wheezy scooter, up, along, with the smokiest trucks in the world , to the border and then the frontier customs at La Jonquièra.

The old twisty road was frightening enough on the way up. Going down was worse.

But when we got down to the Mediterranean, the first Costa's that we found were indeed fun and definitely still sunny. This being in the first real decade of British package holiday travel, £29.00 all inclusive of flights, hotel and all meals for two weeks in the sun, might have been a better option than adventures by Vespa.

The Sangria, before we learned, made us very drunk and prone to more ingesting more Sangria or worse, expelling same.

Of course, the Senorita's totally ignored us. "No speak Inglish."

In reality, and very sensibly, they " No wanted to speak English, with a bunch of scruffy looking long hairs, who seemed to sleep on the beach, who apparently didn't wash, except in the sea..." We did, we didn't and we did. (Beach Sleep, Wash, Sea.)

Remembering this was all before mobile phones, credit cards and in our case, common sense.

The money, we were allowed to take abroad, and in fact all we had, soon ran out, and having totally failed in our ambition to get jobs there. Guess what? Their, 'No tourists winter season,' was upon them also, and so we aimed back to England.

The journey was horrendous,. As the cash got less and less, the need to sleep in bus shelters, barns (why did I always get the cowsh*t bit) became colder and wetter and more and more miserable.

Of course the ferry rockin' and rollin' on the grey greasy looking English Channel made us ill. So much so that it was 24 hours before I could make it back to my village near Staines just outside London. Staines of course later immortalised by Ali G.

Never had my mother's cooking been so welcome.

Even my Sister's, 'I see you still haven't learned to clean the bath properly after you've used it,' seemed music to my ears.

My benign, also a school teacher, like my Mother, Dad waited until the Monday evening after my return to toss me the London Evening News. The paper open at the 'jobs vacant,' pages. "Good idea to look through that son. Winters coming."

I don't think he meant for me to think I'd be sleeping on the snowy streets if I didn't have a job, but I read the paper anyway.

Tuesday Morning.

Gingerly using the phone, with which I was not too familiar I dialed, (rotating circular dial-- tic tuk tik tik - ring.) The London number, FLEet Street xxxx was in response to an advert for: "Editorial Junior Wanted."

Wednesday morning.

I caught the 218 Bus to Staines station. Note it was not then , Staines on Thames, and no 'Staines Posse' seemed to exist. In fact Ali G, or Sacha Baron Cohen wasn't even born till 1971. Train from Staines to Waterloo. 4a Bus to Fleet St.

I hour interview at 11. 00 o'clock. "Can you come back at 2.30 today and we'll let you know."

Home again, on the bus, train, bus and long walk . That evening, as they returned from work, casually reporting to my mother and father, "I start in Fleet Street next Monday. Company called Thomson's. 6 pounds and five shillings a week."

And a bit later in the evening, to my sisters delight," I've got to go to night school and learn Pitman's shorthand."

Pre portable tape recorders, Pitman's shorthand was a speedwriting system needed by all real journalists and secretaries to keep up accurately to talking speed when writing down letters, quotes and happenings.

My wonderful, always kind and very clever sister had already very successfully done the Pitman's Shorthand course and knew full well what it entailed.

Fortunately for me ,Rock-'n'- Roll intervened before I lost the battle with shorthand. But then again, as Ian Fleming and Aunt Sally had deduced, I was hopeless at new languages.

I managed to keep it a secret from my Mum and Dad for about a month that Thomson's published the Beano and the Dandy. My mother said, "Well, I really don't really think that's quite what your Aunt was thinking of when she said, 'Journalism'"

My Dad, just smiled and said. "Do your best, and don't be late with what you do."

Turned out in the end ,that my Aunt was completely out voted, as her husband, originating from Aberdeen, had been raised on a diet of excellent Scots newspapers all from DC Thomson.

I can't imagine he read the Beano though.

3. Whatever Happened to Jackie Magazine's Pop Man Pete Lennon?

Opener: Draft 1. It's a drizzly 1964 evening in Manchester, and just outside the BBC's Top of the Pops studios I am removing teenage girl's underwear.

Well actually, before yet another Police enquiry starts, I am removing underwear that has been tucked under the windscreen wipers of my car and using them to attempt to clean away hearts, kisses, 'I love Pete', 'We love Jackie,' and much worse; scrawled by Jackie and Pete fans over the car and the windows in bright-coloured lipstick...

Opener: Draft 2. The very blonde and obviously KGB lady, (that's blonde except for black smudgy eyelashes), leaned over in the candle lit bar and started to nuzzle my left ear.

Now the beer had been strong, and it suddenly seemed remarkably hot for a Moscow winter's evening. Bars in exotic locations—I was used to. With British pop exploding in popularity globally, I had been travelling widely for some years in the very business of Pop Music...

Fleet Street London. December 1962.

I am a 17 years old trainee journalist, or 'Editorial Junior', as the job was advertised. My first editor, a Mr. Sears, was slightly gruff but kindly, and very busy. After a month or so of me delivering his sandwiches daily, he noticed my existence.

Leaning back in his chair he said: "There's three rules to reporting and writing in this business, lad."

"One. Get 'em in the first few lines or they turn the page or buy another paper."

"Two. Tell the truth and get it right-especially the names and dates."

"Three. Get it in on time, and first if you can."

As I thanked him, in a slightly strangled, nervous voice, and backed out of the room, he glanced up and added. "Oh yes, Journalists write. Sub editors and printers spell."

Given that journalistic 'writing' for me involved three fingered typing, and this was all occurring during the carbon age, (that's the typewriter and carbon paper age), before correctable computer's, let alone spell check, this was welcome news to say the least.

As I type this in January 2016, I use digits and digital help. That's as in, still the same three digits on each hand bashing the keyboard, but thanks to a certain Mr. Gates, my words are now digitally corrected, enhanced and remembered.

Somewhat surprisingly, given it's had fifty years in my memory store, even without the microsoftian help of the aforementioned Mr. Gates, I have remembered Mr. Sears' advice and have just given you a choice of 'Get 'em in the first few lines' opening paragraphs.

This is also surprising, as in the end I spent but a few years in the world of inky paper and thundering printing machines and moved on to an even noisier world: that of the music business...

or as the newspaper headline writers will always say : The world of Sex, Drugs and Rock n' Roll.

Even more surprising, because, as is / was / and always will be, set out by all those very headline writers again: "If you, really lived through the sixties, you are not supposed to remember it at all."

By some mysterious quirk of life, maybe it's in my ~~jeans~~ genes, I do remember it very well....well, most of it.

So if you are of a certain age, and would like a reminder, or if you want to know some of how your Dad, Mum or Grandma really 'lived it up'.... or at least dreamed of 'living it up' back then....read on...

The Soundtrack to some lives.

Now, these days, the veracity of the inky press is often somewhat open to doubt.

But remembering Mr. Sears' advice, 'Get it Right' and with the benefit of my notes from the time, together with some of those anatomical memory circuits—note anatomical, in my head, not even analogue, let alone digital—I can report more fact and detail.

More about those lipstick-wielding and predatorily nubile pop fans, facts about that KGB lady, about her equivalent at MI6—and revered memories about that lunch with Ian Fleming and *Me*.

A lot more interesting than *Me,* obviously, are the pop stars, the hits-the misses, the gossip, the facts, the fans and the frankly bizarre collection of people I encountered as my life progressed after journalism, whilst owning a music company.

I guess this is partly about 'my small part', or was that a quote from the KGB lady, in creating part of the soundtrack to your life. Strictly speaking, that life soundtrack was mostly created for your Mum or Grandma or indeed your Dad.

Many of the musicians and singers of that era may now sadly be gone or have become 'be-zimmered.'

Their music though, with the biggest hits at least, can be heard regularly on most popular radio stations and mostly remains as fresh as the day that it was made.

The hits: Many of them as fresh? Yes.

The Hits: Memorable? Yes.

Catchy and hummable? Oh yes. Or in some cases as bloody annoying as ever they were. Oh dear...

As all too often heard by me, "I hated that song then, and now I can't get it out of my head; again."

Oh, the shame, for someone having the responsibility for so much, 'dad dancing. 'I wonder who was that 'someone' ?

Moi? Surely not.

Never forget though, many of today's 'golden oldies' were once Jackie, Valentine, Boyfriend, Fab 208, Romeo, Rave or Roxy heart throbs , whose posters adorned a million bedroom walls.

Who brought you those posters and pin-up pictures?

Me again! Well, the Jackie Magazine ones at least, but obviously as just one of a team of people way more smart than I.

So never fear. I'm just the link, the messenger, the reporter...

Me? Oh yes. I was 'Pete Lennon' in Jackie from the heady days of 1964.

'Here's all the pop gossip and latest news ' about your heart throbs and teen dreams from Top of the Pops, Ready Steady Go, and much, much more. Enjoy Pete's Pop Gossip, Pete's Pop Picks, and (you can truly blame the editor for this one) Pete's Shorts.

Rather to my surprise, more than 25 years later, I was still often to be found regularly standing at the side of the Top of the Pops studios, as I supplied them with yet another band of musicians or a singer.

With more than 100 Top Twenty hits, owned, produced or published by my own music company, I spent a lot of my life waiting around at Top of the Pops. If it all sounds unlikely to you, to me it's staggering and still surprising—and 'I'm the blokey wot dun it!'
What do you think this is ? The Beano ?
So as Mr. Sears said, "**Get writing, Get the story in.**"
Someone else can sort the ~~spellnig~~ spelling....and I promise not to use that old typo error correction joke again.
London's Fleet Street, famous the world over as being home to some of the biggest selling, most widely read, and most respected newspapers on the planet, was an exciting and heady place to work. I was going to be a real journalist and bring news, scoops and 'All the News that's fit to Print' to the world.

I had been engaged in November 1962 by DC Thomson's to work in their Fleet Street, London offices. D C Thomson's were, (and still are) a much respected and long established Scots newspaper publishers, behind a variety of titles.
Given that my 'trainee' journalism so far had me in a minor role assisting in the London Office of The Dundee Telegraph, The Courier and The Sunday Post, The Weekly News and suchlike, notwithstanding their excellence, obviously I had more than a few steps to take before graduating to delivering 'hot news' to a real national newspaper. Nationals: whose many offices dominated not only Fleet Street ,but also the surrounding streets, alleyways and courtyards.

But I had the ambition. I was even going to night school learning short-hand; Pitman's no less. These days, thanks to Messrs. Gates, Wozniac, Jobs, Brin and a few others, you can look Pitman's short-hand up on your phone.

It's a lot of squiggles—it was then and still is now.
I assumed then, that my key to a sensible future career would be as set out by that first boss, the already referred to, Mr. Sears.

He, who was usually (as I delivered the sandwiches and the horse racing first edition of the evening paper) complete, I kid you not, with green eyeshade, gold expando armbands that held his shirt sleeves away from inky paper, and a very full ashtray.

Today, any movie or TV producer would reject that image as being predictable and clichéd.

Clichéd? I was only almost 18 and we were only just learning what a quiche was—let alone a cliché. This was the 60's don't forget.

"Trainee Journalist," pause for effect, "Editorial Junior actually." I would tell my chums in the pub in the Surrey village where I lived. When I mentioned to them those eminent and 'important in Scotland,' newspaper names referred to above, despite them being (still) displayed in tiles on the side of the building at 185 Fleet Street, it did not impress my chums, or the girls in the pub.

But when I showed them my sample copies of just some of the host of magazines and comics printed on those same newspaper presses, when they weren't busy with the news, impressed was not the word. They were in awe...*Dandy, Topper, Beano, Wizard,* had the boys drooling into their Watneys Red Barrel beers...and they were soon buried in the latest exploits of Dennis the Menace, Beryl the Peril, Desperate Dan, and a variety of football heroes.

When, from my James Bond style briefcase I then produced copies of *Bunty, Cherie, Romeo* and some others, the girls forgot guarding their cherries and their Babychams, and were lost in memories, romantic dreams and fan and fashion fantasy. I was very popular— in the pub at least.

Reference the 'James Bond style' briefcase, should you decide to read on, you might well assume I had ideas above my Editorial Junior status. Err no! Everybody had one, bought cheap in the market!

After a good few months of training, and sandwich delivering, I had started to contribute badly typed pieces about the London pop music scene to the company's Cherie and Romeo comics, which along with most of Thomson's output, was assembled and produced in Scotland.

'The London Pop scene?' Despite an increasing number of honourable and talented exceptions, someplace called Liverpool comes to mind, pop music tended then to originate more in London than the regions, or even Scotland; well, the record companies at least were in London.

Scotland's time would come. Remember this was pre-Bay City Rollers and their soon to be Europe wide tartan army. Rod was still a Mod on London's Eel Pie Island.

The three most famous Scots then, were probably, Jim Clark, a Grand Prix driver, footballer Billy Bremner, and on New Years Eve, (as the real world calls Hogmanay), Andy 'Donald Where's ma' Troosers?' Stewart...but more of him later.

I was encouraged to write, report and submit to Cherie and Romeo by a Dundee based DC Thomson's man called Allan McDougall. Despite my earlier protestation of remembering it all, and recalling my Mr. Sears training, I am now concerned if I've spelled his name correctly. MacDougal, McDougal. McDougall. In Scotland even the names aren't easy.

In fact generally speaking, for a southerner, Scotland was never easy. Even their beer, generally referred to as 'Heavy' certainly wasn't, (easy that is). Scots beer, as I discovered the hard way, was twice as strong as my usual London ale, the weak and wimpy Watneys Red Barrel. 'Scot's Heavy,' made you fall over. Heavily.

Allan, if I recall correctly, often wrote under the name of Alan Allyn, and he really, 'got it' when it came to trends in music and the rest. The general editor of the gaggle of girls comics, and soon to be setting up and then running Jackie Magazine, was a brilliant, creative and very kind man called Gordon Small.

Just as Mr. Sears had taught me stuff, so did Gordon. Although I was based in London and he in Dundee, on the times that we met, amongst other valuable lessons, he hammered home one rule: 'Do not underestimate, and thus patronise your readers, of any age'. Which incidentally was also the main credo of the creators of BBC's Blue Peter.

So, bearing in mind that even today I am firmly following Gordon Small's excellent rule, and not underestimating you dear reader, the following 50 lines or so, are a bit more nuts, bolts, politics and business than dreamboat dating and scurrilous tales of all your fave popstars...*they come later.*

So there were those girls comics. Bunty, Cherie, Romeo, Valentine and the like.

Then along came Jackie Magazine. A Real Magazine.

A Magazine. Not a comic printed on smudgy newspaper paper. This serious step up to magazine quality, was enabled by a massive investment from the remarkably far- seeing DC Thomson's, in new technology colour printing. Helped also, at last, after the easing of wartime restrictions on paper, by the now much wider availability of better quality 'slightly shiny' paper on which to better print in colour.

So Jackie was launched, after much secrecy and planning, with the first issue in the first week of January 1964. On the cover Cliff Richard.

Shock and Awe, has in recent decades become a phrase associated with the start of wars. But Jackie Magazine, a bigger size than seen before in young people's imprints, produced plenty of gasps. All colour, great quality, full-page pop pin-ups, teenage fashion, love stories and some, 'strictly above the waist' answers to readers questions.

Remember this was a world where, teenagers were a newly discovered breed, there was as yet, no all day music radio, no mobile phones, no social networks, not even any colour TV...so colour, well printed, was important. Especially if you wanted to see your, fave pop raves' in the nearest you could get to 'real life'.

So Shock and Awe and much enthusiasm there was: in the girls' schools, colleges, factories, shops and offices. And Jackie was a sell out.

For some of the other newspaper and magazine publishers in and around London's Fleet Street, the Shock and Awe was, Shock and War. Jackie was a powerful declaration of position and intent by one of their provincial rivals, (if Scotland can be called a province). After all, colour printing of that quality was still a big deal.

The recently launched first regular colour supplement to a UK newspaper was the already referred to 'The Sunday Times Colour Section.'

Their content reflected the age of the Swinging Sixties, with cover pictures by David Bailey of Jean Shrimpton wearing a Mary Quant mini dress, and a new James Bond story called 'The Living Daylights.' (Which, of course, became a major Bond movie about 20 years later).

So for DC Thomson's to invest in good colour for teenagers was an early recognition of their market potential.

For London's Fleetway Press, the publishers of various newsprint comic-styled girls publications, including Valentine, the newly styled Jackie was indeed a declaration of 'serious' competition. They (Fleetway), had apparently in some haste, cobbled together a similar rival magazine to Jackie, called Fabulous, later Fab 208. It was war. No pistols, but there would be 'Pop Stars and Petticoats' at dawn. On Thursdays anyway.

It was a new style of modern print success that also rankled and very much annoyed the unreasonably strong London print unions. DC Thomson were famously established as a 'non-union company. They were so exemplary and such paternalistic employers that they had few real union problems within their offices, (and that's even in still famously militant Scotland.)

It wasn't until years later that a maverick Rupert Murdoch, armed millions of pounds, was able to ~~emasculate~~ educate the London print unions to sensible and financially viable ways of adopting new technology.

So Jackie got off to a good start. Newsagents were very happy with 'another letter box friendly' item to deliver or sell on those Thursday mornings each week.

After the first ten weeks or so some concerns about Jackie started to surface. Newsagents were returning unsold issues or lowering their orders. The main problem, and a potentially very serious one, was that the advertising sales department were hearing that, "The novelty is wearing off," and more worryingly, they were also hearing, "For our cosmetic and fashion advertisers, the Jackie content seems a bit fuddy duddy, old style, not very 60's hip and teenage."

In the autumn of the previous year, 1963, Allan McDougall had persuaded me to put together a fictitious band called 'The Modbeats,' for Romeo Magazine.

Throughout the first months of '64, as Romeo reported on their front page, and several more inside, the Modbeats struggles to become famous were recounted in photos and cartoon story strips, complete with photos and drawings of yours truly, and a few mates from the pub!

The photos were even then, embarrassing, although the drawings were fun.

In March '64, just a few weeks after Jackie's launch, I happened to be in Scotland at the Dundee HQ, to talk a new series of Modbeats stuff through with Allan and the others , when what was apparently a crisis meeting about Jackie's future took place. For printing and distribution reasons, Jackie was completed for print about twelve weeks before it hit the streets, so by March they were looking at early summer issues.

At the meeting, along with the company bosses, I learned later from Allan, were Gordon Small, Robin Needham (the always 'bow-tied' manager of the London office), and Archie Hamilton the London based ad man. They, together with input from those of the team who dealt with advertising, sales and circulation were concerned.

Fabulous, from rival Fleetway Press, was overtaking them. Fast.

The advertisers said, Fabulous had better pop pictures and apparently, or perhaps allegedly, Fleetway were on, 'a mission to wipe out,' Jackie with deep discounts for the retailers, and special deals for their advertisers. They were planning a blitz of more cover-mounted giveaways, such as combs, makeup, pop stickers and even extra poster pages.

Such discounting and other tactics did not impress any of them. Needham, Hamilton or apparently Small. A new cover design, with a new plainer print style 'Jackie' layout, more adult, less 'Romeo–Cherie-comic style lettering' was already in hand and coming through the system. A cover mount plan was already well in place to restore regular readership after the summer holidays, but extra pages were not in the budget.

"But what about the content?" they asked Gordon.

Now Gordon, was already regarded then, and is still now remembered quite deservedly as, a brilliant and legendary comics and magazine man. Much of his editorial genius came from the fact that he was rather practically family orientated and traditional in outlook. So he translated the needs, interests and dreams of families into print and the print thrived.

But he was aware that pop and fashion trends were transient and the changes were speeding up and needed specialist input. Not only that, but the input they needed had to come from London, if for no other reason that London was where the record companies, fashion companies and the national broadcasters were located.

Suggesting to the Scots bosses that help was needed from London never went down well.

As Gordon told me years later, understanding that one of their team, Dundee-based writer Allan McDougall, really had a good, up to date feeling about the machinations of the rapidly changing music market, he had already tuned in to Allan's view that Jackie and the other comics and magazines could not just rely on free handout pictures and stories from record companies.

They needed someone to figure out which of the bewildering variety of new popsters being pushed by those music companies was worth page space.

Allan and some of the others felt strongly, and apparently told Small very clearly, that if he wanted Jackie to remain credible—and more to the point not to get crushed by London based Fabulous—Small's team should not end up putting some 'old guy' in a dinner jacket, or kilt, on the front cover just because he happened to have a lucky hit record in the charts.

Too much Andy Williams, Andy Stewart, Frankie Vaughan, or Val 'Rocking Chair and Irish Sweaters,' Doonican, was a distinct negative in this new media market.

There were a few 'almosts' to be considered; possibly, Allan suggested to Gordon, you could feature, The Bachelors, as one of them at least looked quite heart-throbby.

The same went for the slightly folky and older style Springfield's, at least Dusty, the main vocalist, who was a bit of a mascara'd rebel and a genius singer. As it happened, she was also on Ready Steady Go more often than not...

McDougall and Gordon had a meeting, and later the following day Gordon got Allan to repeat to me some of his points. "We need more

Rolling Stones, more Kinks, more Herman's Hermits, Animals...Dave Clark." I agreed 100%.

But the key point that Allan made and Gordon, showing why he was so highly regarded, really grabbed and simplified was: *because we write and print Jackie so many weeks before the readers see the magazine, we need to get a more accurate and true feeling of,* **"What's coming up. Not, following what's been and gone."**

Apparently, Small and McDougall had discussed him (Allen) relocating to London as a free lance, which he refused. (Although he later joined the legendary writing team at London's New Music Express and went to America as a pop music advisor.)

He claimed later to have added, to that refusal. "The beers shite down there in London." But he did add to his ale expertise, "and anyway Harry Buckle has been doing a little good stuff for us. He lives there, he knows all the clubs, many of the bands personally, he's well connected and welcomed at the TV shows and the record companies. He's even been sharing a flat with one of The Rolling Stones."

This was the reason why, Archie Hamilton and Robin Needham (Mr. Hamilton, Mr. Needham or Sir, to me) found me an 8 foot by 6 foot third floor office, a beaten up old desk, an old typewriter, and a phone (calls all via the operator, no direct dial in those day) at 185 Fleet Street. I was now exclusive...blimey! Purveyor of all that was pop, directly to Gordon Small.

Directly to Gordon ?

Me: "But Mr. Small, it's kind of Allan to say all that good stuff about me, and I'm OK with knowing all the people. Most of them I've mixed with for years at Eel Pie Island, various pubs, and elsewhere. I'm happy and getting better at doing the interviews, but when it comes to writing them up my typing is slow and terrible. So making them presentable is taking hours, not to mention acres of paper-producing trees every day. I'm creating bins full of screwed up screw ups!"

Gordon Small: "Send me all you write, with corrections just typed in after the mistakes, or corrected in pen. Don't worry what it looks like. Get it, addressed personally to me at the Dundee office, in the

Wednesday overnight bag from the London office and I will knock it into shape for you. You'll soon get the hang of it laddie."

"Oh yes, and lets a take a few snaps of you whilst you're up here."

A few snaps? Bloody hell, they changed my life. From late spring '64 for the next how many years, my picture appeared most weeks in Jackie. Many weeks it was shown multiple times on many pages, and now and again, hard to imagine these days, there was me as a 'pop pin up, for your bedroom wall.'

One more thing. Gordon hadn't told me, was that I'd have to adopt a pen name, nom de plume, with the writer's, bye line, of Pete Lennon. But hey ho....I had an office...a salary of £6.10 shillings a week (£6.50)...some expenses, one even claimed for bus fares. So being 'Pete' was fine as well.

Then, after a very few weeks, the extreme implications of having your photo regularly in the world largest selling teenage mag started to sink in. It seemed I had a fan following of my own, both as a 'Modbeat', and as Pete Lennon.

Years later, Katy, my daughter chimed "Dad those photos are so terrible, very bad embarrassing, never show my friends." Psst...dear reader, some of those photos may soon be on our web site.

But back in the sixties. Remember them?

That's why we're here and I was then explaining every day, "John Lennon, no, I know him quite well but we're not related", and every week cleaning that indelible Jackie Fan lipstick from my car windows, so I cursed Gordon Small and Allan McDougall.

In truth, those two men and that lady, 'Jackie' changed my life. For the better, and I thank them.

The effects of that change rumble on today, for me at least. Actually, although you haven't quite yet reached that part of this story yet, in some small way they might rumble on for you also.

Much of the music my company made or looked after then plays on. Hopefully with no hiss or rumble—despite some of it being from the vinyl age. As others have said, we ended up creating part of 'The Soundtrack to your Life." (Or more strictly your dad's, mum's or grandma's life).

***But why? Why was, 'Jackie' so important to your' life'
and apparently to the life of 85% of the teenage girls in
the UK?***

Firstly it was yours. For you and your special friends :
Why did Jackie 'touch your heart?" Did Cathy and Claire, not
forgetting Samantha, really give you answers? Did it really inform
you first about the new pop music, find you fashions and initiate or
even ignite your dreams?

In your room, with your pop pictures, and if you were lucky, your
record player, but hopefully without your brother, you had a friend,
someone who 'understood'.

Strong stuff, that claim; and fifty years on, seems a bit amazing.
But as is shown by the on-going media storm of interest in all that
was Jackie, with further flurries of ongoing interest forecast for
later, it really does suggests that actually in this instance :
nostalgia really is, what it used to be.

Overstated. Not really. But how? Why?

Let's remember the real world in those dream-boat days.
No mobile phone. In fact no phone, or if you were one of the few
(18%) who had one, it was on a table in the hall and, "That's
expensive, no chatting now."

Then, the phone had a name as well as a number, as in, "Hello this is
DUNdee 1234....or The Beatles London office number was COVent
Garden 2332.

No internet. Which meant No Facebook, No Twitter, No Line,
What's App, No You Tube, No Google; or a million other necessities
of social interaction and survival.

Apples, plural or an Apple, singular : When in season were
only to be found at the green grocers, and **Galaxy** was a soon to be
launched Chocolate bar.... *I am starting to get nervous about my
spell check. It may be taking over. It suggested 'Galaxy' a soon to
be 'munched' chocolate bar.*

Samsung was something that had happened earlier, in a movie,
around the piano in Casablanca.

No nationwide music radio. The pirate ships, Caroline, Radio
'Big L' London, broadcasting great music from ships just outside
British waters, only covered part of the country.

The much publicised Caroline and rather obviously London's 'Big L' were in the South of England.

Patchy coverage was provided elsewhere by Caroline North, off Liverpool. Scarborough's Radio 270 (with Paul Burnett), was rather exposed to storms off the East Coast.

Scotland had their very own Pirate Radio Scotland. The Radio Scotland ship, which had no engines and had to be towed around, was moored at various locations between Scotland and Ireland. Radio Scotland's real claim to fame, as well as the much loved Stuart Henry, was it's brilliant broadcast mantra: *"Tunes to tickle tartan tonsils,'* and its *"Fan Clan."*

All of which is, as Steve Wright would say in his pastiche of DJ's, "All a bit Dave Doubledecks."

No BBC Radio One: "Welcome to the exciting new sound of Wonderful Radio One". Tony Blackburn, with Arnold the dog's first words on opening the BBC's answer to the popular pirates, were uttered not until late September 1967.

That was of course Tony talking, not the dog. Arnold, whilst indeed a major radio star, and with better hair than Tony, just woofed a bit, reverberating your 'woofers'; to use a then modern and new, 'Hi Fi' term. Actually, Even *stereo* was new! Radio One was in mono. FM Stereo would come later.

Colour TV. Well, of course you could see all your 'fave's' in colour on TV.

Err no you couldn't! Regular Colour TV, receivable across the whole country was still some years away, and anyway there was little real pop music for you even in misty black and white. There was some of 'your Mum and Dad's music' on 'Variety Shows.' i.e.. mixed entertainment shows, 'Our special guest tonight is..."

In fact, as well as no colour TV, BBC TV wasn't yet a 'One'.

Or well actually it was, but not in name. It was was exactly that: BBC TV. BBC Two was only just being launched, to bring up the number of available channels up to three.

ITV was a collection of local stations, Grampian and Scottish TV north of the border, Rediffusion in London, Granada in Manchester and in the northern environs, Southern TV on the South coast, Anglia in the East, etc.

Depending on where you lived, they delivered their own and some other programs to your DER, Rediffusion, or Radio Rentals TV sets—all popular but still in black and white.

Of course they shared programs that they had made locally: 'Coronation Street' for instance, originating with Granada and broadcast by the others in your region.

So for you, and all the girls in your school, your friends and others, Jackie really was a life-line , wherever you were, it was a vital connection with a bigger, real world; a world beyond the confines of your street on the estate or in the village.

A world where there were other teenagers.

Fashion. With Carnaby Street expanding, and the Queen of the Kings Road, Mary Quant hitting the headlines *with skirts so short that your brother (and your dad) read more than just the sports pages,* there was quite a lot of fashion coverage. This coverage, mostly in black and white, suffused the national press. There were a few other magazines also covering the world of teenage fashion. But Jackie had it in colour— *and anyway you trusted Jackie.*

 You needed Jackie's advice, more than the oft heard, *'You're not going out in a mini skirt that short,' slightly gruffly from your dad, or slightly wistfully, from your mum.*

The Teenager had arrived, and that was you !

As people wiser than I have written: Jackie arrived in an era when teenagers and adolescents were suddenly found to exist.

Before then you moved straight from childhood with your Barbie dolls (from 1959) to being an adult in a bra. Admirably put I am sure, but not my words I stress!

Most parents didn't wear denim, and were only just about, mainly thanks to the Beatles, if you were lucky, starting to grudgingly accept some of 'your music.'

'That Paul McCartney or Herman (soon to be Peter Noone) now they are nice boys, but not those Rolling Stones."

O.K. I know I said this a few lines back but the facts cannot be underestimated.

Thursdays were Jackie days.

On those Thursdays—Jackie days—you could retreat to your bedroom, with your posters and pin ups and your music, and share your secrets with Jackie Magazine.

It was rather like the big sister you needed..... and it was always there. Every Thursday. Much to my surprise it seems that along with Cathy and Claire, Samantha and 'The Ed,' I was there as well. In print and picture at least.

Jackie was a friend at a time of your life when you needed a friend like Jackie.

I kind of understood its resonance then, but twenty years later , I was on tour in America with Depeche Mode, who were signed to one of my music companies.

I was in Branson Missouri having breakfast with a great record producer, an Englishman called Kenny Denton who had been producing some recordings in town for my company.

There we encountered a tired looking single mum, working very long hours, waiting on tables in what was a very quiet cafe.

For quite a few weeks, Kenny had breakfast in that cafe most mornings. When we stood to leave, it was the last day of recording, the waitress said: "I'll sure miss talking to you in the mornings Kenny."

As we made our thank you'se the waitress continued, somewhat sadly: **"Sometimes Music is My Only Friend. "**

Only then, truly, only then, all those years later, at that moment did I really understand the privilege and power of communication that Gordon Small had understood so well right from the start. And what DC Thomson's, Gordon and the late great Allan McDougall had given to me.

In no way am I attempting to add 'importance or extra credibility to pop music, of any kind, although those , deriding simple pop hits should perhaps consider the words of that lonely waitress.'

In truthful modesty:

"I hope our music was there when you needed it."

Now: Back to 1964 and on. Now's the real test. Do I indeed recall the sixties?

Again following Mr. Sears' instructions about ten pages and many years back:

Opener: Grab 'em at the start of the story...*It's still that drizzly May 1964 evening in Manchester, and just outside the BBC's Top of the Pops studios I am removing teenage girl's underwear.*

As I said, well actually before yet another Police enquiry starts, I was removing underwear that had been tucked under the windscreen wipers of my car and using them to attempt to remove, hearts, kisses, I love Pete, We love Jackie and worse scrawled over the car- and the windows in bright coloured lipstick..

With 'Juliet,' by the Four Pennies and 'Someone Someone,' by Brian Poole and Tremeloes , still playing in my mind as I left the studio in Dickinson Road, I encountered a very smartly uniformed (always then) and cheerful (always then) and very Manchester (ex forces I think) BBC Commissionaire.

"I'm not sure you're going to be too 'appy Pete, when you see what those girls have done to your car. We try to keep them out of the building, but there's so many waiting it's 'ard to keep an eye on them all at once."

His, "We've asked for more staff, we need eyes in the back of our 'eads," was still ringing in my ears as I turned the corner to find my beloved, old (even then) Red Triumph Spitfire sports car covered in lipstick script. Names, hearts, kisses and more. Again.

I say, again, as the same thing had happened quite a few times over previous months; outside the Aldwych/Kingsway London Studios of Rediffusion, where on Fridays, live on national TV, it was, " 54321 -The Weekend Starts Here—it's Ready Steady Go." Always called, then and now. RSG.

With the honourable exception of maverick genius Jack Good's ground-breaking 1958 pop show Oh Boy! RSG, was the first of the pop shows on TV to really make a credible impact with the teenage nation. It was certainly the first to connect with real relevance to the Jackie readers.

When Top Of The Pops started, from BBC Manchester, in Jan '64, co-incidentally the same week as Jackie, TOTP, whilst welcomed, seemed a little bit tame, a bit parent friendly.

Until some years later when the Radio One DJ's took over as presenters it was a bit condescending compared to the very credible Cathy McGowan and the real teenagers fronting RSG.

For the first few weeks the RSG opening music had been the Surfaris manic instrumental, 'Wipe Out,' but then in an inspired choice they used what became a classic, Manfred Mann's '54321';

The countdown indeed signaling a great start to the nation's teenage weekend.

So Ready Steady Go was for me, an 18-19 year old, very junior journalist, charged with getting some up to date pop gossip, music stories and more for Romeo, Cherie and then Jackie, a golden opportunity.

So many top stars in one place, and most of them, quickly recognising the almighty and very useful promotional power of Jackie, very open to be interviewed and to being photographed, often by DC Thomson's own Eric Huxtable, as well as a whole phalanx of agency snappers and freelancers.

RSG also provided the weekly chance of encounters with a flock of new teenage girls, and was not to be ignored. As I just said, I was also a teenager... so for me and my friends, it became a social opportunity, and was a good place to make new friends.

Back in Manchester, standing in a chilly car park, any flock of teenage girls had long gone. I learnt the hard way that getting lipstick off one's car windscreen was almost impossible.

Despite multiple cleanings, the names, hearts, arrows and kisses, all reappeared weeks later on the windscreen at the slightest sign of rain or moisture.

So 'new fans and even girlfriends' was nice. Weeks later, peering through a seemingly uncleanable and everlasting graffiti storm as one drove up the first few parts of the M1 motorway, then completed, their lipstick mementoes were not nice.

As I set too in the now darkening Manchester evening, scrubbing vainly at the windscreen, thinking about cursing Gordon Small and

Allan MacDougall, a blue Ford Transit van, actually also rather more covered in lipstick than Ford blue, drew up close alongside.

I peered at the driver and recognised, Roy Farrant, a guy I knew a little from Ready Steady Go and the Giaconda Cafe in London's Denmark Street. Roy was the experienced, worldly wise and very affable road manager of the then wildly popular Brian Poole and the Tremeloes, who had been on the show performing their new single 'Someone Someone.'

"Catch Pete, this'll fix the windows, but for God's sake don't get it on the paint work." He chucked me a can of what turned out to be cigarette lighter fuel, and went off to collect his band's equipment from the BBC loading dock.

Luckily, although I was hardly Tom Jones, standing on stage ankle deep in thrown undies, as well as lipstick-graffiti and notes, there were plenty of girls' undies as usual tucked under the windscreen wipers. So putting out of my mind all improper thoughts of the discomforting effects of the cold weather on the owners as they were lacking the aforesaid, 'daytime unmentionables' as my 'very proper' aunt called them, the undies saved the day. When soaked in lighter fuel they did indeed do the trick and cleaned the windscreen.

With both a clear view, and conscience, I returned to the center of Manchester and spent the evening with a couple of the Hollies at a pub, I think called the Rising Sun. My plan was to make an early start next day, off to Liverpool to interview the Fourmost and Gerry and the Pacemakers, and then to check out again what was happening at 'The Cavern.'

So May 21st 1964. Two days before my birthday . The morning after Top of the Pops, and the new life of, 'Jackie's man with the pop stars' continues. I was off to Liverpool, but first to The Toggery Shop in Mersey Square, Stockport, to collect some long awaited (and already paid for) Cuban heeled boots. The style, of course popularised by the Beatles and almost every other band on TV or on the pages of Jackie. Annello and Davide the London makers had a waiting list of over 6 months by then, but somehow Mike Cohen, the dynamic and ambitious Toggery shop owner had a supply.

Whilst London had it's Kensington Market boutiques, Carnaby Street, with John Stephen, Irvine Sellars, Lord Kitchener's Valet, and all the rest, Manchester had The Toggery in Stockport.

The Toggery was supplier of cool shirts, suits and shoes to musicians all over the North Of England. Mike was in his early 20's and whilst most clothing shops were still very traditional, Mike had a good rapport with the bands, and a great feel for the fashion. Graham Nash later to be the star of the Hollies (and of course Crosby Stills and Nash) had worked in the shop, which according to Mike had kick-started his shop being, 'the place to go.'

He also made suits and leather coats for the Beatles. I can recall Jackie doing a fashion photo feature about the shop, but I can't recall when it was used.

Back in my car, there was nothing on the radio. Pirate Radio ship Caroline doesn't set sail for Ramsey Bay until July. I also notice later that some kind fan has snapped the aerial off!

Down the East Lancs. Road and into Liverpool. Stayed with a mate in Robey Road, Huyton. Harold Wilson's constituency. Wilson to be elected Prime Minister that October and then to feature somewhat surprisingly later in this book.

I have lost my notes of whatever we did in Liverpool. But I was there so many times that given the many Jackie pages and stories devoted to The Cavern, Gerry and the Pacemakers, The Fourmost, The Mojo's, The Searchers, Cilla, Tommy Quickly, The Big Three, The Merseybeats; any visit there was busy busy busy.

Of course, the real expert on all that was Mersey and Music was Bill Harry. The originator, owner, editor, reporter and chief bottle emptier of one of the greatest ever music papers. Merseybeat. Bill and his wife, Virginia were always welcoming and helpful.

His eventual relocation to London was London's gain and Liverpool's loss.

On the subject of losses, after its almost 1000 mile round trip and almost home, my car engine suddenly lost the will to live. But fortune was smiling on me. Not, 'The 'Fortunes,' the group, but lady luck. Actually, with one of the Fortune's biggest hits being, 'You've Got Your Troubles,' maybe they're in there as well.

Whatever, whoever, however, the car conks out right by my mechanic mate Steve's house in Sunbury-on-Thames: just a mile or so from home and the pub.

Steve's mum, always blessed with a drive full of cars in bits, was somewhat less than happy at my lipstick covered and very dirty wreck right outside her front door.

To London on the train for the next few days. Usual struggles with the typewriter for several days, but sent off loads of stories to Gordon. Took the train home. The Car was still dead and I needed to wait for payday to get it fixed, consequently Steve's Mum threatened Steve with eviction.

In other random extracts from my diary around that time: Another busy week. Monday to Decca to meet, I think Phil Spector, or Billy Fury. Off to EMI to meet Muriel Young and later in the pub near EMI Manchester Square—interview The Roulettes. To Kingsway Studios to hear the new Peter Noone record, or possibly then, still Herman's Hermits.

 Friday. All day on the train, then boat, visiting the Pirate ships. Horribly rough seas...but good fun. I have to take the photos as the photographer has gone green and can't stand.

Back in the Fleet Street office and meet David Essex for the first time.... his manager seems to be a bloke called Derek Bowman who apparently works or worked just down the road at the Daily Express. David makes a series of good records, but it is a good few years until he eventually makes the charts (1973 with Rock On.)

A week later. Mechanic Steve is forced by his mum to extend car-fixing credit to me. She wants my embarrassing lipsticky car off her driveway. So with car now fixed it's back to Manchester. Pictures with Freddie Garrity, of Freddie and the Dreamers fame, his new house and possibly his old milk float (he'd been a milk man). More with the excellent Bob Lang of Wayne Fontana and the Mindbenders.

Taken out to dinner by Denny Betesh, Rick Dixon and Harvey Lisberg who seem to manage everyone not managed by Beatles manager Brian Epstein.

Back to London; and the EMI press office send junior trainee PR man Max Clifford round to 185 Fleet Street to talk to me about Gene

Pitney. In the pub, Archie Hamilton (Mr. Hamilton to me) and someone from his office, give Max a hard time about advertising in Jackie. Max is in the EMI PR department, not advertising, but nevertheless EMI start to advertise in Jackie; they are the only music company to do so I think.

With Jackie's circulation on the up, some advertising survey in a trade paper says that each Jackie is shared around and read by five people: 93% girls. That's suggesting almost 3 million more teenagers are enjoying the mag each week. They go on to say, that is 85 % of all the UK's girl teenagers. In the pub there are some dodgy jokes about 93% girls and 7% boys. Best not go there in this PC World. And I don't mean the shop.

Home for Sunday Lunch and my Mum asks me, "Isn't it time you got a proper job?" Even having my words of wit and wisdom read by a serious percentage of the nation's youth doesn't impress her. She also suggests that next time I come round for Sunday lunch I could come on the bus. It's the lipstick all over the car causing problems again.

A week later, with car cleaned, 'always listen to your Mum', quite red and shiny, that's the car, not my Mum, Sunday lunch is memorable. Firstly, a schoolteacher friend of hers upset my Ma by asking if I could go and give a careers lecture at their school. To which my mum exploded: "But it's not a proper job."

Secondly, my car seems to drip a gallon of oil over the front garden. OOPs....

Meanwhile, with Jackie seemingly unstoppable , advertising content is up.

Cosmetics and shampoos, Miners, Maybelline, Brunitex and Stayblonde, Clearasil, Linc-o- Lin Beer Shampoo, Max Factor. Lots of adverts.

Lots of adverts encouraging girls to Join the Army. "See the world. Jolly sporting stuff.

Be an Army Kennel Maid. 'Well done Buster. Good dog, I knew you'd be a winner.'"

And then the No Smoking adverts.

Looking back now at a full page advert, that really demonstrates the passage of time since Jackie Issue: 122.: May 7 1966.

The advert: Smiley girl wearing a 'I don't smoke T Shirt'.

Then check this out: 'You'll have more money ,and more fun if you don't smoke'. Sounds fair to me, both now and then.

The ad continues: '10 cigarettes a day costs £30 a year'... and under that, the rather obvious line saying: '20 cigarettes a day costs £60 a year'. Err yes, I think we got that.

But that old Ministry of Health, they really knew how to put a message across!

These days £30 will get you just under 8 day's worth of fags!

Back to the office and all around London every day..

Talking to bands, managers, PR people, photographers, models, would be producers. I seem to be in demand. Breakfast in the Giaconda Cafe in Denmark Street; Coffee in Valotti's in Shaftsbury Avenue; listen to something new in Decca's West Hampstead studio. Back down to Soho for a few beers and Shepherds Pie in De Hems Pub, Macclesfield Street, with the good and the great of the Music Press.

De Hems was the meeting place for writers from The NME, Record Mirror, Disc and Melody Maker. As such, it also attracted all the PR men and promoters, and some 'dodgy geezers' I remember with trepidation, "Mine's a bottle of Beck's please Mr. Kray."

The weeks go by.

Stories are written and filed, photo's collected and sent to Dundee. Chas Chandler, (ex Animal's and now a manager) introduces me to a very nice guitarist from America. Seems very shy, and talks to me about Croquet. Croquet! We wonder what Chas is thinking of. We soon find out with a flash of fiery licks and indeed a flaming guitar. It's Jimi Hendrix! (Find the origins of the flaming guitar idea, later in this book)

We realise then that ex-Animal Chas is still one to watch; even though he's now off stage. Sure enough, he went on to manage and guide Slade to hits a-plenty.

I attend various song festivals in Europe. Peter Meaden, a hyperactive PR genius introduces us to The High Numbers. We go and see them play in Shepherds Bush, West London. They soon change their name to The Who.

Scooters, mods and rockers—and we avoid Brighton, Clacton and Margate for a while. We do go on several Cross Channel Ferry trips with Rock n' Roll all the way. And I don't mean the sea state.

A big Biba opens, a small one closes.

One Marc Bolan, with help from a stylist called Chelita Secunda , reinvents himself almost monthly. Jazz at The Bluc Posts. Every one at The Ricky Tick's Windsor, Guildford, even Hounslow.

Every day we talk to, write about: The Fortunes, The Trems, The Others, Dave Clark, Cilla, Dave Berry, Dusty, Twinkle, Chris Farlow, Georgie Fame, Paul and Barry Ryan, The Virgin Sleep, Brian Poole, Crispian St Peters...

And of course, the visiting Americans: Sonny and Cher, Gene Pitney, Stevie Wonder, The Beach Boys, Roy Orbison, Edwin Starr, P.J. Proby, Kim Fowley, Scott Mackenzie, Canned Heat, Bruce-'Hey Baby-Keep On' Channel.

Someone takes my photo sidewalk surfing in Park Lane. First time we'd seen roller skates on a sidewalk surf-board.

Now they call them skateboards. Why didn't we think of that?

To Pye Studios, R.G. Jones in New Malden, The BBC Paris Theatre; then off to an East End pub to see a terrible singer...phew...

It really was a proper job, (sorry Ma); long hours and for the most part, not really embodying the glam and exciting world of showbiz. Of course it was a dream for most, and better in many ways than working outside in all weathers, or heavy-duty work in a factory, farm or fishing boat.

I was very privileged and in many way's my chums in the pub where I lived envied what I was doing. For their part, some were also starting to work in London in various careers.

 Seven of them were at Hamble Flying College learning to be Pilots for BOAC or BEA. Mechanic Steve was fixing and selling cars (and still filling up his mums drive with wrecks) His brother Paul was a builder and filling up the rest of his mums drive with skips and cement mixers!

Lots of the girls seemed to come and go with the seasons.

Many of them studying at various universities and teacher training colleges. Others were in offices and shops.

So despite my mother's concerns, a very real and full-time and full-on job. Just keeping up with the fast-evolving music scene and doing my small part in keeping Jackie up to date.

The full A for Animals – to Z for Zombies. And I wouldn't have missed it for the world.

But what next?

National newspaper reporter? Oops, I'd failed to complete the Pitman's course.

By request from some BBC radio producers, I ventured deep into Broadcasting House, and did an audition to be a news presenter on a, 'radio news for young people,' program that BBC were apparently planning. I failed the audition: *"We'll let you know."*

The program did arrive a few years later, as Newsbeat. But without me!

With my hopes of Radio fame dashed, what next was next.

The problem was, I was hooked.

Hooked, not on the glam and the glitz. Hooked, not on wacky baccy pills or some evil injection.

I was hooked and completely caught up in the creative process.
Standing in a studio, and hearing, seeing, feeling a memorable recording taking shape around the basic foundations of a song that someone had strummed to me just a few days before, was magic.

The studio process :Bit by bit, track by track, various instruments, all skillfully in tune, all in time. Not clashing with the other parts being played. Painting an audio picture.

Adding rhythms. A tad more guitar, a little less drums, How about if the piano played a pounding rhythm to add some body and power? How about if the drummer played on an old cardboard box to get a special sound?

And then the skill, the nerves, the talent, the anxiety the sweat and effort as with repeated and repeated and repeated breath straining attempts, until he, she, they got the vocals just right. That's it! Perfect, just right. But let's try one more.

And once more with feeling—this time with tears or joy in your voice. Brilliant. That's the one. We knew you could do it.

And then, late late night now: The lights dimmed, the musicians often snoozing in the now vacant studio, as in the control room, the engineer and the producer are selecting the best parts. Putting a puzzle together. A puzzle *where sometimes, what isn't there is as important as what is*. A millisecond's extra pause before... half a beat of silent anticipation, and then the song starts to build and tell a story. Feel the emotion.

The producer has got the best he can from the skilled musicians. Now it's up to him. With tape machines and the mixing desk. Play and rewind. Play and rewind. Play and rewind.

Stop. Stop. Hear that. That's what's wrong. Cut that bit. Only one bad note, but the rest is very special—we have to keep all the good part. That cut—now it's a digital instant, then it was skill with a razor blade taking out half an inch of recording tape from the 1000 feet on the reel.

Take out one wrong note—put in a good one. The band will get it right when they play it live.

The hours pass.

Then, a final cigarette, stubbed out in an overflowing ashtray or worse in the last coffee cup. "I think we've got it. Come and hear this one."

Everyone stirs. A grey chill dawn is coming up outside, but we don't know that in our timeless and soundproofed warm cocoon of a studio room. The engineer pushes a button- we all gather behind him to listen.

We listen again. Mostly we enjoy...but the guitarist would like to hear a little more guitar, the piano player wants to be heard all through. The singer says she/he can hear them selves breathing, stop me breathing with your magic, Mr. Producer.

With as much diplomatic skill, as audio magic, the producer fine-tunes. He pushes the volume faders up for the guitar, and down for something else. Micro moves, two hundred times or more in the three-minute song.

No computers back then. So much and so complex that sometimes they even need an extra pair of hands just to push a button on the control desk at the right millisecond.

Oops, Sorry.

Lets try it one more time from the top. From the start...

And then: and that's it: We've got a master. A master? A master-tape from which discs can be pressed. Is it a master-piece? Time will tell. A hit? A miss?

Time and promotional luck in finding radio airspace to show off our efforts to the world, will make or break the hit or miss.

It will be listened to by millions, or lie silent in a box of unplayed tapes and over-stocks. Possibly a memory only for those who were there...

We spill out into the early morning.

Around us, the city is waking up and people are yawning to work. I stand outside the studio in the fresh morning, blinking a little.

It's been a long night, with talented individuals being encouraged together to produce a fabulous, brilliant, catchy, and emotive piece of recorded music.

As I walk to my car, a postman passes on his bike. He's whistling. I know that tune. We made that one a month ago, and with enthusiasm at the radio station, now the nation—now the world—is whistling it.

The UN says, more than 1,500 million people 'Sing in English.' And 50 years on, some of them are still singing, or indeed whistling, or more likely just listening, to the music we captured that night in our studios.

 I wrote that description of the recording process back around 1970 having watched yet another recording session. That one, as one of the most talented recording engineers and producers Kenny Denton, had woven his magic over through and around the proceedings.

His job, a mix of audio and acoustic expert and engineer, musical maestro -ears alert for every transgression and moment of magic.

But perhaps the greatest skill of all, in managing, encouraging, correcting, and building a team- work from a group of highly skilled, and often highly strung creative individuals.

I learned very soon, that there were many more skilled than me in the studios, and so I stepped back a little from that.

But I also discovered that I did have a certain knack in finding and choosing the songs.

Finding and choosing the tunes.

The melodies. The musical stories that those with more musical skills and technical talent than me could make with their magic, with hard work, into something that postmen, and quite a few of those millions who need music, would, could, might enjoy....over and over again.

So I was hooked...and the rollercoaster ride of starting my own music company, with no money, had started...

4. A brief note about the team behind your tunes.

As Kylie says ,'You should be so lucky': You just have to listen, and hopefully enjoy the music that arrives in your ears- from a live performance, from the radio, by disc or download.
But all that music usually has quite a team behind it.
We start with the performers: Musicians and singers.
They need something to play and perform so we have the composers putting together the melodies and the songwriters (lyricists) bringing us appropriate, often meaningful words - or lyrics.
Original songs, are the property of the composers and authors and are referred to as song copyrights.
Original recordings are the recorded copyright of the performers.
They use a 'record or music company' to take care of their material.
A music publisher takes care of business for the writers and composers and they are usually assisted in most parts of the world by, 'collection societies,' associations of writers and publishers who keep track of the radio stations and other users of the copyrights.
To record and then reproduce the songs accurately we need a studio, with engineers to do the techie bit. For instance, there's no point in putting the main singer's microphone next to the very loud drums and cymbals or they are all we'll hear.
An in most cases it's best have a producer to encourage and ensure the best possible performance, and to act as referee between the players.
A record or music company can then bring together the techie world of manufacturing (discs or downloads) together with the music, and with some appropriate packaging and graphics then promote and try to sell the productions in a crowded market.
The music companies also have responsibility to ensure that the various creative persons get paid for their work in a fair way.
Keeping an overall eye on all the interacting deals there's usually a manager as quite often specialist business affairs are not usually the strong point of those creative types.
Agents, take care of finding the work and promoters hire the halls and put on the shows. So now you know who to thank or blame!

5. It's Good News Week...until...

*It's Friday January 14th 1966 and we are enjoying the warm
Spanish evening, me with my arm out of the Taxi window. There
had been flurries of snow as we departed London on our BEA flight
to Gibraltar. The flight was on time, and although the border with
Spain has been long disputed, I seem to recall getting through and
finding a Spanish Taxi quite quickly.*

The taxi took the coast road (I suspect the bigger inland highway
wasn't built then) and we drove through some small, then very
wintery quiet towns, but with familiar names.
Even then, in 1966, when package hols. were just really getting
going, we had seen the adverts for Estepona, Fuengirola, Marbella
and Torremelinos.
On the plane I'd noticed an advert for Vernon's or Littlewood's
Football Pools with the headline being, 'It's good news week,' and
now in the taxi, I couldn't get the catchy refrain from the
Hedgehoppers Anonymous hit out of my mind.
'It's Good News Week,' had been a big UK and then US hit in the
previous November.
Remembering song lyrics has never really been a specialty or skill of
mine, but the world and his wife all knew the insanely catchy
opening lines of that Jonathan King written and produced hit.
Surprisingly all sung rather cheerfully despite the ominous words:
"*It's good news week,
Someone's dropped a bomb somewhere.
Contaminating the atmosphere and blackening the sky.*"
I had met the Hedgehoppers—ex RAF men—nice guys, and written
about them in Jackie the previous November. I had learned that
their name, fairly obviously, came from the RAF slang for flying very
low.
That evening, as I tried to erase the melody from my mind, I was
travelling with a mate of mine, Tony Cowell (no relation) T.C. to his
mates, and we were on our way to meet up with a Spanish pop group
called Los Brincos, the following day.

Los Brincos were usually called, at least by the Spanish press, Los Beatles. They were Spain's top band. I had met them in Barcelona the preceding year and Fernando Arbex their drummer and founder was keen to enlist my help in helping the band to record in English. Their recording manager had sent me two tickets to visit them in Spain to discuss the project.

Two tickets to sunny Spain in January sounded good. The disappointment was that my girlfriend, Corina , was still at school so had no time off. Before you start tutting again, please remember, I was only just 20 and she was 17.

So my neighbour and good mate from the pub, T.C., after about .0009 of a seconds thought, agreed to come with me. I say .0009 of a second, as I don't think 'nano- seconds' had been discovered then. After all Mork and Mindy didn't start until 1978! Nanu Nanu.

But first, an overnight in Malaga, circa Jan 1966.

Dinner with an English friend, who lived there in the winter. In the summer, in his uniform blazer, he was a Costa Del Sol holiday rep for Horizon and later Clarkson, holidays.

Later that night, after a great seafood dinner we were still, helped I am sure by the quantities of white and red wine consumed, happily basking in what seemed a warm evening. The Spanish though, were all well- wrapped up in thick sweaters. Lots of those squashed square golfing patterns in evidence.

The following morning and we are , as instructed, on time at 10.30 waiting outside Malaga Town Hall for our rendezvous (or whatever the Spanish is for the French word rendezvous) with Fernando.

 Time keeping, when playing music, as in keeping the tempo, the rhythm, is vital for drummers.

I was already aware, that time keeping for musicians, including drummers, of the, "See you at x o'clock," variety, was a great mystery to many of them, and a skill not mastered by most.

Thus it was, that TC and I had time for morning coffee and a walk around the square followed by a full on early lunch with wine, whilst we waited.

 And waited. With no mobile phones, waiting, of course, was the only option

At around 2.00 pm, a remarkably large and fairly battered American car screeched to a halt, partly on the pavement, as near to the town hall as it could get.

We suspected that was our ride, when a 'dude' in jeans and dark glasses exited the drivers seat. He lit a cigarette and then stood in the door frame looking around. I walked over, and as I approached, smoker dude leapt towards me, grabbed my hand and unleashed a torrent of rapid (as always) Spanish.

I raise my hand, shrug and and say, 'No speak Spanish.' What's wrong with me ?

I always do that. 'No Speak.' Why not say ? 'I am sorry but I don't speak Spanish.' I follow that up with a questioning "Fernando?" Now that one was also stupid, as Fernando is about the most common name in Spain, after Jose. As I say "Fernando," I am making furious drumming gestures with my arms .

One of those has worked. "Si Si." and "Come, we go, Fernando." The dude opens the front passenger door for me then he leaps into the driver's seat, Tony into the back, and we swoosh off. It turns out that he doesn't speak English, but it also turns out that in the back seats there are two great looking girls. One of whom speaks English, with an American accent. Tony is looking more than happy. Optimistic even.

So as swoosh turns to hurtle and we rocket through the dusty countryside, I learn we will meet Fernando in Cartagena.

"There will be a show." "There will not be a show."

"There may be a show, but the money has no arrived."

Three different opinions from my three travelling companions.

But Fernando: "He knows we are on our way. He is mucho 'appy to see me."

I sit back and start pondering how Fernando has divined this updated information. No phone. I hadn't observed the release of any pigeons with messages. Smoke signals—that must be it. Dude and the Senorita's with their new found best friend Tony were smoking non stop. But hey, again, no problemo. This is Spain, and smoking I don't mind. It's ashtrays I hate.

I learn that Cartagena is, 'One hour,' no, 'Four hours. Stupido.' I start to think well, four hours it is. But no! There's a late bid from the back seat and it's now six hours.

I lean back and start to doze. Wine at lunch does that to me, but it's taken me fifty years to learn to reserve my wine intake until the evenings. I am just nodding off, eyes closed, when, with a jukebox style hiss and a loud click, the car fills with music.

Dude's got a record player in the dashboard. Plays 45's and he's got all the latest British hits. I learn later that they had been late to pick me up as Dude had been to Gibraltar to pick up the discs from a mate in the Spanish customs there.

I learn that, whilst on the receiving end of a lot of nods and winks, so I guess there's a deal been done with the customs guys. Pity really, I could have brought the discs with me and saved them the drive.

Drive time rocked on with the car-shaking soundtrack of Keep on Running' by Spencer Davis. Now that does sound good at high speed, high vol., with max. bass, as does ,'Yesterday man,' by Chris Andrews..

Meanwhile, as the music keeps on coming, 'My Generation,' by the Who , we zoom along towards Cartagena. Lots of DJ work for me in the front seats, and Fontella Bass with Rescue Me' is up next, I am not sure about what is incubating in the back of the car, but Tony doesn't sound as if he needs rescue. Lots of giggling at least. We drive on as the day turns to evening, sometimes with views out of the right hand side windows of a sparkling or at least blue Mediterranean sea.

Dude the is feeding me the discs, and has treated us next to 'I hear a Symphony,' by the Supremes, and then, 'Turn Turn Turn' by the Byrd's.

Six hours passes fast and we soon enter the narrow streets of the old city of Cartagena. The Spaniards in the car, that's all three of them, are in hysterics at the Sandpipers version of Guantanemara. I assumed then, wrongly, that it was a Spanish song, learning later that it is in fact Cuban. But we have enough about Cubans in this book, so we move on...now down a very narrow side street.

With a swoop into a flurry of Los Brincos fans, who seem to be
squeaking in the street, Dude stops the car, blocking the road
completely, and we are ushered into the lobby of a hotel.
Dude disappears, presumably to the loo, and returns quickly and
settles at the bar ordering coffee. As it is by then around 8 at night,
T.C. and each of the others order a beer and receive not only beers
but room keys also.
So, small bags in hand, we brave the standard shaky Spanish lift,
negotiate the dull lit corridors and I find my room. Tony ascends
further.
I open the door and there's a lady lying on the bed watching TV in
Black and White. That's the TV in B&W, not the lady.
I start to back out of the room apologetically and she rolls off the
bed and whilst finding her shoes says. "No. Is your room. I am here
to speak Spanish for you." I nod, somewhat surprised.
She continues, pointing at what is presumably the bathroom door,
"After you are freshed we go to find Fernando."
I nod again, squeak a bit, and indeed go and fresh my self.
Suitably 'freshed,' I re-enter the room and madam, or I guess,
Senorita, stands up from her preferred place on the bed. I am then
really shocked. With her shoes now on, she's well over six foot,
possibly almost seven feet tall.
We adjourn to the bar, and I make the introductions to a very
surprised Tony, "Tony-- Carmen", "Carmen--Tony."...
"Bloody hell Roddo, that was quick work."
We sit at the bar and are now all about the same height. You didn't
have to be El Sherlock 'olmes to figure out she had very long legs.
I start to order beer and and she says, "No. You are in Espana; we
will have sherry." Actually what she said was, "Herreeth."
Now I am reasonably travelled. I had spent two weeks in Callella De
La Costa and Barcelona the year before... so Sherry I knew, was not
going to be a Frankie Valli and the Four Seasons track.
After several ice cold and wonderful dry Hereeths, Spain was
starting to look rather good. Carmen was funny, and once I was
tuned in, she had good English. She was a basketball player.
"But in England I play the Net's Ball." I nod...you do a lot of nodding
in a non-English speaking part of the world.

Carmen continues, "I have been to school in England . In the Benendon, with your Priceless Anne." This turns out to mean that in Carmen's last year in the UK, Princess but not priceless, Anne had joined the school.

'Priceless Anne'—we still use that name in our family, but I have a feeling it is better applied to Fergie.

Suddenly there's a flood, no a torrent, of Spanish, and about twenty of us exit and cram into the Dude's car. It's about 11, or nearing midnight, and of course that's the time the Spanish go out to Dinner. A very jolly dinner too. I assume obviously "no money 'as arrived, and therefor no show," and we get twenty or so opinions and variations of yes, no, maybe, a show. But a very jolly for evening for T.C. and I surrounded by Senoritas—all keen to practice their English.

Some hours later, about fifty of us cram into Dude's Thunderbird, and we seem to arrive at a farm. Lots of old buildings and high fences made of plaited bamboo, with some fairy lights.

"Fernando, he come to see you soon." Turns out to be an outdoor club, with a glitter ball, a spotlight and a massive, for then, sound system. Lots more Motown hits, or as we Europeans knew it then-Tamla Motown.

Johnny Walker whisky and ice is placed on all the tables. Now I can drink anything...even Chinese Mai Thai. But never whisky, not even in Scotland, or not even whiskey if it's all Shamrocks in the garden. Mind you in Shamrockia why would you drink whiskey, when you can have a pint of Guinness or Murphy's.

A slight delay, and some surprised discussions, and I am served red wine. In those days, it seems, wine went with food and that was that. To obtain it in a club, even in Spain, was unusual.

I start to get a lot of, "Fernando, he come and see you after he make the show." I think I dozed a bit, several large Sherry's, sorry Hereeths, a lot of good wine, and then a lot of not good wine, and a feast of suckling pigs, salada and chips, will make anyone sleep.

I don't think it is possible that I slept through any show that may have occurred, but you never know. Well, I didn't anyway. Know that is.

I awake, still in the crowded, noisy, and very smoky bar. Still lots of Motown, a few fairy lights and Spanish chatter at both hi speed and high volume. I wander outside, for some air, and, using my new favourite phrase learned from Carmen just hours before, I have a fresh.

Having 'freshed', I stand taking the air, and realise that T.C. is sitting on a bale of straw nearby, also taking the air. He has been having a great time with his back seat senoritas, whom he seems to be keeping in fits of giggles.

Me. "I didn't know you smoked, T.C.?"

T.C. "I don't "

Me. "I didn't know you spoke Spanish."

T.C. "Nor did I."

My watch says its four am. At least in England it's 4 am. But thanks to the 'Herreeth flood' I cannot recall if in Spain it is 3. Or possibly 5. Or even 4. But it's getting light and I am knackered.

I may well be in my early twenties, but Spanish life has done me in. No siesta, or too many of those killer Hereeths. Tony agrees and we approach a taxi, of which there are many.

We then realise that, neither of us have any idea what is the name of our hotel. But no problem. The taxi man says." I think you the friend from Fernando."

Nod. Nod from me. Nod. Nod from T.C.

"OK. We go. I know your hotel." From him. And he did.

The following day, Carmen arrives just before lunch time, and announces. "Fernando, he very busy, we write some Spanish words to an English song. He say I must take you to a special restaurant. Is his favourite." Now I had thought we were meant to be writing English words to Spanish songs. We await instructions from Fernando.

So Sunday passes in a blur of good food, a deep siesta and later a simple supper of Tapas. I manage to stay on the wine, despite the wonderful Herreeth on offer. At about midnight, Dude appears, after another torrent of Spanish, Carmen tells me I have to be in the lobby for a six A.M. departure as it's about 500 Kilometers back to Gibraltar.

"Oh yes. Fernando send's his apologies he's working on some songs, he will, 'Catch you later.'"

T.C. departs for another music club, and I retreat somewhat thankfully for an early, by Spanish standards, night.

In the morning. No sign of Carmen. T.C walking wounded-but there.

"Is no bill to be paid...Fernando he happy to do for you."

Dude has three double espresso's and we rocket off towards Gib. This time with the sea on the left side. The same two sexy senoritas are snoozing in the back, but not before telling me that they, TC and the Dude, have come straight from the club.

I refrain from asking if there was a Los Brincos show and how it was?

A few hours later suddenly we're in a cloud of dust. Shortly after, the traffic all stops and then about thirty minutes later in amongst the cars , tractors, and trucks, there are lots of Police, flashing lights. Ambulances and Guardia Civil in their funny hats.

On several occasions, dude winds down his window to enquire about the cause of the problem. Is, a problem, apparently. Dude winds up the window. Now he knows. Is a problem.

Eventually, about an hour later and we have wriggled, with the long line of trucks and tractors, through clouds of dust on farm tracks, rough roads, and after a while through a village called Aloe Vera, (that's the kind of name you remember after all these years!) and back towards the sea. There, we soon find ourselves back on the coast road.

About an hour out of Gibraltar, Dude demands music to "keep him away the sleep." I start feeding 45's into the record player.

Unfortunately, it seems that Fernando, "He has taken the best of the discs."

So we are stuck with three discs.

Keep On Running, by The Spencer Davis Group, sounds good for the first five times.

The Carnival is Over, by the New Seekers is indeed over after two plays.

Spanish Flea by Herb Alpert produces some Spanish lessons for us; for some odd reason I can still remember the words for Flea: Pulga or Liendre. But in keeping with the double entendre of the title there was another word, but I think it's not for use in polite company. Silence falls. Three records doesn't take you far.

Then one of the girls finds another disc in the back of the front seat...and we listen endlessly, to Hedgehoppers Anonymous...all the way to the border at Gibraltar.

'It's Good News Week. It's good news week, Someone's dropped a bomb somewhere. Contaminating the atmosphere and blackening the sky.'

'It's good news week.'

I was still humming the song as we checked in for our London Flight. The girls and Dude having hoped we had a good time with Fernando "Wasn't he a great guy?"

T.C. and I agreed. "Fernando? Great guy. Very kind. Please tell him again, Mucho Gracias."

A few days later , and I am in my flat in East Molesey, Surrey, when there's a morning knock at my door. My neighbour T.C. offering me a lift in to London. Fleet Street calls and all that. Back to work at Jackie.

Tony is a bit of a sports fan, so he has the morning paper delivered daily. I sit in his car and casually study the paper.

On an inside page I spot a small report. It seems to have been a plane crash that caused the traffic problems in Andalucía on Monday.

It's not until the end of February that the headlines or at least the real story starts to emerge : The US Airforce drops Four H Bombs on Costa Del Sol. Three on land and one lost in the sea. Radiation a major risk.

I run out and get every paper and read on. The Spanish and the Americans, whose plane inadvertently dropped the bombs after a mid air re- fueling accident, have flooded the area with Army and Experts. Whole areas of tomato fields and other land around Palomares have been cordoned off.

I go cold, and scrabble through the papers to find out when this appalling accident happened. Monday 17th . Morning. I go even colder, and scrabble to find page xyz where there's a map of the area.

Christ. Exactly where I had been on that Monday. Exactly at the time.

Another chart, this time pointing out that each H bomb was 1.5 Megatons. Each therefore about 70 times stronger than the bomb that devastated Hiroshima .

They had, 'luckily not exploded thermo-nuclear-ly but had split asunder on hitting the ground.'

The following day the Americans owned up to an, 'accidental, minimal release of Plutonium,' which turned out to have been many kilos.'

The fact that one micro spec, nano spec in todays terms, of weapons grade, radioactive plutonium, could cause humans terrible problems, and that it stayed deadly for 24,000 years or more was a worry.

Especially for the Spanish farmers pictured helping the clear up in no protective clothes.

There are press mutterings about it no longer being , Costa Del Sol but Costa Armageddon. Spain's tourist industry is threatened, and their agri exports.

But the US have a secret weapon to reassure the world.

They get their Ambassador for Spain to have a much publicised swim, in billowy swim shorts, off a beach in Palomares. "Hey look, no problem."

This is not the place to document further the fact that for a month dozens of US Navy ships and submersibles, 14,000 skilled operatives, failed to find the fourth bomb which had, as they were told by an old Spanish fisherman, splashed down in the fishing grounds, "Right there, amigos.'

Eventually, with the world starting to sniff at the US Navy, at the beginning of March, a Spanish speaking US navy officer goes on a discrete trawl through the few fishermen's bars in Palomares area. He's looking, very casually, for an old guy, who a while back, said he saw the bomb hit the water.

Eventually they locate the local fisherman, Francisco Simo. *He then, using navigation techniques in common use 1000 years earlier, suggests where the US fleet might care to direct their awesome technology.*

They find their missing bomb two days later. Then lose it again and eventually retrieve it. Even the very staid US magazine Newsweek, is taunting the US Government. They print a rhyme:

" Where oh where, has our H Bomb Gone?

  Oh where, oh where can it be?"

As the story unfolds, and dreaming of my big journalistic moment, on the 18th of March I type up a short, 'I was there,' piece and put it in the 'news in' tray on Mr. Sears' desk. And wait. And wait.

But there is no request for, 'Write this up son. Get it in quick.' Despite a few reminders from me, the call never comes for me to 'File my big report, Exclusive. From our man on the spot in the bomb dust storm.'

Mainly because, Also that day someone in London has nicked the Jules Rimet World Cup football trophy.

Now that's a real story.

I get back to the world of music. Less stressful than atom bombs are falling on my head.

Years later my friend T.C. and his wife Elise, bought a small sailing boat and spent their retirement sailing around the Mediterranean. Now and again I'd get postcards from Tony. "Am in Majorca, or Ibiza, or Gib, or Marseille,'" and always with the line, "Nice here, Sky not falling on our heads."

On one occasion a card arrived from Sardinia.

Tony and Elise, "Roddo, Understand busy in the music business at Radio Stations. Suits you. You being radio active after all."

Which then was funny.

Not so funny is reading now that after 50 years, the US have only now at last in 2016, just agreed to properly clean up the Palomares accident sites, where a considerable acreage is still, no go, with high fences all round. Not so funny are the regular radiation checks required on some living in the area.

I also learn that, the official military name for the clean up, 'designed to be re-assuring to the public,' is 'Operation Moist Mop."

I think I'll stick to. 'It's Good News Week.'

Still a really good record, although for me now, a bit chilling.

Having written all the preceding words for this book, I then recall that somewhere I have a copy of that January '66 Jackie Magazine in my files.

Of course Jackie, issue 107, dated January 22nd 1966 was written and printed back in mid November.

Front cover, Cliff, back cover, Donovan. Stories and picture of me on page 11. More stuff by me on page 7.

Center of the page, my story about Hedgehoppers Anonymous singer, Mick Tinsley, liking mushrooms.

Goes foraging for them at all opportunities.

I wrote then, two months before the US bombs fell, *'that the Hedgehoppers band say they help Mick: By eating the mushrooms. The headline is Mushroom Addict.'*

For the country folk around Palomares, on the Spanish Andalusian Coast, Mushroom Cloud, might have been more appropriate.

As for some in the local villages, the old simple country pleasure of foraging for mushrooms in their fields, they'll have to wait 24,000 years before they can enjoy that simple pleasure again.

It's good news week....until.

6. The Birth of a Band. The Rollin' Stones.

Before you start complainin' note the header for this story. The Birth of A Band. When the Rolling Stones started, and before they became a brand, they were in fact called the Rollin' Stones.

For most of us, there's a, 'Special Band.' Usually associated with our teenage years, if you were lucky they were 'local', and then went on to bigger things. Or perhaps they were a national name, but back then you hopefully saw them once or twice, and followed them from that time. For me that 'local,' band happened to be the Rolling Stones.

Geology : My son Tom is a Geologist, and over his university years I observed him lugging around and studying huge piles of books. Apparently there are more books about the origins of million or even billion year old rocks than there are on any other science subject. I suspect that number of books will one day be overtaken by tomes about The Rolling Stones.

Science Note: Rolling Stones. Formation early European R&B Period. Circa Dartford, West London and Cheltenham. AD 1962. At the time of writing just four original examples are popularly known to exist. Although somewhat weathered looking they have survived the ravages of time, with erosion by liquids (various) and dust (various) rather well. As with other giants of the standing stone type, viewing them is very popular.

Gee-ology. The late and very much missed Mike Raven, originally a Pirate DJ, then a respected and much-loved fixture on BBC was a good friend of mine, even after he stopped broadcasting and moved to Cornwall to pursue a career as a sculptor. He was very knowledgeable about music of all kinds—from Flamenco guitar (which he played) to the ever-developing world of the roots of black music in R and B. (Rhythm and Blues).

Over the years we had fun discussing combining my modern knowledge (then!) with his roots histories and producing a series of Radio, maybe TV, programs, tracing the development of modern music.

Our plan was to call the series: Gee-ology...The Origins of Rock. Sadly time passed and other aspects of art and business took precedence for both of us ,so we never put that series together, which is a pity as these days there is a huge, and growing interest in the subject.

Geography. It is from New Orleans that we can pretty much trace the origins of almost all styles of pop and rock music. Over the past few hundred years, the port grew (and grew rich) from the exports of cotton and almost everything else exported from the USA to the Old World and much of what was imported.

Like most sea ports, New Orleans had a lively bar area. In taverns and 'red light' bars and clubs, music would be played and would evolve: Songs, culture and people from old Europe ,meeting the naughty drum-based Rhythms of Africa (arriving with the shame of the slave trade) and the sensuous sounds of the South American tropics.

All mixing together via the islands, especially Cuba and Haiti, and coming ashore in the The Big Easy, as they called New Orleans, in the southern state of Louisiana. *US of A.*

Actually, it took a while in becoming the fully *United* States of America, as the end of the British colonialist rule, (we walked) the exit of the French (they sold) and the resolution of the North South divide took time.

But generally speaking, from around 1776 until about 1812, various areas were added on to the 1776 part which eventually, with the addition of a few other bits, (such as California), became the USA. Then of course everyone had to wait for someone to invent Coca Cola so they could propose a toast.

They had quite a wait as actually old Doc Pemberton didn't invent Coke didn't until 1886.

Whilst New Orleans teemed with musicians back then, it was lucky that my old and sadly missed chum 'Lemmy' from Motorhead was not around in those days.

According to the bottle label he could have ordered his much loved Jack Daniels any time from 1866.

Even with Lemmy's style and laconic 'dry ' humour, waiting 20 years to get the Coke invented and splashed in to make his favourite drink, would have been a bit too much.

I mean the ice would have melted...

... and before you write in to point out that fridges and ice making didn't arrive till the 1880's...ice was shipped to New Orleans in sailing ships from New England winters as early as 1820.

In fact, rather amazingly, Fred Tudor's Ice company successfully sailed a load of crystal clear ice to Calcutta, India in 1833. But India brings in a whole very different style of music so we'll leave those stories to the George Harrison-Ravi Shankar anecdotes. If I have time!

We'd best focus on the origins of popular music as promised.

So in New Orleans, from those early times, the food, life, language and the music were already a mix of those European, African and South American styles. All of which then received another shot in the cocktail with some musical memories and styles seeping in from a new generation of very poor French speakers. (They probably spoke French very well, but were very poor, OK!)

The French colonists of Louisiana, were later joined by several thousand French speakers, who had made the long overland trek from Canada having been displaced by the British when we took over the French parts of Canada, (this time the French walked). This made, that often referred to Cajun region of Louisiana, one of the few places where many of the rural Whites were poorer than the rural Blacks.

(Please note I refer to White/ Blacks here in a very simplistic, non-judgmental purely historical context. Todays, understandably preferred, African American is it seems more correct, but I'm trying to get over the way it was then.)

Over time, many of the established blacks, with small farms and businesses stayed in Louisiana and the south. Many though, in search of a better world, and a life beyond farming and cropping cotton, went north towards the allegedly golden paved streets of Chicago.

Of course they took their music with them.

Very generally speaking the various routes took them generally North via Memphis, Tennessee, Georgia, Alabama...and as is the way, as they passed through they picked up a few more musical influences on the road.

Then from the states around Virginia and Kentucky, those influences came from the Irish and Scots living (and often working as miners) there. Blue grass by name, nature and musical style, became the name of that local mix.

So What? I hear you ask what's all that guff got to do with the Rolling Stones?

The answer lies in some foot-tapping music.

In the sweaty confines of the crowded Eel Pie Island or Ricky Tick clubs of West London, almost New Orleans temperatures actually, the Stones played Memphis Tennessee. They played songs originated in New Orleans , moving on towards Chicago they played Bright Lights Big City and Hey Bo Diddley.

Then later, at most gigs they finished, with us all going mad, clapping, arms waving, singing, girls dancing, guys not dancing (the problem being the full pint glass) as they played Route 66 and Johnny B. Good.

The fact being, not realised then by most of us in the audience, that most of those classic songs were pretty accurately tracing the journey of the music and many black musicians as they progressed north through America to a more modern urban world.

A geography lesson indeed...especially when we knew the words of Route 66 as it recited the list of towns and states on the road, in that case, to the West.

Or in the case of , Chuck Berry's still popular, Johnnie B. Good, it evokes an interesting picture of rural life.

'Johnnie' carries his guitar in a gunny sack, and goes and plays by the railroad track.' A kid, way out in the country, learning to play on a beaten up old guitar, probably with a few strings missing, all alone, not with any mates with drums, needed some rhythm.

Maybe once or twice a day he'd hear the distant whistle of a train coming. Pulled by one or more mighty steam engines, some of those freight trains were over a mile long, and depending on their speed could take five minutes or more to clickety click—clickety clack over the joins in the railway tracks..

A perfect, regular rhythm for some guitar practice. As the song tells, 'the engineers would see Johnnie sitting in the shade.....strumming to the rhythm that the drivers made.'

Chuck Berry, I can tell you from personal experience, was not an easy guy to deal with, but as a modern poet painting pictures with his lyrics he's the genius of a generation.

Much inspired, I add, by his piano player, Johnnie Johnson. Many Chuck Berry songs, famous for featuring guitar are equally wonderful when performed on piano.

But back in the day, as we supped our pints and tapped our feet, and guarded the girls' handbags, we didn't think about all that clever stuff. We were just having a good time.

Geography lessons. Who'd have thought.

"They don't make music now like they did in my day."

I have a very clear view on this having had that phrase thrown at me weekly for 50 years.

The favourite music of most people is the music they heard and enjoyed in their teenage and possibly college or university years.

OK. I hear you again.

You agree, and we're all having a good time BUT this is all about London's Rolling Stones, and indeed they were 'Our Band' as we lived around London.

But what about your band?

Of course there were many more millions of you, from the real world of Birmingham, Manchester, Liverpool, Newcastle, Ireland or even Scotland—or that place Tom Jones comes from.

We all have (or had) our own memories. Our favourites, our own, 'special band.' Yes, that music we really remember from our own teenage or student years. Especially the ones we saw live.

In the early Sixties we were still living in the shadows of a world of trad. (traditional) jazz. Complete with trumpets and other brass instruments , usually with a stand up double bass.

Influenced by imports of discs and rumours from New Orleans a younger team of British Jazzers started filling in during the intervals from the main Trad Jazz bands with what today would be called-fusion music. Then they called it Skiffle.

And with a varied mix of acoustic guitars, banjo's, rhythm from an old washboard (a corrugated metal sheet used to rub clothes clean) Often with a bass improvised from a big old wooden box, a broomstick and string. A fine time was had by all.

Don't let the ramshackle selection of musical instruments fool you, these guys could play and in Lonnie Donegan they soon had a chart topping hero. Without upsetting the musicologists - skiffle was a blend of Jazz, Folk and various country styles.

And it worked, and with a few pints of beer and a Babycham or two it was fun.

As electric guitars had become more accessible skiffle was closely followed by the excitement that was Rock and Roll. Electrified and amplified. Suddenly both Bill Haley and Elvis both borrowed from the roots music of the Southern States. (Elvis somewhat more than Bill—the accidental Rocker)

In the UK , Cliff with the Shadows arrived, and with varying originality-or not- a bonanza of beat groups followed them, Tommy Steele and a host of macho named rockers, and brought in the twangy and over- echoed beat group era.

Then in the early sixties, along came another generation of bands. This time, still electric guitar music, but very much more musically influenced by those mainly black roots music that grew up along that winding road from New Orleans to Chicago.

Spearheaded by Alexis Korner, Cyril Davies and popularised by the Stones, the Animals and many more. R and B, or sometimes, R&B, had arrived. As it happens often by boat, and it's arrival not very much to the surprise of legendary and inspired Jazzers, Chris Barber or Ken Collier who had seen it, as with skiffle a few years earlier, evolving out of the sounds of New Orleans.

So, although at the time they (the tradsters) were a bit grudging in their acceptance of change, in a way, the electric R & B of the Stones was slightly more to the Jazzers' liking, or at least leant a little in the right direction.

Now it was the Cliff and Shadows fans who were heard to say: "They don't make music like in my young days any more...."

Of course Cliff and the Shads didn't say that themselves, they knew and well respected the roots of their style.

I guess you also are likely to have uttered those words, "*They don't....like they used to in my day*"

But they do. These days there's plenty of music out there, although the Apple avalanche has killed the forty years old music industry business model. A set up that had worked so well and provided a real potential career route for new musicians who could find original and talented ways to stand out from the other starters.

But we can with luck, skill, or a young guide, find some still original good stuff to Zimmer to.

But I agree: So far, too much London...but read the Header, 'Birth of a Band'. The Rolling Stones.

They evoked the smells and sounds of America but underneath it all Mick was a Cricket fan and Bill Wyman an ex erk, but you and your, 'special' bands from elsewhere around the UK are not forgotten.

Of course, as you will no doubt remember as is set out in Charles Darwin's 1859 book, On the Origin of Species.'

Life started and evolved in many ways; it did so in many places at the same time.

Local and regional conditions made for slight changes...Stay with me dear reader, stay with me!

Rock and roll resumes shortly...

The Darwin evolution proposition, of course explains why Guinness can best come from Dublin.

Scrumpy from the apple orchards of mainly West England, Herefordshire and Norfolk ,and all drinks called 'Mac' something that make you fall over come from Scotland.

It's those, 'regional conditions' that will do that.

Clever man that Charlie Darwin, although I have to say that with his big white whiskers he looks more a Trad. Jazz fan than an R and B enthusiast.

Of course, ever since Darwin wrote that book there's been controversy. *It's never good to upset the vicar.*

Should you be reading this book having grown up in some parts of America you won't know much about Mr. Darwin and his theory as the schools in some states are apparently not allowed to teach about The Evolution of the Species.

They choose to believe it *was all the work of the Almighty.*

Who am I to argue for or against on either side...so I won't.

If the Almighty happened to create the Rolling Stones on a quiet Monday that's fine by me, or if they evolved out of the primeval swamps around Dartford Kent that's also fine by me. You choose— and I'm happy for you.

So, for the many millions of who you who evolved from the swamps way away from the Big Smoke (Smog in London's winter was still very normal then) or suddenly woke up one day, fully formed, in Stoke On Trent, Aberdeen, Yeovil, West Bromwich or Swansea, I mention here just a few of your own musical heroes from 'your' clubs and pubs.

'Your bands' from at least the time the Rolling Stones were becoming special to a generation of Londoners.

Spencer Davies having introduced Birmingham to the world of R and B, and left the door open one black sabbath, allowing the escape of some Ozzie's. Then some Moves who begat some Wizards. Some very Moody Blues, and Elo Elo Elo. (That Jeff Lynne of Elo, he loved a bit of echo.) Rocking Berries, Slade and of course Jasper Carrott..although in that later case it may have been Mr. Darwin's day off.

Shout it from the rooftops Lulu. Starting in Glasgow, Alex Harvey with his ever changing and growing band was on the same mission. (Mission? Oops! Sorry Mr. Darwin).

In Newcastle the Animals were belting out the best of Chuck Berry, John Lee Hooker and other gems from the roots of American home entertainment at 'The House of Rising Sun.'

Manchester had Hermits, Hollies , Mindbenders and many more. Liverpool is so well reported on we won' t repeat the Liverpool list.

I have a slight problem with listing the best of Ireland, as despite many visits there with wild good musical times, the good times were indeed so good my memory is a blank !

Tommy Scott (Jones) and the Senators, or Crazy Cavan in the Green Grass of their Wales homeland, were a bit more rock n' roll, but later as the bar closed, no more Brains, they did a mean version of Johnnie B. Good that sent us singing home up the valleys.

For those of you not overly familiar with the principality, Brains is their leading local ale.

Dundee, as well as being home to Jackie magazine, was home to a countless great bands, of which one, to name four, were, the Johnnie Hudson Hi Four.

Like many of the great bands from Liverpool, JHH Four were mostly playing the same stuff. They had also fine-tuned their musical skills playing in the red light bars of Hamburg, Germany.

Hamburg, Liverpool, Newcastle, Dublin, Cardiff, Glasgow...Guess what? Big Ports. Some of them even getting boats in from New Orleans.

The danger of naming the names is everyone is disappointed. "This guy's useless, he left out...all our favourites: The Poets, Marmalade, The Downliners, Thin Lizzie, Them, The Others, The Troggs, Peter Jay, The Rockin Berries, The Searchers, Simon Dupree, The Virgin Sleep, Dave Dee, Dozy etc.

Joe Cocker, Various Berries-Rocking', Dave,or Mike . Simon Dupree, Joe Dolan, Margo and the Marvettes,Victor Brox, The Paramount's ....Adge Cutler and the Wurzels...any and all bands with Chas, Dave and Clem Cattini in. ~~The Saint Winifred's School choir~~.. Enough. Enough. Please Enough.

So whilst teachers in those days, generally seemed to approve of the Mop Top Beatles and rather disapprove of the Rolling Stones, it was more the Stones that were teaching American musical geography in clubs and bars right across the UK.

Ah yes. The fab four. The mop heads. The Beatles.

Whilst their stage act in Hamburg and at Liverpool's fabled Cavern Club featured the usual selection from Chuck Berry's American Geography lesson, their Parlophone EMI recordings were mostly of their own songs.

I am sure there have been books written and university courses taught on the Beatles' choice of songs to put on record. I suspect and detect the sensible and creative hands of producer George Martin on that choice.

Their own songs were and are brilliant stuff obviously, but on the 'Please Please Me' LP, released in March 63, they did sneak in 'Twist and Shout' and 'Anna - Go to Him' (an Arthur Alexander song). The Stones liked Arthur Alexander's songs as well and recorded his song, 'You'd better move on'.

The Fab Four's second LP: 'With the Beatles', came out in November the same year, amazingly just six months after their first one. This was again mostly original and great Lennon and McCartney songs. Chuck Berry, did get a look in, with George Harrison belting out a good version of his song, 'Roll Over Beethoven'...so maybe Music History not Geography was the lesson of that day.

All that's a bit specialised, and luckily for you, unlucky for me, when my Vespa was stolen they took my Anorak with it...so lets get back to basics.

As I said, many trees back in this rambling reminiscence: there are, have been, and doubtless will be so many more, documentaries, films, stories and learned books that recount in every detail the Stones' story, so I am not going into each and every detail here.

So no Mick meeting Keith at Dartford railway station (place now marked by a plaque). Nothing about the eventual joining of Bill Wyman (They were happy he had some big equipment. A phrase, that considering alleged scandals in his later life, should perhaps be re-written). Zero about the Cheltenham origins of the sadly missed, very talented but then quite pushy, Brian Jones.

Nada about the final addition of drummer Charlie, whose stone like visage and relaxed but implacable manner, conceals a brilliant creative wit and fierce artistic talent.

Sadly nada also of the ousting of the piano genius, and original engine room of the band, Ian Stewart. Known to all of us as Stu. Without whom. Etc. ..etc. Etc.

Stu was a good few years older than the rest of the band, he had a job and thus kept them fed. He was well respected as a great, legendary piano player in the few clubs and venues that offered opportunity for their style of music around London.

The slight problem was he, Stu, tended to wear a suit (slightly crumpled) and he was constructed like a Rugby Scrum front row player. In fact his bulky frame and large hands belied the fact that as well as boogie woogicing with the best, he had a delicate and sensitive touch on the piano keys when needed.

The Stones, eventually agreeing with their Manager, the then apprentice Svengali Andrew Oldham, that Old Jazz Man Stu didn't quite fit the Rolling Stones' image, and he was out. I talked to Brian about it at length at the time, and he said Andrew's action almost caused them to break up.

In later years, Stu was quoted as saying, "I don't like Andrew as a person. But I think without his initial influence and vision the Stones would have not lasted as long as they have." An honest view from a very straight guy. We missed him. They missed him and it is a clear example of their appreciation of his talents that they retained Stu as faithful tour manager, in some business roles, and most importantly he played piano on almost every Stones recording until his untimely death in 1985.

There are many thousands, if not, tens of thousands who have claimed to be there at all those early Stones shows. I make no claims to perspicuity or 'Wasn't I hip and clever.' I just happened to be in the right place at the right time. Even more luckily, I ended up in a job that required me to go to some of those shows...*and then clock in the office on time in the morning.*

Thousands...at the early shows. No way. Impossible.

The reality of it was: for the first year or so, there were only a few hundred of us at most of the gigs, we stood, crammed in shoulder to shoulder, beer glass in hand, listening to the band and looking at the girls; those girls, many of them Cherie, Romeo readers, fortunate enough to live in London. OK and there were lots from Valentine, Roxy, Mirabel, Boyfriend.

No Jackie or Fab Mag girls? I hear you ask. Well, no actually, the last of the Stones Ricky Tick gigs was in Autumn '63 and at that time Jackie was still a baby in Dundee...not to be launched until Jan '64. On the subject of girls, our Cherie and Romeo girls had something to look at as well as the band. As by then the fashion leading style and glamour of supermodel sister Chrissie Shrimpton and the Linda's Lawrence and Keith seemed to be at every show. It took about 7 days, and suddenly the eye make up of the entire audience changed. Fringes were in and skirts became even shorter...and the eyes way darker and heavy heavy lashes. And that was just the boys. (I'm kidding)

I am really not trying to be disparaging or a smart arse about the thousands claiming to have been there but *the reality is the venues that they played in then only held very limited numbers.*

500 on Eel Pie Island (950 when no one was checking) Even then it wasn't easy if you needed to breathe, let alone get to the bar or the loo!

There was simply no more room to squeeze more people in.

The Old Ricky Tick upstairs in Peasecod Street, Windsor had room for 250 (400 when no one was checking) I know because I had booked bands into that very place myself.

The Stones played 'The Ricky Tick' more than 40 times in various locations. And some of the places were even smaller than Windsor! Despite my best efforts, you'll still need a lot of your imagination to try and capture the awe, the magic, the sweat, the floor sticky with Newcastle Amber beer .(always Newkie Amber-never Newkie Brown then) The relatively 'not so loud' music, with the surprising brilliance of Bill's bass thumping through, now we understood why they wanted him.

 Hard to describe the exhausted sweaty elation as we watched and listened in the increasingly crowded confines of Eel Pie Island, on the River Thames in Twickenham, West London.

Or also in West London crammed into The Station Hotel in Richmond or eventually just across the A316 Chertsey Road at the Crawdaddy Club in the bar of Richmond Rugby Club.

We liked upstairs, at the back of The Star and Garter pub at the top of Peasecod Street, Windsor- right by the Castle walls. It was little bit further out of town, so not so many newcomers attracted by Norman Joplin's excellent stories in the Record Mirror, and I confess, many other stories written by me in a variety of publications.

Attending the Windsor Ricky Tick needed a little courage, as with Windsor being an Army town, there were a few potential gauntlets of rather threatening cropped head guardsmen to be run as we indeed ran—down through the town to get the last train back to our homes.

Oh, the relative joy and feeling of control, when on the days that it worked, travelling on my Vespa Scooter we had safety from Her Majesties Palace Guard. Even without their huge tall bearskin busby hats they seemed big enough to us!

These days, demographics now being a more detailed and researched science, they would have a field day ascertaining as to why soldiers seemed to be rockers and somewhat disapproving of us Stones fans.

I can understand a little as we were mostly wearing our Anti Nuclear War CND badges, and we had more hair than the army allowed.

The soldiers liked Elvis and the beat groups, and played him and them on the pub jukeboxes a lot. Maybe, Elvis having been a soldier himself is what attracted a million men in uniform to his fan base.

Interestingly, or maybe not, there's always been a big argument about how the name Ricky Tick started. I got about ten variations on the story at the time from John Mansfield and Phil Hayward— the music promoters behind it.

These days some get all literary, and refer to the excellent Kipling. Ricky Tiki Tavi and all that Jungle Book stuff. (No dearest—not cake) At the time, as expressed in the simple but brilliant graphics used to identify the Ricky Tik shows, we believed the words to have some deep south of the USA meaning. That's deep as in Deep South and deep meaning. I don't think any of us knew exactly what the meaning was, but we weren't going to be the first to admit that. We'd nod knowingly and take a long swig from our beer.

But it was, 'The Island' that we liked best.

Eel Pie Island felt great from the moment you paid your few pence to the old lady perched on the little footbridge to the island. Rain or shine, winter and summer, she always smiled, and took your proffered coins in her gloved hand. Those gloves with no fingers...I don't mean mittens...I mean fingers with the ends missing so she could count the coins.

Eel Pie seemed a different world. Although it was only about five miles up stream on the River Thames from central London. With a couple of boatyards in the vicinity, and about 30 houses, mainly wood construction, perched on raised foundations hopefully above the winter high waters.

Many were, even then, rather dilapidated. Some had pretty little well-tended gardens, and were obviously occupied by far seeing folk, appreciating, despite being in the middle of a busy London suburb, the peace and serenity of life by the river, *during the day at least*.

Then there was the large and crumbling, once elegant, Eel Pie Island Hotel.

Built 100 years before— in its elegant days home to croquet on the lawn that sloped down to the river. Once a gentle afternoon row in a skiff, and in the evening a jitterbug or Charleston with a Pimms or two to the backbeat of a genteel Jazz band was just the ticket. But by the sixties, the building and the glamour— but not the appeal, had faded.

Whilst I was using the miracle of modern technology and digging around on the internet to check exactly when The Eel Pie Island Hotel was actually built, I happened by chance upon a great description of the Island in it's Rolling Stones, Alex Harvey, The Others, Rod Stewart, Long John Baldrey, era.

The following evocative words, which as I say, I found today by chance, were written a while back by a guy I know called Bob Wagner.

Then an art student in Twickenham, he became a talented and much in demand designer...you won't realise this but you'll have seen his work on everything from airplanes to exotic tropical bottles of rum! I was fortunate because when I opened my own record company, Bob, as a music fan really understood what we were doing and thus designed many wonderful LP sleeves for us.

Remember, throughout much of this book's era it was , pre-cd, pre-downloads era, and your music came on 12-inch size discs.

They beautifully packed in card sleeves—sometimes with many pages.

The art and graphics became a vital part of the creative work and really added to the concept, understanding and the enjoyment.

I quote what Bob Wagner wrote a few years back.
'As a student at Twickenham Art College my friends and I spent so much time and money at Eel Pie that we decided to work there! We worked in the evening on Wednesdays, and all day on Saturday, or at least all morning and all of the evening to boot.

We saw all the famous bands, blues men and Jazzers for free! Only having to collect the occasional beer glass for the privilege. I have many behind the scenes memories, the hotels tattiness, the famous sprung dance floor, which we swept on a Saturday morning, it had so many holes! Convenient for us as, all the cigarette ends and rubbish went into them!

Jazz nights, (Sat) were harder work, and seemed to attract heavier drinkers! Collecting the beer glasses from the mud of the river when the tide was low (thrown in by the punters), they were covered in green slime ... scrubbing them and hanging them back up in the bar. Emptying nearly empty barrels of beer into other ones (it was served later!)

Working on the door and refusing 'Rod the Mod' (Rod Stewart) entry when he said he was "with the band" (Long John Baldrey). People at various times jumping into the river then being pulled out and thrown out of the club. A clubber climbing onto the balcony of the hotel only to leap off as the Alsatian dog that lived upstairs decided to see him off!

Later I was told by a friend (I had left by then) that the club had been closed because a girl went into the toilet, pulled the chain and the cistern fell on her. I don't know if that is true but it would describe the general state of the building.

I later designed record sleeves for many record companies and musicians, some of whom very well remembered playing at Eel Pie. I have student drawings of that time still in sketchbooks. The club was a dump, the hotel dilapidated, BUT the bands were great and it belonged to us... A great place to be in your youth, a place where I made many lifelong friends ...Cheers to the Eel Pie ...Bob Wagner.

You betta move on. As 1963 moved on so did the Stones. With singles recorded and released, the shows and venues were getting bigger. For them theatre tours with other bands were now the thing... they played their last shows at the Crawdaddy Club, by then in Richmond Rugby Club pavilion.

Then last one at the Ricky Tick and—for me—the emotional one—their last gig at Eel Pie Island.

As '63 became '64, on January 1st, they appeared on the first ever edition of Top of the Pops (from Manchester). They didn't feature in the first Jackie also out that January. But they popped up in March—when issue number 10, had a double page Stones poster; but we made up for the late start in future issues.

Through the Spring and Summer of '64...the Stones roller coaster, now looking unstoppable rolled on. More TV. More theatre tours. USA TV and more—even a recording session in the legendary Chess Recording studios in Chicago.

Those Chess studios, the very place much dreamed of by many of those musicians who had trodden the difficult track from New Orleans and elsewhere in the deep South to the Windy City.

For most, sadly the streets weren't paved with gold. But for the very talented, the fortunate few, they made wonderful music there. Music so good, that it was enough to make you believe in your dreams.

Recording at Chess, Stu and the Rolling Stones could hardly believe their luck.

They were also quite surprised at having just topped the UK Charts with: 'It's all Over Now'. Back then, on August 7th 1964, sitting back stage chatting with them in a very large tent on the Rugby ground at Richmond, just across the road from the Station Hotel where it had partly started, it plainly wasn't all over now.

They could also hardly believe that their first LP release in the USA had climbed to number 11 in the Billboard charts. The great and the good, in their suits, of Decca America having titled the US release as: 'The Rolling Stones: England's Newest Hit makers."

Much teasing and merriment backstage, about 'England's Newest Hit makers.'

That year in Richmond, at the 4th National Jazz and Blues festival, actually on The Richmond Athletic ground, but always referred to by us as the The Rugby Club, in a tent holding several thousand, just steps away from the Old Station Hotel , capacity only a few hundred the Stones are top of Friday night's bill.

It was clear to the national Jazz Federation, even if renamed The National Jazz and Blues Federation, that this was the year when Electric R & B took over. As it happened, none of this would have happened without the intrepid genius and vision of Jazz-men like Chris Barber, Ken Collier and a few others.

As the light faded the Stones didn't, and we were treated to a rolling and tumbling performance of most of our favourites. But alas it had to end ... as the echoes of the encores and the cheers died away and the tent slowly emptied.

Even then we felt a sense of loss. Our band. Our Rolling Stones, belonged to the world now— not to us anymore.

A week later—we Islanders were again enjoying shows at Eel Pie: Jeff Beck and the Tridents, Long John Baldrey—sometimes with Rod Stewart, The Yardbirds, and not forgetting The Others: the best band never to have hit the big time.

And then on the island some bands from out of town, John Mayall, The Animals, Spencer Davis, Alex Harvey— some new and all great— for us...*but I guess, somewhere in Glasgow, Birmingham, Newcastle ... there were tinges of sadness for you.*

Your local bands had moved on...gone to London and beyond... But we've still got the memories and the music.

And the Rolling Stones, pensioners all,and their Brand belongs to the world.

7. Jimi Hendrix...It's All Balls.

There are certain superstars whose names resound right around the world such as Elvis, The Beatles, Bob Dylan, Prince, Michael Jackson, David Bowie, Madonna and certainly Jimi Hendrix.
In music company terms, those were the artists, where, if you were lucky enough to be releasing a new record by one of them, you knew every music store in the world would need at least one copy for their stock, which kind of gets your sales off to a good start.
Now of course with the world being online the rules have changed.

When friends and colleagues learned I was writing this book, they immediately said, knowing that I had known Jimi, and rather a lot about the mysterious business dealings around him, "Are you going to write about Hendrix."
The answer is yes and no. So much has been written about him, fact and mostly fantasy, it seems a waste of space, and my readers' time, to drag it all up again on the repeat setting. But there are a few tales here not usually told.
Jimmy as he was then, was spotted playing guitar in New York by Linda Keith, onetime girlfriend of Keith Richards, about whom Keith wrote the Rolling Stones hit, 'Ruby Tuesday.'
She alerted ex Animals bass player Chas Chandler to Jimmy's talent and Chas, who was moving to a career as a manager, agreed with this assessment. In mid September 1966, he bought him to the UK, which is when I first met him, over a pint in De Hems pub.
He seemed like a very nice guy, a fact much agreed on then, and reported on later. It was that week that Chas persuaded Jimmy to change his name to Jimi!
Very polite, modest in fact, such a quiet guy we wondered what Chas had seen in him. After all, with Eric Clapton, Jimmy Page, Alvin Lee and the most legendary of them all Jeff Beck, there were plenty of great guitarists around.
After some brief rehearsals, Jimi together with bass player Noel Redding and drummer Mitch Mitchell, debuted as a trio on some support gigs in France for Johnny Halliday.

In the second week of October, he recorded some songs for Track Records in London, and the first single, 'Hey Joe', was released just a week or so later.

In mid November he performed at one of the UK music industry's favourite London clubs, The Bag O'Nails. Much has been written about this show, attended by 'everyone who was anyone: Pete Townsend, Mick Jagger, John Lennon, Brian Jones, Paul McCartney, and whizzo guitarists Eric Clapton and Jeff Beck amongst others.

I was in that 'amongst others,' category. Bill Harry, the founder of Merseybeat (and by then a De Hems regular) wrote a wildly enthusiastic piece for Record Mirror. Over the years most of those there have claimed, 'to have seen the light and heard the oracle that very night.'

I was there, and it all seemed OK to me. But not more than OK. An average night, *and remember I liked Jimi,I wanted him to do well.* Most of the other musicians were busy talking, as was usual in London Clubs then. Brian Jones did sit entranced, of which I wrote at the time. But the others were just, 'The guy's pretty good'. Next please...or at least, next drink please.

I can remember Chas, in the following days, being very down about the show, not quite knowing if it had been worth all the effort. Then came Bill's piece in the Record Mirror and the roller coaster started. Hey Joe, charted, on Dec 29th, in a week when record sales were traditionally very low, and after much in shop promotion by the Track guys.

But Hey Joe had the legs and did pretty well following it's rather contrived sales launch. It was followed swiftly by Purple Haze, which also did OK. Of course these were hit singles by an artist who looked more like an LP style of guy, and indeed an LP followed later that spring.

In March '67, on the 31st in fact, at Finsbury Park Astoria ,North London, Jackie Magazine's greatest rival in the magazine business took a hand, and to some extent changed the future for Jimi. Journalist Keith Altham had been my equivalent at Fab 208, and later worked on the NME. A whole crowd of us were standing backstage at the start of a tour for the Walker brothers, on which

Jimi was also booked. Keith was talking to Chas Chandler about Chas's wish to get some extra PR for Jimi.

They discounted smashing up the equipment as being old hat now that the smashing antics of Pete Townshend and the Who were regularly boosting the sales of guitar and instrument makers.

Keith, only partly joking suggested "It's a pity you can't set fire to your guitar whilst playing."... the roadies rushed around and eventually obtained some cigarette lighter fuel...and the rest is history.

The audience went crazy, as did the theatre's firemen.

The Walker Brothers were miffed to say the least, particularly Scott. But Jimi was all over the front pages and incidentally in the local A&E with burnt fingers!

Now two things—dear reader. Firstly, many books and newspaper stories are written about the above...as taking place at London's Astoria. Wrong, that, 'London Astoria,' was in Central London— Charing Cross Road.

The conflagration and fiery coronation of Jimi as a performer, was up in North London's, 'Finsbury Park Astoria'. Also home to the Beatles' Christmas shows— and later to be called The Rainbow.

Secondly, alert readers will be aware that as I was regularly having to clean Lipstick traces off my car windscreen, I could have saved those roadies all that rushing about finding lighter fluid for Jimi; I had a can in the back of my car all the time.

So well done, Keith Altham. Credit where credit is due. In the Jackie office we often referred to our rivals as, "That flaming Fab Mag. Look what they've done now." Now we knew.

Over the next few months Jimi set the world, and on occasions his guitar, alight. The rest is history, legend, and becomes a sad and cautionary tale and partly an over-hyped hysterical myth. Many of the stories don't do any justice to the memory of a very talented and nice guy.

Much of the myth and mystery surrounds his unfortunate death, and is compounded by the fact that Mike Jeffery, originally partners with Chas in managing Jimi, was himself a man of self- declared mystery.

Jeffery, like Chas, also from the North East of England, was ,*unlike* Chas a rather *un-straightforward guy.* Mike claimed to have worked for the CIA. He deliberately liked to create mystery, and confusion, almost in a way to boost his ego and image.

Mike set up, with an English lawyer called John Hillman, a web of companies in the Caribbean, *much like the recently publicised secret companies in Panama,* designed to focus there, world earnings for Jimi (and some others) and thus minimise taxes paid on four aspects of music business earnings:

-On live income from performances. Tours and individual shows.

-On the royalties received from the sale of records featuring Jimi.

-On earnings from the use of songs written and composed by Jimi.

-On income received from the sales of merchandise—T-shirts and more.

The latter was a far-thinking move by Jeffery. The music merchandise business was in its early days, but the scale of Brian Epstein's total mismanagement of the Beatles' merchandise business had already started to wake up the industry to the real opportunities.

For those Bahama's companies to trade they needed to own something, before they could, license out, sell, or earn from Jimi. So Hillman and Jeffery got Jimi to transfer various rights for existing songs and recordings, mainly by signing new contracts for older songs and recordings and for any new ones directly to the Caribbean companies.

All this took place with Chas Chandler's involvement as I discussed with Chas at the time. Although I am not sure the actual terms of their deal as Chas and Jeffery split their business's around that time. Chas then focused on building up the career of Slade, whom he also managed.

Much mystery surrounds the affairs of Tamiko, the first Caribbean company Jeffery and Hillman set up. The web of tangled intrigue and dispute over who owns what still rumbles on today, all these years after Hendrix's death on September 18th 1970.

Knowing most of the individuals concerned, and their lifestyles, including Jimi's, I am firmly convinced his death was a sad accident, caused by a mix of too much red wine and drugs.

But of course the many, who have cashed in on that death and in many cases made a good living out of their proliferation of baseless rumour and lack of facts, will disagree. Their cashing in with pirated recordings, boosted with yet more rumour, is beneath contempt.

That intrigue, mystery and rumour mill was then much compounded by Mike Jeffrey's ongoing bizarre behaviour and his death in an airplane accident on March 5th 1973.

All of which clouds the memory of a brilliant guitarist of a certain style, an interesting song writer, a great showman—and a croquet fan.

1966. I'm standing in De Hems chatting to Jimi and he suddenly asks me about croquet. I assume he means cricket. Given that complete books, poems, songs and even a musical have been written about the Rules of Cricket and how to play, it was an interesting question.

Soon to be founder of Charisma Records (Genesis, Hawkwind, Peter Gabriel ,The Nice and others) Tony Stratton-Smith, an ex sports journalist and De Hems regular, starts to explain.

Jimi is listening politely and intently. Tony and I are then thrown by Jimi's next question. "Do you have to play the different coloured balls in a certain order-like in pool".

Tony and I grind to halt in mid description of the deadly cricket enemy Australia, playing against England, not for a massive gold or silver trophy, but for a thimble-full of ashes from some burnt equipment.

We realise then that Jimi is talking about Croquet. Croquet usually presented as being played by genteel men and ladies, in hats and cravats, on the vicar's lawn; perhaps followed by tea with cucumber sandwiches, and then Pimms.

In reality, croquet is a game of strategy, as with skill one is able to wack your opponents ball off in to the shrubbery, as you make you way around and through the six hoops.

Over another Becks beer, (DC Thomson/Jackie expenses, put down as a taxi fare!!) we gave Jimi a brief run down of afternoon sport at the vicarage. Tony and I were much more intrigued to learn where Jimi had seen the game.

It turned out to be at a very exclusive country club somewhere in Kentucky or South Carolina. He had observed ladies and gents in white clothes, playing—the ladies carrying parasols. Sadly at that moment, Chas, and his mates Henry Henroid and Terry the Pill, needed Jimi to go back to their offices and so we learnt no more. Both knowing very well how, relations between black and white were still at that time very separate and much troubled in America, particularly in the southern states, Tony Stratton- Smith, (Strat, to his friends), and I, often wondered about the exact circumstances of Jimi's sporting discovery.

I mentioned earlier that I have considerable knowledge of the background to those Caribbean contracts set by Mike Jeffery and Mr. Hillman. Indeed I visited the area at the time, and met many of the locals involved. I also spent some time with Mike Jeffery in Majorca. There's another story to be told there, one day...

8. Thanks Chuck...and Dan

"If you tried to give rock and roll a different name, you might call it 'Chuck Berry.'"
-John Lennon.

Chuck Berry, classic US songwriter much referred to herein, and composer of probably more hits than almost anyone else, seems to have had a considerable influence on my career. Or at least his songs have.

First of all let's list just a few: Johnnie B Good, Brown Eyed Handsome Man, Nadine, Sweet Little Sixteen, Roll over Beethoven, Little Queenie, Maybelline, No Particular Place to go. And of course Memphis Tennessee and My Ding a Ling!... I could go on.

Through the sixties almost every band I went to see was performing some of the above, and in fact their Chuck Berry cover versions were probably what first attracted me to the Rolling Stones.

In the seventies, very late one night, having heard some great sounding Chuck Berry-style sounds coming from a bar in San Francisco I went in and was completely blown away by George Thorogood and the Destroyers.

I thought they were the best band I had seen since my early Eel Pie Island Rolling Stones days. (I know, I know, your all time favourite music is very often what you enjoyed as a student!) Introducing myself after the show, George, Billy and Jeff were somewhat disinterested in some very late night enthusiasm from,' yet another fan.'

When they learned that I was the European licensee (distributor) for Bruce Iglauer's legendary, but rather specialist blues label, Alligator they paid a little more attention and we shared more than a few beers together.

Having established that George and the guys, were working with an excellent Boston Mass. based label called Rounder, I made strenuous efforts to make a deal with Rounder to get the rights to release their recordings in Europe.

Having succeed in gaining those rights, and over the next four or five years, having backed up my personal enthusiasm for the band with just about all our UK company funds, we managed to set up, (for set up -read subsidise!) extensive tours across the whole region, and the band's brilliant stage shows soon rewarded our risk taking. We sold well over a million of the first two LP's, which was an amazing achievement for a blues based band, and real tribute to their live shows, and their very visible European success helped them grow in stature in the USA..

It was their version of Chuck Berry's 'Nadine' that I had heard echoing across the street in San Francisco that opened that door for me.

In 1979 my Chuck Berry luck struck again.

This time, somewhat bizarrely for me as I was a bit of a blues buff and 'real music fan,' it was a twinkly little synthesizer version of Berry's Memphis Tennessee recorded it seemed by a band called the Silicon Teens on the Mute label.

No drummer and no guitar. All synths. very much removed from being, 'your real authentic blues band!'

After some research I traced the Silicon Teens to one Daniel Miller, then working, or at least hanging out, at his distributors Rough Trade music.

It turned out that the 'Teens' didn't exist as the whole project was set up, by Daniel as a 'virtual electronic pop group.' An interesting and arty project from a pioneer of the early days of synthesizers.

Nevertheless I really believed in the recording, and managed to persuade Daniel that I could - and eventually actually did- license the record to some good companies around Europe.

The plan being to raise some monies for Daniel to further develop the Silicon Teens and maybe some other Mute projects.

The creative ethos of Daniel and his Mute label was interesting. Although they viewed us, or me at least at part of the old style, 'music establishment.'

I viewed them as being a modern version of us... given that we had struggled and survived to make and produce cutting edge music of the day, and wanted to beat the old style music companies at their own game.

Somehow, with more than a degree of patience from Daniel, we managed to work together rather well.

After a few months when Dan came in with some hopes to sign Depeche Mode I saw them very much as a potential pop hits factory, but only provided that Daniel could accept the idea of using some very 'pop style 'promotion and marketing.

That promo style not really fitting in with his general plans and ethos for Mute, but fortunately for all of us he agreed and with some full on promotion from a guy called Neil Ferris, together with and instore marketing from a team at Bullett - Stewart Coxhead and Barry Evans and Depeche were soon on their way.

All backed up with well connected press PR from Chris Carr. Chris ,a retired snake catcher from Southern Africa , was credible and thus respected, which was exactly what Depeche needed to help their journey from fashionable 'New Romantics' to the brilliant stadium filling band they became.

On their way of course thanks to them being a great and very smart band , Daniel's production of brilliant songs, from Vince Clarke in those early days and equally good ones from Martin Gore after Vince moved on to Yazoo and then Erasure.

Fortunately with my reputation for good music and reliable business delivery, I was able to quickly set up a great team of international licensees to invest in Mute and fund most of the above. For their investment they gained the rights to promote and release Depeche Mode and then later Assembly ,Yazoo ,Erasure and many more Mute artists in their territory.

What really worked was the fact that, I had a strong appreciation of the importance to Daniel, and the Mute artists to retain and express their creativity and artistic independence with the minimum of interference from their international distributors.

From 1979 to 1990 the Mute and Sonet team worked very well, with hundreds of hits, both singles and LP's (Cd's) in almost every country where music was sold. The hits of course then providing the key to brilliant touring careers for many of the bands.

I could quite appreciate their original concern about us, especially as they were in the forefront of modern credibility-whilst we, thanks to some very middle of the road pop hits, were to their eyes -not hip at all!

I was pleased to note that over the years, Depeche and the other Mute bands kept encountering people, journalists, D.J.'s, people at other record companies, who spoke very highly of us. Eventually once they discovered our stock of meaningful blues, jazz, folk, world music and other genres in our basement they regularly left with arms full of samples.

The detailed story is covered in several books. The Depeche Mode part in particular is rather well told in Simon Spence's book, Just Can't get Enough.

(for more information see, 'recommended reads.')

Looking back, it quite amuses, amazes me really that the cutting edge, and very advance electronic Mute music connection with us was triggered by a very new style version of an old style classic Chuck Berry song, Memphis Tennessee by the Silicon Teens. .

So, as they say in Coronation Street, 'Thanks Chuck.'

9. 'Well of Course, We All Know He's Gay.'

*Or actually, back in the sixties and seventies, the comment I heard
from about nine out of ten cab drivers, pub landlords, and more
than few friends, was, 'everyone knows he's 'a poof', or 'a queer'.
 The words sounding very strong all these years on, and I use them
in context, not to shock.*
*Notwithstanding the changed nuances and acceptability, or not, of
the various phrases, the sentiment was the same.*

Over the centuries the accusation- for the words were usually
spoken in an accusatory tone -had been applied to actors, popular
musicians, poets, painters and artistic types in general. And very
specifically to all ballet dancers, those who went to boarding school
and members of the Royal Navy (no pun intended).
This is not the place to detail the various stages of change to the
laws of England that have brought us to the position of today.
But back in the late 60's, even after the 1967 reforms, there was a
still very much a fear of prosecution, and a widespread 'stigma,'
attributed by the public to any and all homosexual activities.
This, clumsy writing, by me, is not attempting to specify in any
detail the nuances of the changes made then or later, but to try
and convey the overall tone expressed by, 'Yer average bloke in the
street,' as cab drivers in London used, to try and attribute their
views.
London cabbie "I mean I'm as broadminded as the next man guv,
but many aren't." Real meaning: This is actually what I think as
well!
In my place then, as the, by then rather well known, 'link between
the fans and their idols,' I was expected to provide answers to the
accusatory questions.
So , secrecy or at least discretion, were the norm, for both gay and
extramarital activities. Given the government of the days squirming
embarrassment just months before over the newspaper stories of
Christine Keeler, Mandy Rice Davies and Government Minister
John Profumo, it is now revealed that much political pressure was

used to try and kill any scandalous story. The real world of, TV's wonderful, 'Yes Minister,' come to mind.

I am not sure if it's true but a much quoted line at the time had the French President saying, "Of course here in France, we only worry if our ministers don't have a mistress or two."

Whilst spending time lecturing in the Far East on music and copyright matters, I have spent many years in Thailand, and indeed I am now married to a Thai lady whom I have been with for ten years.

There, where the beautiful girls and general tabloid image of the country belie the strong modesty and moral code of Thai women. Married is married for them.

But with a somewhat practical attitude, they tend if necessary to tolerate the existence of what is called there: The Mia Noi.

The literal translation of which is, 'extra wife.'

The rules of engagement for having a Mia Noi are remarkably detailed and way beyond me.

(Not that I am thinking of seeking one.)

But practicality and tolerance also makes Thailand the country where, 'lady boys' are not only usually the most beautiful looking in the room, but are very much accepted as part of usual society.

Then there's *the completely different question* of gay men in Thailand...

Back then, over the years in the UK, as the publicity and rumour mills regularly exploded so did the inevitable questions to me in my local village pub about the private lives of pop personalities become yet more than somewhat boring.

On a personal level, I had long observed what seemed to be knee jerk auto reactions of green eyed jealousy, from males in general, and indeed my mates ,whenever their girlfriends, discussed or showed their admiration and affection for a new magazine pin up pic of Mick, Paul, George or one of the David's.

Such jealousy inevitably manifesting it's self as," Well of course he's queer as a coot."...usually followed... as he (it was always a he) received nods of agreement from his mates in the pub , with an appeal to me, as the acknowledged link with all that was showbiz- "That's right isn't it Rod?".

Mostly I didn't know, mostly I just didn't care.

Then, as now, as far as I was concerned, people could do what they wanted, provided there were absolutely no children involved , and those participating were able to make up their minds and were definitely not being forced into anything.

So my responses were usually more than somewhat disinterested. But I had noticed, more than paying attention to the private lives of the artists, that in many cases, the managers, who showed the most skill in picking and promoting photogenic singers were themselves gay.

So that created another source for the ever strong rumour mill. From the 1950's with former dress shop owner, then pop manager, Larry Parnes who regularly appeared on TV and in the press promoting his Stable of Boys, providing, for London's Cabbies at least , clear evidence of their claims.

Parnes favoured 'strong names' for his singers, Tommy Hicks became Tommy Steele, Reg Petterson became Marty Wilde (father of Kim), Billy Fury was actually christened Ronald Wycherley. Vince Eager, Johnnie Gentle, Dickie Pride, and many more were known by their mums and school teachers under other, more usual names. Clive Powell became Georgie Fame, and under that name graced the pages of all the best magazines of the day...and ever since.

Pete Dello of 'Can't let Maggie Go' Honeybus and Nimble Bread advert fame, told me he was once under pressure from a manager to change his name to Wayne Thrust.

A final word here, not on, 'Is he? Isn't he? - but on stage names: Much loved London cockney, and one of the UK's most respected guitarists, Joe Brown, tells that he managed to avoid a name change to: Elmer Twitch!

A good career move that, I feel.

10. Methinks the weeping Virgin doth Protest too Much.

Virgins are supposed to be vestal. Pure and chaste. This one certainly isn't chaste and this, the Branson one, is far from the whiter than white that he claimed later! In fact it's down right murky.

Although much like those mysterious statues in Italian and Spanish churches, this Virgin icon was also apparently prone to tears , don't worry we're not getting into dangerous ground, with emotional personal affairs, way deeper than those legendary advice columnists Cathy and Claire were ever allowed to advise or comment on.
This is business. But business that is far from immaculate, and is in its early years downright sinful. That's if you count as a sin, the deliberate defrauding of the British Inland Revenue and Customs and Excise of tens of thousands of pounds in Sales Tax.
In reality, it was rather more than a sin. It was a crime . And where there's a crime discovered there's usually an arrest...and in early summer 1971 there was.
But first: It's June 1984. *"Hi Rod, Do you know where all the Swedes are, we need to raise a million dollars or so very pronto?"*
The caller's Virgin Music—or more correctly a contact at Virgin Records HQ just around the corner from my Notting Hill Gate London office.
Now I like Virgin.
My Swedish business partners liked Virgin.
We like Richard. We like him more when he leaves the choice of music to his more musically skilled colleagues, Simon Draper, Nik Powell and Steve Lewis, and mostly when he leaves the business in the very capable hands of a genius called Ken Berry.
But we like him. We like his get up and go—he can do it style.
We know most at Virgin rather well, as my Swedish partners in Sonet Sweden, have represented Virgin for Scandinavia since Richard started the company.

To get those rights to represent them, we have had to regularly lend – or advance, ever growing amounts of dosh to Virgin UK.

The advanced monies are recovered by our deductions from any and all income received from sales of Virgin's records in our part of the world.

Advances are a very normal music industry incentive to encourage hard work, but still a risk for the lender, over which one has to take some professional care.

Representing Virgin over the years means that we've had the pleasure (and the risk) of promoting marketing and distributing a pretty continuous string of hits, starting with their very first set of releases that included Mike Oldfield's Tubular Bells.

Tubular Bells was a great record, but a slightly lucky hit for Virgin. But hey, we all got off to a great start selling hundreds of thousands of copies. Then on top of that the whole Tubular Bells epic got a second boost when the track was featured in the hit film The Exorcist.

Virgin went from strength to strength. To our satisfaction and now we learn, usually to their relief, they delivered hit after hit.

The Sex Pistols in May '77, had moved to Virgin records, with 'God Save the Queen,' their second release after 'Anarchy in the UK.'

They found a home at Virgin after various well-publicised scandals had upset EMI and other labels. Like 'em or loath 'em, we all shifted a lot of records.

Other hits followed but it was then the global chart topper by The Human League in '81 with 'Don't You Want Me?' that made us even more liable to succumb to Ken Berry, as with charm and skill he re-negotiated regular renewals of our deal to represent Virgin in Scandinavia.

When in '82 Culture Club dominated the charts, tabloids, radio and television in every country of the world, up in Scandinavia they obviously worried slightly less about recovering our advances—and our local costs—those being at our risk in that part of the world.

As the world resounded to Boy George and the wonderful 'Do you really want to hurt me?' *we wondered why the titles of the Virgin hits kept asking questions.*

We also worried slightly more about Richard's apparent adrenaline death wish with exploits involving several fast boats and hot air balloons.

That was, even if the Balloons tended to have a skilled Swedish Pilot: Per Lindstrand.

Actually, by '85, with Simple Minds', 'Don't You Forget About Me' the questions in the Virgin record releases song titles had stopped, even if concerns and rumours about their financial position hadn't. That million dollar call in June 1984, or to put it another way the call for a million dollars in June 1984, had gone out to the Virgin music division's subsidiaries licensees, publishers and associates with some urgency.

Obviously liking being 'Up There,' Richard had just some months before embarked on what his critics, and privately many of his associates thought, was his riskiest venture yet. As one of his people put it to me, "It's not a balloon, so this time the only hot air is from Richard. We've bought a 747."

Or more accurately they had leased one. And Virgin Airlines was preparing for its inaugural flight on June 22 1984. LGW-EWR. That's Gatwick to Newark USA. Just across the river from New York. They had a serious promotional party planned as the plane progressed at thirty thousand or so feet over the Atlantic.

The airplane graveyards of the world are scattered full of old planes from bankrupt airlines. Many with fading paint on their tailfins showing the once familiar litany of those beaten by hi finance and hi politics: Pan Am, Laker, British Caledonian, Court Line, Branniff and many more.

Richard seemed to be embarking on a business with much potential appeal and with his flair for PR, some potential upsides.

But the much discussed view, at the time was, that we admired him taking on the challenge, but the hi-finance required needed deeper pockets than he or Virgin, probably had.

Sadly that seemed to be the case even before Virgin got the legally required CAA certificate to get their first passenger flight off the ground. The CAA being the UK's Civil Aviation Air worthiness regulators.

Two days before that much anticipated and eventually publicised launch flight, Maiden Voyager, their leased 747, had been on a routine CAA airworthiness 'Fit to fly,' check over the South of England, when one of it's four engines exploded in a mass of sparks, with some rather concerning smoke.

Not a huge immediate safety issue: 747s can fly on two, or even at a pinch, one engine.

Hardly Richard's fault. Provided a replacement engine could be installed, there was still time for the CAA to approve them before their planned celebrity-filled launch flight set for just two days later. The slight problem was their slight lack of a spare engine.

A slight secondary problem was a slight lack of cash.

Their bankers were it seems not likely to extend further credit, and with a replacement engine costing a staggering £600,000 or so, the slight lack of cash was not so slight at all.

There was a real potential for a slight lack of flight.

Branson's gang did what they'd always done in a cash emergency. They called the distributors of their music around the world to raise further advances—to be repaid against earnings on future sales. There was one slight problem.

Such were Ken Berry's negotiating skills that most international companies, even their own new subsidiaries, already had their local margins squeezed to the pips.

The other slight problem was, at least for their Scandinavian plans, that when I took the call that day in June, it was Swedish Midsummer. As I explained to them, with the Nordic winters there being long, cold and very dark—midsummer in Scandinavia was a special time. The festivities usually extended to a week.

For the first ten years, we'd handled all aspects of local business for Virgin in Scandinavia, but now by 1984 they were setting up their own business in some countries, including ours.

So we're still working together, except that Virgin's own Swedish company is now taking on responsible for some aspects of the business, whilst we handle the rest. Good for all of us, and that day I rather assumed from my position in London, likely good for us if they needed an extra advance.

I explained that I knew my partners, and doubtless all the Virgin staff, would be out of the offices, on these special long summer days; likely to be on islands somewhere around the Swedish Archipelago. There they would be celebrating with traditional Crayfish, *krefta* parties. Good food and of course much alcohol. Mainly beers and ice cold and very strong aquavits.

Even if mobile phones had been around then, which they weren't, I had learned by experience over the preceding fifteen years, that communication, function, work and Swedish business efficiency were never in much evidence over the Midsummer weekend and the ensuing week.

In fact many times, adopting the usually good plan , "If you can't beat them, join them," I had enjoyed many a crayfish feast, and suffered the hangovers the next day.

This didn't seem good news to my caller. My, "anything I can do?" produced a baffling waffle about, "Just needing some cash input for the airline project rather pronto."

I promised to send and or leave messages to any and all persons who might be able to find a sober Swede or Scandinavian Virgin and request they call Virgin HQ.

As I replaced the phone, I smiled to myself, not because the plane problems gave me any pleasure, but because I knew what the project, or more accurately named 'problem', was.

Not only had I got a hint the night before from my father in- law, "I think your mate might be in a bit of trouble getting his plane off the ground."

My father in-law? Oh yes. He worked at the CAA. The very licensing organisation that Virgin needed to impress. He, of course, always 100% professional, said very little with no names or details. The details however were being discussed in the pub near my house where I had been for a drink with several Gatwick aircrew who seemed very well informed.

Having completed my early morning call from the Virgin office, and passed on faxes or phone messages to various Scandinavians to try an find some Virgins in Scandinavia for their London office, I myself was on my way to the Airport. Not Gatwick for Virgin Airways but Heathrow for an Alitalia to Milan.

On the plane I thought about Richard's plight.

I liked him. Despite us, as I have said, representing both his publishing and record companies in Scandinavia for all those years, I hardly knew him personally or socially.

But I had recently had lunch with him on his houseboat, as he picked my brains about the chances of Virgin buying Mute records. Mute were rivalling Virgin with consistent global hits at that time with Depeche Mode, Yazoo, Alison Moyet, Assembly and later Erasure. I had very much helped Mute owner Daniel Miller, get the label started.

Not only that but all the rights to the label and all the recordings, and most of their songs were exclusively handled by my Sonet UK company for the world with an agreement stretching ahead some years.

I had explained to Richard that I didn't think Daniel would be interested in selling Mute as his company was profitable. Apparently more than Virgin was, although to the best of my knowledge Daniel Miller didn't harbour any *Biggles style piloting* ambitions.

More to the point, Mute was very much a 'co-operative effort' between very similar creative types: Daniel and his profit sharing bands were on the same wavelength.

He, Daniel, was keen on making the records.

So not only did he leave the worldwide business to me, but his then 'innate modesty, shyness almost,' left me to do the sales presentations also. If I say it myself, we did a good job and Mute records were topping the charts in almost all markets of the world, and the deals we had were the envy of the industry.

I had learned a lot from my Swedish partners, in particular a brilliant man called Dag Haeggqvist.

After the brief lunch, as I departed the Branson boat, Richard, almost with a knowing wink, said, "Of course Rod, we'll take care of you. There'll be ten per cent of what ever we pay for Mute for you, and a job at Virgin."

Richard obviously had assumed that I was an employee of my
Swedish partners and not a part owner of my company...and had not
even considered that working as a Virgin employee might be less
interesting than having my own business or at least part of it.
More to test him than anything else, as I shook his hand I said. "20
per cent sounds better to me," to which he said with a Branson
shrug, "Whatever it takes Rod, whatever it takes. I want Mute as a
Virgin label."
Some days later, a little further along the canal from Richard's boat,
in the Mute offices I recounted the conversation to Mute owner
Daniel Miller, including mentioning Richard's attempt to 'bribe me'
or at least, as they say 'offer inducements.'
I also told Daniel, that I had told Richard, he should always call him
Danny –which Daniel absolutely loathed. This was a standing joke
with Daniel and myself, and he spent many an evening in parts of
world, explaining to people that I had 'got at,' that 'Danny,' was not
his preferred moniker. On occasions, Fletch from Depeche Mode or
Yazoo's Alison Moyet, would join me in the, 'let's annoy Danny,'
game.
Richard Branson and Daniel Miller did meet on many occasions but
Mute stayed out of Virgin's clutches. They mainly met due to the fact
that a year later, for various reasons, I was seeking a new
distribution deal in France for our joint Mute Sonet company.
One company we spoke to were Virgin France.
Virgin France, were a great company taking care of their own sales
and promotion, but paying EMI (Pathe Marconi) a chunky
percentage of the sales price, to handle the stock, deliveries and
billing to the shops.
Their Virgin contract said if they went over X million in sales
turnover in France, then in future, EMI Paris could only charge
them something much less than they were then paying.
Virgin were several million French Francs short of that vital trigger
to lower all the EMI fees. Now, my Mute Sonet France company was
needing new distribution.
We expected to turn over about more than a few million then.
So we joined in with Virgin for distribution, and by adding our
millions to their turnover dramatically lowered all their operating

costs in France. We shared in the benefit with a great deal also for Mute Sonet.

It was the type of deal I had learned about when Virgin's Ken Berry had done the very same thing to us in Scandinavia! So Richard did well out of Mute in the end.

At least in France.

Back in that June, '84, in Milano, I had dinner with Guido Rignano. He was the chief executive of Ricordi, one of the oldest established music companies in the world. Ricordi having been, like us at Sonet Sweden, a long time Virgin licensee and like us, observing and assisting Virgin's progress as they built their own company in Italy.

Guido was urbane, wise and artistically immaculate; along with Dag Haeggqvist, one of my most respected heroes.

But that evening Guido is apoplectic with indignation. It's about Virgin. He has heard enough about their airline. He has heard enough about engines.

"My dear Rodney. The Balloons were bad enough. The Boat's insanity. But an Airline. No . No . No." It seemed that Virgin licensees from various countries had been talking to him. He was after all was one of the wise ones.

I had rather assumed that presumably Dag Haeggqvist, the other highly regarded 'wise one' was probably snoozing under a pile of Midsummer Crayfish shells on a Swedish Island somewhere.

Guido repeats. "An Airline. No. No. No. In the end it will eat his record company." Guido was never visibly angry. A gentleman of senior style. But I could see he was upset.

He went on "I like Richard. He has had more than some style. A big vision, and thanks to some good people of his," he stopped, grasping for names....I offer, "Ken, Simon, Nancy, Nik, Lisa, Tessa," he interrupts, "Yes, Yes and of course Luigi Mantovani , Richard could do so much."

As he insisted on me enjoying a final Grappa, I innocently say, "So he won't get the urgent money that he needs?"

Guido, finishing his own Grappa with a flourish barked "Of course he will. Of course he will. No one has a choice, and you know. Richard is brave...I just hope he's not stupid."

And he did...and he is...and the jury is out on the last one.
Richard got his cash. And sure enough, as predicted by Guido, eventually the needs of the airline took precedence over Richard's only real success, the music company. And Virgin's music division was sold to EMI in in 1992.
Was that sale of their music company, as predicted by Guido's, 'Stupid'...or a genius Branson Virgin Vision?
Did he foresee the internet causing the global changes coming in the world's music industry and get out in time?
Or was he still just an impetuous chancer? Who in his very early days in the music industry, 1971 actually, had taken one chance too many for the time.
The chance. The Chancer. That crime—that tarnished the birth of a Virgin. The crime that required, deserved even, arrest.
And arrested indeed our Richard had been.
Arrested for defrauding Customs and Excise and held for a while in Dover nick.
Up before the magistrates and released for a while on £30,000 bail. A hefty sum: reflecting the fact that his was a real fraud, not a youthful error.
Not a student jape, but a way to cheat the system. A way, as even Richard admitted, discovered by him personally, when driving a van full of export records.
Having been to the Dover Customs office and got the usual stamps on his paperwork confirming a load of record had been exported, and were thus not liable to UK sales tax of 30 per cent when sold abroad, he should have proceeded to drive aboard a ship to indeed export the discs. Various versions of how and why the discs were not exported have been given- the sailing was cancelled, Richard claimed at one time to have had the wrong paper work to transit France . Whatever the reason Richard drove back to the Virgin warehouse in London.
In the van, many thousands of records on which he no longer had to pay tax.
He quickly realised that if he now sold those discs in the UK, without owning up to the customs/tax authorities, he'd get an extra 30% to put in Virgin's pocket.

Given that most of us in the business were usually making about 10 per cent on every sale, making *an extra 30 per cent* was a real bonus. For Virgin.

Richard tried the export trick again a few days later. Drove to Dover. Got the export stamps and simply didn't get on the ferry.

Brill. Great. What a wheeze, and pretty soon their van and other vehicles are regularly making the round trip from London to Dover and straight back filled with the records that were supposed to have been exported. The discs in the back never actually likely to make it to French or other shores. A useful extra margin for the new young Virgin company, enabling them to start to open a chain of shops. But highly illegal. Criminal.

Following his arrest, an admission of guilt saved a long and formal trial, and with time given to pay the hefty fine of £20,000 and back tax of £40,000, Richard was back on his own two feet in no time. Or possibly on his houseboat.

And Virgin Records, with it's never-been-overseas discs , exports now properly regulated, was back in business.

Those of us in other companies, genuinely exporting records to Europe at the time and doing our best to also sell in the UK, thought he had gotten off very lightly.

 For smaller amounts of money, caused by simple and genuine book keeping errors or simple late payments, some of us, in similar, but honestly run businesses, had often been threatened with imprisonment.

Virgin, by avoiding having to pay the 30% Tax, had hugely improved their profit margins, and their cash flow. Whilst operating in that ruthless way, they had also crushed a lot of others by offering to trade at lower prices than could be afforded by more correctly run companies. We survived but some good people didn't.

In later years, his memories of bad days excised by the passing of time, he gradually adjusted the story from the reality of it being a deliberate scam, originated by him, actively...perpetrated...by...him. 'He only drove the van more than a few times'... 'It was a mistake'. 'He had not understood'.

Hang on Richard, you boasted about it before.

A few years later he changed the story again, claiming that he drove the van just four times through Customs in Dover. Even more years pass and the story is now reported that he claimed was selling worthless junk as exports, and also some confusion about empty boxes.

Most of us in the industry liked Richard. We well understood that he actually knew nothing about music, but that with his shop, soon to be shops and his record label, he had some good people, in both the creative and the business side.

But that unfair start rankled with many. We were surprised when we learned the extent of the secret Customs and Excise investigation. 24/7 observation from a building across from the Virgin warehouse. Midnight visits to an EMI factory marking discs in sequences of invisible ink, later revealed when those very marked discs turned up in mail order cartons at customs investigators' homes and in Virgin shops, whereas the Virgin documents showed those very discs to have been sold for export.

Those of us in the know had expected the authorities to also act over thousands of copies Virgin had sold, and was selling, of pirated-bootlegged LPs.

The Virgin shops, and the export company would happily supply bulk copies of the most popular white label bootlegs of the time: Bob Dylan, Simon and Garfunkel or Jimi Hendrix at the The Isle of Wight Festival.

I can recall then being very pissed off when one of our export customers, Nico Mertens, who used to come over from Belgium in his van each month to buy from record companies and wholesalers, asked me if he could leave a load of stock with us over the weekend whilst he went to a folk festival.

He'd been to his usual customers: Transatlantic, B&C, Island records, Caroline Exports, Virgin and a few others. He wanted to leave his van empty over the weekend.

So we obliged and on the Friday he deposited the records from his van in our stores, and collected them again on the Monday.

What pissed me off was that after he had gone, I discovered that many of the boxes we had stored, were bootleg LPs. He had just that afternoon picked them up from Virgin, in Chancery Lane or Paddington.

Now if the authorities had come round to my office that weekend I might today have a criminal past. Like Richard. Then again I might have ended up with my own Island with Palm trees.

Am I motivated by jealousy? No. I even accept that most entrepreneurs have to, 'duck and dive' a bit sometimes to survive. But does he deserve to be Sir Richard?

Had you asked me back in the early seventies when Virgin were definitely not playing fair, I would have said, 'No. For me, he's just an unscrupulous and opportunist Dick.'

Now I'm not so sure.

Good promotion man, although, considering the ten years or more of broken promises and target dates with his Virgin Galactic project I'd rather someone else gave me a lift to the moon.

11. Ding-Dong: "Would the person who ordered dinner please identify your- self."

I'm leaning slightly back into my standard economy seat as the plane climbs steeply but slowly out of New York's JFK Airport. The plane's pretty full, but I've got an empty seat next to mine in the four- across middle row. It's Autumn 1977, and I'm quite happy, as I've only paid about £65.00 for my flight to London Gatwick. With the usual price on BA or any of the US carriers being almost £200 I have reason to be happy. In fact I could have paid just £55.00 for the flight but had coughed up the extra for some headphones and a meal.

It's 20 or so years before Easy Jet, Air Asia, Air Southwest, Ryan Air pioneered the no -frills, seat only, pay for extras way of travel to which we are now so accustomed.

I'm on Skytrain, the wonderful brainchild of the ever-smiling Sir Freddie Laker. A much loved national hero, and man with vision. Ding-Dong again. The voice, slightly exasperated this time: "would the person who has ordered dinner please identify themselves by pushing the overhead call button."

Not thinking much about it, I indeed push the button, and the little light comes on above my seat. As the plane levels out, I observe that not many of those little lights have come on. In fact on a closer look I can see that no lights other than mine are on, at least over all the seats in front of me.

The voice again. "Ladies and gentlemen the captain has extinguished the no smoking and seat belt sign." Before you ask, you could smoke in some seats on airplanes until 1988.

With the 'seat belts' announcement ,there was the usual flurry of activity. People as usual rushed off to the loo, stewardesses appeared at the front of the plane with trollies, and in what seemed a lot more action than usual, about half of those on board started getting stuff down from the overhead racks.

A tap on my shoulder. A stewardess. "Mr. Buckle?" I nod and she hands me a standard airline tray with a foil-wrapped package on it.

As she stands up she calls forward a few rows to one of her colleagues, "It's OK, I found the guy who ordered the meal."
In some embarrassment I sit back, and surreptitiously look around. I am indeed the only one with the little tray, but all around me people are unwrapping wonderful looking picnics.

I then realise the stewards and hostess' are only selling drinks. I buy a couple of mini bottles of red wine and poke a plastic fork into my plastic-looking food.

All around me I can hear snatches of conversations. "Hey any one need some smoked salmon?" "You want it on a bagel with or without cream cheese?"

"Who's got the mustard for my pastrami?"

I realise that indeed I am the only one with the meal...and sit back in my seat, more than a bit pissed off with myself.

Another tap on the shoulder. Another passenger this time— "Hey buddy, this your first time on Skytrain?" I nod sadly.

As the people around me also nod and say "We guessed so," I am being offered a share in this picnic feast. The best that New York's famous delis could offer: corned beef, pastrami, bagels, wonderful breads, big dill pickles-mustard, mayo, horse radish and various cheeses.

I start to offer wine in return—to no avail. Most of them have chilled bottles in their hand luggage. Good stuff as well.

Introductions were made and friendships created. On later flights, when I knew the drill I arrived suitably equipped.

Sadly, the same airline politics and fear of competition from the big boys on both sides of the Atlantic that had deliberately delayed the start up of Laker's vision, killed it off as well. *The service closed in 1982.*

In 1996, reacting to popular demand, Sir Freddie re-started a weekly service to and from Florida from Gatwick. His flights went into Fort Lauderdale, which was convenient for Disney World and the Islands, and more pleasant than the very overcrowded Miami Airport.

Having to attend a conference, actually in Fort Lauderdale, I booked a ticket, and for the price of an economy return got a big business class reclining seat. Good stuff if you want to get to work as soon as you arrive.

My father-in-law, who had worked for many years for the CAA—The British Air Safety and Licensing Department—drove me to the airport.

" "Freddie Laker," he smiled, "he caused us all sorts of situations. Not about safety, he was 110% on all that, but he was always at war with all the other airlines as he found ways to cut fare prices; or they were always trying to stop him."

"But he was such a great man: honest, always concerned for his staff and very straight so we liked his approach. We were sad to see him go; all those Laker planes were parked outside my office for a while." He continued. "You know, whenever he flew anywhere, he used to do the announcements on the plane, and then he always spent the whole flight walking round the plane talking to the passengers. Then, after landing, he'd stand by the door and shake hands with them all when they left. No wonder people loved him."

An hour or so later we are taxiing away from the gate at Gatwick, and amazingly it's Sir Freddie's voice on the PA making the usual announcements. Recorded I assumed, as I settled back in my very comfortable front row seat.

Then, as the engines started their windup, the curtain in front swished and Sir Freddie, looking smiley, as he had the last time I had seen him on TV, quickly buckled himself in next to my seat.

I told him about my first Skytrain flight, which amused him, and he said. "Actually, we made a mistake there. We thought the flights would be full of backpackers and tourists, all buying bargain meals from us. But it was a big success with Wall Street and big business right from the start."

"They were the ones who started to order picnic packs from the famous delis around New York. The bad news was, we lost money by not selling food, but I got great snacks as I wandered around the plane meeting people."

And with that, he said, "Have a nice flight," and set off towards the back of the plane. Ten hours later he returned having spent the whole flight talking to the passengers.

And he shook hands with us as we disembarked.

12. Ready Steady Go –The Weekend Starts Here'...

RSG arrived in our living rooms in the early evening of Friday 9th August 1963, from a surprising source. Rediffusion TV. It's operations HQ and Aldwych London building run very much on Naval Lines.

Uniformed Commissionaires, on the door, "Ready Steady Go office? "Certainly Sir, up to the fourth deck and along on the starboard side all the way to the bows." or on Fridays, for the privileged few allowed through the excited throng pressing for entry on the glass doors, at street level .

"RSG Studio. Certainly Sir, that's down below, two decks-use the lifts or there's a companion way (stairs!) over there."

The main company had been established as Broadcast Relay Services back in the 1920's to deliver radio programs , and in later years TV, along cables to housing estates, towns and blocks of flats. During the war it had become involved in flight simulators and naval communications equipment, hence the ongoing Navy style in many of their buildings.

As TV became more widely available most people in the UK rented their sets, paying weekly and Rediffusion were one (with DER, and Radio Rentals) of the major rental companies. Then they got a licence to make and broadcast programs. They started broadcasting in September 1955 ,having won the right to broadcast TV -with adverts- to the Greater London area.

Having explained the Naval traditions that surprised us 'pop' people on our first visits, *as I reported back then*, John Lennon said to me at the time, 'I thought we'd joined the Navy.' Maybe it was those magnificent Commissionaires uniforms, mixing with the mods and the rockers, that gave him and Peter Blake the idea just a few years later for Sgt Peppers clothes!

A greater surprise, even allowing for it being the Sixties, where anything and everything seemed possible to us, then young, creative people, is quite how such a traditional, old style TV company could suddenly deliver such an advanced and cutting edge program.

Looking back, from now, maybe it was in fact exactly because the bosses of Rediffusion, 'were of a different age' and all at sea in the new world that was all teenage, that enabled 'Elkan Allen and Francis Hitching,' advised by Vickie Wickham, to get away with packing the basement with credible music and fashion.

With real up to the minute dancers picked by trendy, 'Mickie the Mod,' from London's clubs. So the dancing and the look were cool. Ready Steady Go had real, pill popping, all nighter, groove bustin style. Not only that, but almost for the first time the dancers were there, right amongst the cameras. You, the viewer were there as close to the action as you could be.

This a change from the old BBC style, where ,some years before, after them first seeing the audience mixing with the cameras on their 'Six Five Special' show, a 'mix of music and information for young persons,' BBC bosses had forbidden the, *potentially uncontrollable mixing of cameras and audience, in case a camera was damaged by uncontrollable jive dancing'...'Uncontrollable Jive dancing-there's a BBC phrase to conjure with.*

At RSG, in the small basement studio of Rediffusion's central London, Aldwych offices, and later in their larger Wembley studio's it was, " *Take care, mind the cameras, we don't want you getting hurt.*"

RSG was also, when it started 'Live'. That is the show was transmitted and seen by the nation as it actually happened in the studios. TV folk liked the cutting edge risks that involved, and believed it created for better programs.

Despite the freedom, the need to keep the broadcast network right across the country functioning properly, meant timings on a 'live show,' had to be down to the split second. So whilst cool, RSG still initially had to accept the mandatory avuncular presenter. Keith Fordyce.. there to hold it all together in case the exuberant but very hip and informed Cathy McGowan or Michael Aldred lost the plot. Cathy in particular could witter for England when consumed with transparent excitement about a new band, recording or similar. And we loved her for it. Valentine, Mirabelle, Marilyn, Jackie, Boyfriend readers loved her for her cool, hip up to the minute style. She became, along with model Twiggy major style icons, and teenage girls followed their every move.

Standing backstage, talking to Peter Noone, (Herman of Herman's Hermits), he said to me, referring the navy style of the building operations, " I don't know what Lord Nelson would have made of all this?"

Some few years, for another magazine story, I decided to ask his Lordship himself and went up and asked him, right at the top of Nelson's column in London's Trafalgar Square. It was an interesting climb up with a photographer called Trevor Jones, and a long way looking down...but that's another story....you'll find the pictures of me up there, with the others out there online somewhere.

13. Winning on Miss World. Coo! Or Coup?

It's 1975, and for the second November in a row I am sitting at my office desk counting out big piles of cash. I have so much that I am able to go out and buy my wife a new car. I have won a lot of dosh betting on the Miss World contest.
November 1976 comes around and again I am able to put in a heap of cash to buy a new car, this time for me. Again I have won, big time on the Miss World Contest.

The music business is indeed a proper business. From the outside, and to be honest, from my narrative in this book, the 'image of sex drug and rock and roll fun,' is more referred to than the mundane reality of early starts in the office, and late nights finding or promoting singers and songs. Followed by early starts again, and again, etc...

Not only that, but just having or creating a great song or recording is no guarantee of success. It's mostly repeated radio plays that get you the sales. Sadly, quite often very same the week you arrive at the Radio Station to try and find some scarce airplay space for your new, and genuinely great record and there are a lot of other, also good, rival new record releases queuing at the DJ's desk.

As described in some detail elsewhere in this book, with space for only four or five new records added to the play lists each week to be chosen from the hundred or so new releases—the odds are not good. So, often, and with genuine regrets, the DJs and program producers simply can't find any airtime spaces for your masterpiece of money-making music. It never gets heard, and thus never sells, or even has a chance of selling.

So the industry, despite professional business planning, budgets and all, is a roller coaster. There's not, as is the popular view, much, 'luck' involved but even with good planning and a skilled pilot—it's still a roller coaster. And in the eyes of your bank manager it's a gamble. So generally, you don't find many music people in Casino's. Their day job is enough.

Back to 1970. Definitely no piles of cash on my desk back then . But we're making almost enough money to take on our first employee. Until then it's been me, me, me and the answerphone...plus an eager and helpful team of mainly underemployed musicians, who needed a few quid to hang in there and survive in the world of rock n roll. Those musos' , like me, had ambitions of a musical kind, except theirs usually, and hopefully, involved making a successful record and then performing on stage in front of enthusiastic and adoring crowds.

I'd had enough of being recognised in the street or the pub, and definitely enough of, 'Lipstick on your collar, tells a tale on you,' except Connie Francis' 1959 number one hit single, should in my case be, 'lipstick on your car-er !'

OK, OK, I know. That's exactly the kind of thing that my old editor Mr. Sears, would have edited out.

 At least we avoided rhyming lipsticks and dipsticks: Rodney.

Of course, with all the regular personnel changes in up and coming groups, plus the slight lack of well-paid gigs, for anyone not in or around the charts, survival was a struggle.

So the market for 'paid by the day' or 'buy you a few beers if you could help around the office with this' was rather oversubscribed. Many were the vital record company skills learned by our erstwhile musician recording stars. Coffee and Tea making. Deliveries and collections, stuffing hundreds of records into envelopes to be mailed to Radio DJs. Ditto with leaflets for shops and clubs.

I soon learned that sending our 'part time gophers'—as in, 'go for this- go for that' —on delivery missions to recording studios was a guarantee of not seeing them again for the next week. We then on occasions noticed when the bills came in, a few 'extra' late night hours of recording work carried out on our account!

One musician became a millionaire in the seventies when, expanding his part time job, he started up a delivery company that ended up going nationwide and was sold on the stock exchange.

Of course traditionally, and rather deservedly, most musos had a habit of not surfacing until lunchtime. In most cases they stumbled into the office soon after. They were welcome of course. Partly of course because you never knew who would get that lucky break and be the flavour of next month's Top of the Pops. So welcomed they were. Mostly. Welcome to help them selves to tea and coffee. 'Plenty of sugar', they never know when the emergency need for an energy-sapping ten minute drum solo might arise.

Coffee for them of course also meant, "Coffee for you boss?" Minutes later, and remember our hero has been up and about only for an hour, and getting to the office whilst avoiding ticket inspectors on the bus or London Tube train was energy-sapping. So, within minutes, "You wanna sandwich boss?"

I dig in my pocket for enough petty cash to get sandwiches, for two. Muso: "Err, Boss, I need a another couple of quid, my girlfriend's outside in reception, best get her one as well."

Sure enough, lounging on the office sofa just outside my door, reading Jackie magazine, would be an impossibly gorgeous girl. Usually waif-like, slender with a neck hardly looking strong enough to carry the huge weight of black eye make up that was a required style of musicians' girlfriends.

These days that fact makes me wonder if that was the origin of our modern 'Panda Fixation.'

Please remember in this PC age, (noting my Mini Skirts and Hot Pants comments and some others herein), that at that stage, late '60's early '70's that I was the same age as most of the musos, and their girlfriends.

I make no judgements here—I was just the reporter, don't forget. Then wolf-whistles were allowed if not welcomed. Coarse, of course. But usually whistled as a complement and usually, with a sigh and a shrug, taken as one.

P.C. then meant a blokey with big black boots, a blue uniform, a hat like a Taco sign and, "ello,ello,ello, Dixon of Dock Green 'ere." PC George Dixon, whose exploits about the life of an affable traditional P.C. (Police Constable) in East London had been popular Saturday TV viewing since 1956 and was still going strong until 1976.

I also soon learned then that most of those slim waifs could pack away more food than an entire Rugby team at a kebab stand after a night on the ale. So sandwiches would, eventually arrive and be consumed. More coffee then offered to me, as it was obviously and urgently needed by the un-hangovering muso and his now slightly fed girlfriend.

"Boss, we're almost out of coffee, again. If you give me a bit more dosh, (Linda, Pat, Susie, Megan, the names changed weekly, and on occasions daily), she'll go and get some."

Dosh handed over to smiley, but usually silent girl. I instruct: "Big jar of coffee please. Be sure to get Maxwell House." Maxwell House instant coffee, then a powder, had only been launched in the UK in 1969. Maxwell House. 'Good to the last drop.'

In the meantime I am wondering why I am not getting any phone calls. Of course, with just two office lines, 'Mr. Muso' is using one to call round and find the next step to superstardom, and bloody Flossie in reception, whatever today's name was, had been calling her mother in York—or worse, New York.

Whilst the coffee, "Don't forget to get some milk," is being found and purchased, I unplug the phone from reception and hide it in my desk drawer. I am at last able to connect to the world, (most international calls via the operator only, no direct dial yet), and seek ways to indeed make Mr. Muso, or one of his mates, a superstar.

With stocks of coffee and milk replenished. No change offered. None expected. Flossie /Linda /Pat, has of course used the change to buy new tights and eye makeup from the shop next to the coffee shop. She doesn't notice the missing phone, as she then spends at least the next hour in the 'only' toilet.

 She was presumably, adding new make up (visible) and also presumably updating her tights. (Didn't look, didn't notice, Sir, honestly, it was 50 years ago).

I think Jackie Magazine did a fine job with the pop pix and stories. I would think that wouldn't I? Cathy and Claire were also exemplary in the advice they gave. I guess the fashions were good...at least as far as we were concerned in the sixties, they all seemed to be mini skirts, and then hot pants. Remember them? Both styles were certainly still in with muso's girlfriends.

So, whilst Jackie was on the case with the fashions, it seems to me that the make up and beauty advice was mainly ignored—in the case of London's trainee Pandas, black black eye make up stayed as the in thing for ever. Not only that, but the office cleaning lady, a jolly

Jamaican, who came in very early in the morning, and thus never saw our visitors, started to demand overtime: "Mr. Rodney, it take me ages to clean your eye makeup off the basin and around."

I hardly looked like Marc Bolan, Bowie or a member of Sweet, but she still considered the 'indelible, waterproof black mascara' (just as Maybelline advertised) as coming from me.

Our offices were on the second floor of 37 Soho Square in Central London. We shared the cleaning lady with another record company on the ground floor: B &C records. They specialised in Jamaican Music, which had been Blue Beat, blended into similar Ska and was becoming Reggae. It turned out that the Jamaican cleaning lady knew more about where to find the hits than we did!

Enter Mr. Mac.

One of our wildest, also nicest, regular, 'Help you out in the office' musos, was the always cheerful Tony Mac: Tony Macintyre—one time drummer with Steve Marriott, he was louder than John Bonham (Led Zep) and wilder than Keith Moon (The Who). Tony Mac claimed, when Steve Marriott's band became the Small Faces, to have been replaced in the band because he was too big—nothing to do with his drumming excellence.

Mr. Mac, always broke, always on the verge of a, 'great deal,' was much- liked. Musicians, superstars, agents and managers of the biggest artists, multinational record company bosses, all were always pleased to see Mr. Mac. He was never considered a sponger or hanger-on, as he always knew something or someone useful.

So despite us all knowing he could never afford to buy us a drink in the pub, or return a lunch, ourselves and half the industry, always included him in all our outings, plans and promotions

He really was so well connected, he knew about deals, before they were made. Hits before they were hits. Bands hiring new singers or guitarists, before the current incumbent of the job had a clue the 'axe' was going to fall. Above all he was honest and earnestly good fun. He could never become a good promotion man, hired to tell Radio producers or DJs how great a record was, as he simply couldn't lie!

In addition to all that, he had a gorgeous long time girlfriend called Veronica, (or Ronnie to us all). Daughter of a Covent Garden Opera singer, she was tall, lithe, with long blonde hair and a shy and very appealing manner. Many a superstar, chatting up Ronnie and not used to rejection was indeed rejected. Ditto smooth looking, smooth talking execs, or hunky looking promo guys. Ronnie was a patient, loyal, and lovely but never dumb or downtrodden fixture at Tony's side. We wondered why and considered him very lucky.

She was also remarkably, and regularly skilled at delivering a very inebriated and increasingly rowdy Tony Mac home in a taxi.

Mr. Mac, somewhat slurred and slightly less than vertical: "Boss. I need a tenner, boss. Ronnie" (note Ronnie) "needs to get home."

So Ronnie became my first full time employee.

I could just about afford her wages, but hadn't really factored in that Tony Mac's, coffee, sandwiches, and phone bills would just about double the costs. But then again every week he turned up in the office with musicians or producers.

"They just signed to xyz Record company," who would be looking after the recordings just made. But that new band needed someone to care of the songs that they wrote. (Songs and recordings needing different care, promotion and accounting.)

Now, my London company couldn't afford a lot of the deals that Mr. Mac alerted me to, but the main brief from my Swedish business partners was to sign up good upcoming songs and recordings for their part of the world.

With Tony Mac nodding in the background, me to the new band. "Well done for getting your recording deal. Now those guys you have signed with are brilliant. The best. They will do a good job for you. But of course they don't have an office in Sweden, so you might end up not being released there. They may get a deal to have your great record coming out with a big company like EMI or CBS over there".

"They are also good companies in some countries. But very busy...hundreds of new releases every month, in fact counting all their offices around the world, hundreds every week. So you can easily end up at the bottom of their promo pile, even with a hit here."

" But sign with our company for that part of the world and we'll do a great job for you."...and many did. As it happens, my Swedish guys, were great, hardworking and so honest that some of those old deals are still being respected today.

Not quite made in the same way, but deals made for the same reasons of creative empathy, hard work and honesty, meant that U2, Paul Simon, Bruce Springsteen, The Police, Pink Floyd and hundreds more ran with us in Scandinavia—Sweden, Denmark, Finland and Norway—for thirty years or more.

So, back to 1971. Gorgeous glam Ronnie, has now been running the office for almost a year. The upside: better organisation, tidy office, reports made, accounts done on time, postage costs down, never run out of stamps or loo paper (bit of a personal agenda there I think). Downside: always more lurky muso's coming in to vainly flirt with Ronnie. Ditto photocopier salesmen, insurance sales guys, printing reps. The lot, we got 'em. One of Ronnie's most persistent and unrequited admirers owned and ran a pretty good music magazine, International Musician. He always wanted me to buy adverts I couldn't afford.

He seemed so taken with Ronnie, that in an unheard of gesture he offered us a discount. His name was Richard Desmond. Nice guy, but we thought he was too pushy as an advertising salesman to go far. He only ended up owning Channel 5 and The Daily Express! So we were right (Not!)

By August '72, with Ronnie's organisation leaving me free to get on with production and promotion, my company had created it's first home produced hit. 'Seaside Shuffle'— by Terry Dactyl and the Dinosaurs had made it to number 2 on the Radio One /Top of the Pops Chart. It stayed 11 weeks in the top 40 and was kept off the top spot by another summer-flavoured hit—Alice Cooper's "School's out For Summer."

So busy, busy for me. Seaside Shuffle became a hit thanks to a lot of excellent work on distribution by Jonathan King and his UK Records company. So we've proven to my Swedish partners we can make hits, but not yet shown we can distribute them ourselves.

But a great start, and the recording and the song scored well right across Europe.

43 years later as I write this in December 2015, I have just heard that classic and wonderful Christmas hit; Stop the Cavalry. A slightly unusual and off the wall hit—by one Jona Lewie.

Jona Lewie? Who's he? Well his first hit song and recording was: Seaside Shuffle.

Ronnie in the meantime has news. She's been somewhere in the provinces and has become the runner up in a beauty contest. Given her innate shyness and modesty, we (the males in the office or The White Lion, The George or De Hems pubs) hadn't even been able to imagine her in a swimsuit, let alone walking around on stage in one.

But then *with less and less* and very soon, *no time* in the office, it seems that there are a lot of people out there who thinks she's as pretty as we do.

On the 15th of March in 1973, live on BBC One, from London's Lyceum Ballroom, in a show hosted by Terry Wogan, she wins and is crowned Miss England.

A month or so later in sunny Blackpool on August 15th, again hosted by Terry Wogan, sponsored by Walls Ice cream, and Ronnie is crowned Miss United Kingdom. Except now we have to revert to her given name. Miss United Kingdom-Veronica Cross. Mr. Mac, Ronnie's mum and many others are besides themselves. The Times calls it, 'A Cheesecake Spectacular'. Not only has Ronnie won some cash and a lot of work, but she's also assured of a place in the Miss World contest.

The landlords of our regular haunts, the various pubs around the office, moved from, "Who'd have thought it?" to a smug, "I always told you she was something special."

The pub landladies *who didn't know* Ronnie were to a sniff, "Well she's doesn't look very special to me. Look at her hair."

The ones *who did know* Ronnie, were 100%... "Brilliant, so happy. Always was a lovely girl, very nice with it..." And she was. Although I haven't seen her for years, I am sure she still is.

So November 23rd 1973, finds Ronnie at London's Albert Hall with 50 or so other contestants and about 5000 other people including me and Mr. Mac (still her boyfriend) in dinner jackets and bow ties.

My wife Mandy (new frock), Ronnie's Mum, shiny frock I think, looking like the Opera singer she was.

It's the Miss World contest. The big one, and every year for about ten years, the biggest or second biggest TV show in the U.K. After three hours of preliminaries, intervals, cabaret, and eliminations, 'the deciding vote is held by Eric Morley, the Chairman of the Judges.' We're live again on BBC 1. The hosts are David Vine and Michael Aspel, and we're down to the last six contestants, from around 60.

Ronnie, sorry Veronica Cross, Miss United Kingdom is still in there. We are in awe and agonies of nerves. She's in the last six of the Miss World Contest. My wife and Ronnie's mum can't hold their champagne glasses without spilling them. Tony Mac for the first time in his life is silent, and rather looking is if he is going to burst. Sadly, burst, our euphoria is, as Marjorie Wallace, Miss United....long pause................States, is crowned winner. Miss Wallace was later to be made to resign over some tabloid publicity with George Best and later Tom Jones.

As Mr. Mac keeps informing us through the year, for Ronnie, even though she had to deal with the "almost but just missed situation," the year went well; with plenty of appearances, sponsorships, modelling and the like.

Tony's music career, despite his affable style and considerable talent makes it's now rather usual roller coaster run of ending up where it started. He's helped a lot of people along the way, they had a good time, but eventually he's back at the starting point. Although he's also been busy helping Amnesty International, the human rights charity on their fundraising ambitions with the music industry.

It's now November '74. A year has gone by and my company has been busy. Things have really changed for us. We've had our second first big hit record in the UK with 'Yviva Espana,' by Swedish singer Sylvia. In fact it amassed 28 weeks on the chart, reached number 4, and was that week just dropping out of the top 40. Happy days.

By the time we'd paid all the old debts, Sylvia, and moved to a slightly larger office, we didn't have much left. But I had proven, as much to myself, as to my Swedish partners and possible new sources of material that we could take on the big music companies; and win—on our own.

Mr. Mac appears in the office. As usual he is full of news, stories, jokes and gossip. He has a request, one which is unusual even for him. "Can you lend me a thousand pounds?" I pat my pockets, (a predictable joke even then) and say, "Sorry Tone, don't have that kind of cash hanging around." In reality we didn't have that kind of cash in the bank let alone lurking for lending!

I casually ask, "Sorry mate, what was it for?"

His response-was unpredictable even for Mr. Mac, "I wanna go to the betting shop over the road and put a bet on."

I sit and consider this response. Mad: yes. Stupid: yes. (The question, not the response), but as ever with Mr. Mac: an honest and frank answer.

With his rather obvious Irish background I say, "Don't tell me you've become a Bloody Mick Tipster. Got a tip about a horse have you? Sure winner?" Before the Irish Nation and the P.C. brigade get too excited about my well meant and much-used, 'Bloody Mick,' insult, I should point out that thanks to my Mum's antecedents, I too hold an Irish passport and an English one.

The response from Tony is not what I expected. We'd been so busy that I hadn't noticed that Miss World time had come round again. Tony: "No horses boss, but I've been down at the Albert Hall and I know who's going to win this year's Miss World contest tomorrow."

Gambling on the results of the Miss World contest had become quite a well-publicised annual story.

In fact there was usually a short piece on most TV news shows, where Ladbroke's Ron Pollard (also regularly seen on TV at Grand National Horserace time or quoting on the likelihood of a White Christmas), would declare the odds.

So TV news coverage of the event, over the years, fell into a pattern. Shot of last year's girls in swimsuits of course. Shot of rehearsals. Shot of chalked up odds. Miss France 10-1, Miss UK 5-1, Miss Iceland 100-1, etc. This was usually followed by pictures of the girls at the hairdressers, or in later years admirably promoting a worthwhile cause.

So 1974. And I don't have a £100—let alone a £1000 to lend. For lend, read lose, to Tony Mac. He says, genuinely: "Only trying to help boss. The landlord of the pub's putting a £1000 on in the morning. He's got such a motor mouth that I'm sure his mates will do the same, and of course that may lower the odds."

So, idiot that I am, I dig around in the postage stamps box and find £200 reserved for tomorrow's big mail out of sample records. "Go on then Mr. Mac. I can't lend you £200...but nip across the road and put this on the winner and I'll split the winnings with you 50-50."

He rockets out of the office with me yelling after him, "Bring me back the betting slip!" which he does, and at that stage tells me who we are gambling our hard-earned cash on.

The following day is contest day, and I'm not in London as I am getting my car fixed in Sunbury-on-Thames and then going to a local travel agent who is organising a trip to Moscow for me.

At lunchtime, still waiting for my car, I am grabbing a bite to eat in a pub called the Admiral Hawke in Thames Street, and I notice that the Landlord, Joe Pegram, has got some kind of sweepstake going on the Miss World contest. I put my 50 pence in and select Miss UK—Helen Morgan.

I tell them all in the pub that I know that she will win. A friend, Sandy Sneddon, delivers my car, and gives me some good news, the part replaced was still under warranty so I've only got to pay £50—not the £200 I am dreading.

That means I've got £150 in my pocket. So, for some insane reason, I go into the betting shop next to the pub and put the £150 on Helen Morgan to win. I have to wait in a small queue as the Landlord and some pub customers are also putting on bets; some on my tip.

Of course later that night Helen Morgan wins, and the next morning I am collecting a pretty big pile of cash from the bookies in Sunbury, and my £50 for winning the pub sweepstake.

On Monday, Tony Mac comes into the office with a huge bag of cash for me...more than £1500.

I say, "Hang on that's more than there should be," and he says, "No boss, I put on your (or our) £200, and I actually had a pocket full of cash, because I knew she would win, so I put on another £200 for you. Thanks for all your help over the years."

Helen Morgan was later forced by the organisers to resign as it turned out she had a son...and in those days contestants were supposed to be unmarried! All of which is a rather long and convoluted tale about a lucky win.

Except that it's not.

Tony Mac then went on to predict or give us the winners in advance for the Miss World contests in 1975, 1976 and by default in 1977. Each time on the day before the contest, he gave us the winning name—not a list of names—just one.

And somehow, he was correct.

That first betting year of '74, Tony had also told those working in our office, and a couple of visitors, about his "sure fire, winning tip." They had almost all become very enthusiastic and started to call friends, and ask for advances on their salaries to bet with. We now had an accountant and copyright expert, Alan Whaley, working for us—and like me he had tried to calm down what we saw as the potential for disaster.

We lectured, "You know Mr. Mac, we all love him, but he's one of those who gets everything slightly wrong nine times out of ten." We both strongly suggested that some people had a flutter, but only with a small amount that they could afford to lose.

Thus it was that on Monday morning in my office my staff were very pissed off. Alan and I having lectured caution and "Don't gamble more than you can afford," their winnings were thus less than their Friday dreams. I didn't own up to my out-of -town winnings and luckily for me I had a Tuesday flight to Moscow, to embark upon even more bizarre adventures, which are recounted elsewhere in this book.

1975, and we keep in contact with Tony through the year. Come November, and he calls me in the office. "I can't get into the Miss World rehearsals, my mate's left the company." Us: "Was he the guy who told you the result in advance?"

Tony. "No." Go figure!

A day later, Tony calls again. "It's all O.K., I'm in the hotel. I'll call you tomorrow." Well, given that there was an intruder, journalist and paparazzi-proof ring of secure steel around the contestants' hotel, in the office we all agreed, "Only Mr. Mac could get in there." Around 11 on the day of the contest, Tony calls and says, it's Miss put a grand on for me." And puts down the phone.

I have decided that having won several thousand pounds the year before to gamble £1500; so even if I lose, the average over the two years will mean all was not completely lost. The story though, has spread and various mates have given or pledged us money to put on for them. Not only that but some of our foreign contacts have also got in on the act.

We have by then moved offices to Needham Road, Notting Hill Gate. West London. We now have my old mechanic friend, Sandy Sneddon, working for us. We dispatch him with £3500 cash in a bag, to go to a few betting shops in the area, and put on bets for the staff, our foreign friends and myself.

He puts on some, but then calls, from a phone box at Notting Hill station to say, "They are limiting how much I can put on. For big bets they have to call their head office." He says, "I'm taking the tube to Soho as there's loads of betting shops there. With, "Take care of the bloody cash," we wish him well.

But all is not well. He calls again about half an hour later. "Quite a few of the shops here won't take any more bets on Miss World." Having realised that they are all near our old offices, and more to the point the pubs where Tony's musician friends and landlords still work, we tell Sandy to return to the office.

The staff are still being lectured by Alan and I to, "Take care it's probably just a rumour or story," but they are calling their boyfriends, wives, family et al. to go out and put bets on for them around the country. In another complication, some of our foreign customers and friends are sending us even more late instructions to "put some money on for them."

With the bag of cash now up to £4500, Sandy and I drive out of town placing bets in reasonable amounts as we go. £100 here and there, while Sandy suggests we say it's the office sweep stake and also spend £5 in small bets on other contestants.

Making it look realistic seems to work as we exit London through Ealing, Chiswick, Hammersmith, Isleworth, Hounslow, Ashford and Staines.

Eventually, we have placed £4500 of bets, £1000 for Tony and the rest for ourselves and friends. Sandy and I sit in my kitchen, sorting through the bag of betting till slip receipts, a few of which are a printed a bit blurry or faint. But eventually we get them sorted. Many of the betting shop names were from the big companies: William Hill, Coral and Ladbrokes, whereas others were local companies with a few shops.

Well, Mr. Mac triumphed again. My phone rang late into the night after Wilnelia Merced won, and it took Sandy and I until Wednesday to collect all the winnings, and then share them out with the winners.

Incredibly, I bought my wife a new car. Not her getting a new car being incredible, but how we afforded it.

On the subject of winners, life changed dramatically for Puerto Rican Wilnelia. A year of success as Miss World, she then became a successful Dior model. In 1980, she was invited to join the judging panel of that year's contest. Also on the judging panel, one Bruce Forsyth. They married in 1983 and remained together.

Interestingly, there's a YouTube clip floating around out there in which she talks about betting on the contest, saying. "I was so surprised, when here my chaperone explained to me about the betting. In my country, Puerto Rico, we only have betting on the horses."

In 1976, very much the same story, except that our pot of cash is getting too big. I tell the office staff they have to sort out their own bets, which results in almost no-one coming to work on November 18th 1976.

They are all at home fingers crossed, waiting for a call from Tony Mac. But Sandy and I are in the office, with a bag of about £7500 in cash, made up of readies from both our foreign business friends and us, in case that call comes in.

To put it mildly we're a bit busy. We have two—yes two—big hit records in the UK Charts.

At number 4, just dropping down from holding four weeks at Number

One is: 'Mississippi" by Pussycat, which stayed 21 weeks on the charts...and ended up selling an incredible, 4.5 million copies.

At number 29, on it's way up, we have another of our very own records: 'Spinning Rock Boogie.' by Hank C Burncttc, which stayed a respectable 8 weeks in the UK top 30 and went on to chart in 24 countries. Not bad for an insanely talented but stay at home Swede whose real name—as opposed to his 'on disc' name, was Sven Ake Hogberg.

So, November has been and is busy. At about 11.00am Tony calls, breathless and nervous as usual. It's Miss Jamaica he says, but goes on, "I can't believe it, she looks OK, but the bookies have got her at 100 to 1," and he's gone.

Sandy and I make a few calls to Alan our accountant and royalties man who is at home in Dartford, and to a few more close friends. We leave our receptionist calling various staff members to tell them, "Take care, it's apparently Miss Jamaica, but Tony's not sure."

Sandy and I know better than to try in the Notting Hill betting shops and take another, even more circuitous route through South London: Tooting, Wandsworth, Wimbledon, Kingston, Epsom, even Guildford and Woking.

This time we're organised with a file. While he's in the shop I note the exact address and staple the betting slips to the appropriate notes.

In the car we are talking about a conversation I had the previous day. A firm of lawyers has moved into offices next door to ours, and in the pub across the road I have had a private conversation with one of the solicitors.

My concern was whether we were we doing anything illegal, in our betting activity. My wife was very concerned. Phrases abounded like 'insider-trading,' not applicable in reality, but we were worried.

The lawyer's informal opinion, in the pub: unless we were stealing private information, or seeking to alter or to fix the results—no we were in the clear.

He then went on to say, "If you get the name tomorrow, let me know and I'll put on a couple of quid."

Legal or not legal, as Sandy and I progress through South London and then the suburbs, the odds on Miss Jamaica winning are shrinking rapidly. From about 80-1 when we started to 40- 1 by the time we hit Guildford and Woking.

Watching the contest that evening on TV, with Sasha Distel and Ray Moore as joint comperes, it seemed to be interminable, nail-biting and eventually unbelievable as: "The winner is ....Miss ....Jamaica. Cindy Breakspeare was crowned by the previous year's Miss World: the wonderful (especially then for us, and eventually for Bruce) Wilnelia.

The phone at home rang for hours, and it was hard work to get the office gang to focus on their work during the following week.

I do remember some guy from the local council calling in, wearing a suit of course. Our promotion girl came downstairs and said, winding me up, "There's a guy from Mecca betting shops up here boss, some kind of problem." Which, as the office gang hid their laughter behind their papers, caused a somewhat disjointed conversation, as it took me a while to figure out that he had actually come in about our license to have a sign across the front of the office, which was a converted shop.

A week later I bought a Range Rover from a dealer in Guildford with my winnings. A Range Rover! Blue-grey! Unbelievable even now; shockingly unbelievable then.

Now before you can't be bothered to read on to 1977...I should tell you that Tony Mac's call that year was disappointing.

"I don't know the answer boys."

"Are you sure? No clues, can't you guess?" I asked.

"No I can't, I have never guessed, I get the info but this year I haven't been told. I don't know the answer." Click and he was gone. The mood in the office sank, and there was a degree of people being pissed off with Mr. Mac, which in turn pissed me off, "Oh come on, we had four lucky years."

I had a conversation with a friend at our Swedish office, who had for fun collected some cash from the staff there. "No can do I am afraid. Tony hasn't got the answer." His response, "Oh well, I can't be bothered to go round giving it all back. Put it on Miss Sweden."

So I gave Ronnie Remnant, our general gopher and tour manager, the money from Sweden, about £150 I think—adding as an after thought £350 from my self, and told him to try and find a shop that would accept a bet and put it on Miss Sweden.

Having concealed the bag of now not-needed cash, in the office I left early that Thursday, as I was going to America the next morning. That being the first long trip I was making abroad since my second son Joe had been born, I took my wife out to dinner locally in Surrey where we lived. We returned not too late, and as is the way with very young babies in the house, crept quietly into our own bed.

I left home about 6.30 am and drove to Heathrow, and by about 9.30 the following morning I was checked-in for my New York flight and sitting in the lounge. I opened the paper to see: Miss World. The winner. Miss Sweden. Mary Stavin.

When I called the office, Sandy Sneddon, said, "Good job you're not here today boss. I think there would be a coup, or at least serious silence in your direction." I was the only person who had won, apart from the Swedish office syndicate. I think I had won about £1800.

Having considered the matter on my flight to the USA, on my return I put £150 into each of my children's Post Office savings accounts and shared the rest with the staff.

In total, over the years '74, '75 and '76 Tony's tips had earned us and some close friends and colleagues at least £90,000.

I was asked then and have been asked 1000 times since then, was it a fix? I don't know. I didn't know then and I don't know now.

Certainly, the innocent and always fragrant Ronnie, Veronica Cross, our very own Miss England and Miss UK knew nothing.

In fact, Tony swore us to silence, never to discuss our bets with her. And we never have.

Did the TV people need to know in advance to ensure a good show? Over the years I met many technical and other staff, who worked for the BBC or other broadcasters. They were shocked at our betting coup.

In the early Eighties, at a Music Therapy Charity fund raising lunch in London's Hilton Hotel, Sandy Sneddon and I had a conversation with both Terry Wogan and Ray Moore about the Miss World

'Game' and Terry was as shocked and surprised as I guess he should be.

Ray Moore, with fond memories of hosting many such beauty shows did say, "Well of course they always used to say Eric Morley, the Chairman of the Judges had the deciding vote." He went on, "I think I have made that announcement a few times."

Invariably, the conversation continued over a few more drinks into them trying to figure out who had hosted one or another beauty contest the most.

I think it ended with Paul Walters, Wogan's much loved Radio 2 morning show producer suggesting that they blame Michael Aspel. All good fun, nothing said with malice.

In 2005, I was in New York and met up with our Miss World Winner tipster Tony Mac, for the first time in twenty years.

He'd been living in the USA, apparently originally working with Amnesty International, and then advising American bands about potential licensing of their products in Europe.

We had an early dinner in a slightly dodgy looking Italian Restaurant in Weehauken, New Jersey. Just across the river from the famous New York skyline.

Fairly predictably, Tony, who still looked the same but had had heart troubles, had managed to get on the wrong ferry but we found each other.

His first words were *"Sorry I'm an hour late boss, but you're about twenty years late."* The reality of that was correct. With a whole host of big hit records in the USA, from Depeche Mode, Yazoo / Yaz, Erasure and many more, I had been in and out of the country many times every year for the preceding 20.

But in addition to me being genuinely rushed and 24/7 busy, Tony had developed some problems with his alcohol intake, and had been pestering my office for money. We had helped a little bit, but after a while I had called a halt to the drain on our cash.

Tony, in 2005, was fine. "Sorry boss, I was out of line hassling you for dosh at that time." He went on proudly, "I haven't had a drink now for three years, so things are better now."

He insisted I drank some wine as we had dinner, "just to show you I can go without."

After much discussion about years passing and the like, regarding the Miss World contest, he claimed that, "Eric Morley tipped me off every time."

When I asked why, Tony said "I really don't know; possibly an ex-East Londoner seeing a younger one hustling and ducking and diving to make a living. I really don't know."

He carried on "His first tip-off was in '74. He just said to me, as we stood together looking at the final rehearsals, 'I'd put a couple of quid on Miss UK if I were you.'

He told me the results for all those years. He did say one time, '76, I think, could have been '75, when he had said put on a few quid...'but don't do it in a Mecca betting shop.'"

Tony finished by saying, "I have no idea if he, (Mr. Morley) knew the answer, or if he controlled the choice of winner with those 'deciding votes,' or if he had just, after all those years, had a gut feeling about the outcome.

Whatever the reality however, Mr. Morley's tips, delivered by Mr. Mac, bought me some new cars, paid for some of my staff to take holidays abroad, and made us not welcome in many a-betting shop around my office and home.

Mr. Mac, who was apparently making a living as an apartment and dog sitter in Manhattan, then borrowed a few hundred dollars from me, and caught the early evening ferry from the Sheraton Hotel Pier back to the city.

Apart from the odd occasion when seeing a new Range Rover, I hadn't thought about the Miss World contest much then and certainly not since seeing Mr. Mac in New York.

For me, I am just happy that Mr. Mac, with his intuitive guesses or with his claimed guidance from Eric Morley, made a lot of people very happy ...including the Range Rover Garage in Guildford.

For me, the business of trying to create music success has been enough of a roller coaster, and I've never gambled again, except with coins in various exotic Casinos that I have been visiting for other reasons...

14. Modern Tabloid Tales and Worse.

In the main this book is supposed to be a collection of sunny recollections of people, places and pop and but not really about the problems. However recent events and sensational news stories have to be mentioned at least briefly and very generally.

This book is not about Jimmy Saville or various others recently accused, or in some few cases convicted. Enough is being written elsewhere about that vile business, and *facts are better kept up to date by the news media.*
I can say, in the 60's, we observed nothing untoward about Saville, We just thought he was generally creepy, bizarre about money, and we disliked him and certainly avoided socialising with him.
I bumped into him regularly then at Radio Luxembourg's London Studios in Hertford Street, where he recorded his Teen and Twenty Disc club programs. I was there to report on other shows.
On occasions, knowing I was returning to Fleet Street he would give me some notes to drop off at an office for his newspaper column, then running in, I think the News of The World.
In later years, at Top of the Pops he was viewed by most in the music industry as an out of touch irrelevance, and mostly avoided for the above mentioned reasons.
His 'Jim'll Fix It' TV series had some promotional value for the record business, but he had no control over the music featured in there, so for me at least, our paths never crossed.

The sad point about the vile (but in that case correct) taint of Saville and some of the other wild accusations is that, although usually referring to a very few individuals, and mostly equally few incidents of impropriety, that the repeated and repeated publicity has overpowered many pleasant recollections of the Swinging Sixties.
And generally speaking that was a fun time to be a teenager.

Neither is this book a rehash of much told tales of television's flying out of wrecked hotel room windows, mostly in the USA, or the choice of a swimming pool in which to park one's Rolls Royce.
It's not even about wild and presumably drug and alcohol fueled 'ten in a bed' shenanigans, again mostly in the USA, which were the News of the World's favourite fodder before they started to tap into targets nearer home

Given the current wave of tabloid allegations about inappropriate behaviour back then, I was advised that it could be considered risky for me to write about those days , and could even invite problems. But I think not enough has been said about the general fan culture prevailing at the time.
A publicity agent had originally suggested the phrase, 'Predatory pubescent teenage girls', to be used as major part of the cover design of this book.
In addition to my son Sam, who did the final cover designs, *advising very correctly, that they were inappropriate words to use* , it also gave the wrong impression of the nature of the contents of the book.
Having said that, I have many recollections of, 'wild offers and amorous suggestions,' made to me as I barred the way into various dressing rooms, on some occasions giving the pop stars inside time to get changed from their stage clothes, or even escape through the window to their waiting vans.
These days personal security is more professionally organised than just asking a journalist mate to bar the door to five hundred or so panting fans!
So I try below, to report a little on the general reality as it then prevailed. The facts and truth as observed by someone who was there. In the case of Top of the Pops I was there as a journalist several times a month throughout the sixties.
 Following on from that, as a manager, producer, publisher, music company owner I was probably there 10 or more times every year through to the nineties. That's 40 years or so of hanging around various studios, waiting for rehearsals, lighting to be adjusted and in more recent years for sound and audio to be sorted.
So, believe me I had plenty of time to I observe the realities.

Lets start by absolutely confirming that any forced behaviour on anyone, by anyone for anything, is appalling.

Of course any such events, as many are now alleged , if they are true even in the most minor way in, <u>need realistic and sensible-not sensational, investigation.</u>

I have to say, from my observations and experiences, in the sixties in particular and on through the years, **that on multiple occasions predatory behaviour was usually more originated by girls than by males.**

By predatory, I do not mean, 'forcing anything,' I mean originating or instigating an approach to someone.

But please, please, don't simply say 'Well he's a bloke, of course he'd say/think/write that. I have nothing to excuse, justify or apologise for. I am trying to report on reality.

I wasn't famous, but I was 'well known' and recognised in the street (Thank you Gordon!)

I saw the picture from the fans position, 'Oh Pete can you get us an autograph,' and over time as a professional journalist I became friendly with most of the stars.

 I was very much a welcomed insider. Someone who was admitted to the dressing rooms at all times, not just for interviews or photos, but a fellow professional just to chat to or share a coffee or a beer with. So I then saw the situations from the, 'stars' angle.

When I moved on to have my own music company very much the same rules applied, so again most doors were always open to me.

From my impressions then, for sure the sixties and then the seventies were increasing liberated.

But in the main it was all very consensual, and a very different world from the lurid tabloid tales we have been deluged with.

With opportunistic headlines suggesting unwanted approaches and inappropriate behaviour being the norm then.

What must also be noted is the general lifestyle, culture and conditions prevailing at the time, not the headlines.

Certainly in the sixties, and through the early seventies, very few girls were on the pill, certainly very few teenagers.

So in general youth culture around the country , as well as in Swinging London, there was still very much a general nervousness, fear even, amongst both males and females about the danger of unplanned pregnancies.

I can clearly recall words of caution and concern being bandied about at parties, in pubs, and indeed sitting in pop stars vans.

There was also a pretty clear understanding of the age of consent, particularly as the publicity surrounding proposed, and indeed recent changes to laws on homosexuality often referred to the, potential for variations in the rules for consensual sex between men and women.

The laws concerning abortion were also fiercely debated then, in the tabloids and elsewhere, and those stories also usually mentioned the ages of consent.

So as our friendly London cabbie would have said, *'Most kids know how many beans make five.'*

Having said that, telling the age of girls was never easy. The primary objective of many-if not most teenage girls -(and boys)- was to look old enough to get served in the pub.

Figuring that out was a daily nightmare for pub landlords attempting to enforce the alcohol service rules.

My local landlord, Joe Pegram, always said, *that many students sent their girlfriends in to buy the drinks as they could usually get away with looking older than their boyfriends.*

There were no 'show us your I.D. if you look younger than 23' rules then. 18 was then, and is now the age required to buy alcohol under most circumstances.

Bringing in the 'must look 23 or so' was a clever move to assist and defuse confrontations with bar staff.

So girls, mostly looked older than they were, and concern over that again was a natural control factor in the lifestyle of the day..

What I mostly observed, pretty much weekly, year in year out, at pop shows, be they Top of the Pops or a touring package show, was overly enthusiastic fans, *almost all female*, in almost hysterical fervour, needing restraining, from pushing into dressing rooms, jumping into cars, and generally ripping the shirts, and more, from their personal idols.

Such popular fan fervour is nothing new.

From the days of black and white movies, Rudolf Valentino made 'em swoon in the Kinemas. Old books write about ladies of the court keen to meet masters of the joust ! (Bit of innuendo there Mr. Chaucer and your Chums).

I am sure scholars can tell of hieroglyphs and inscriptions on Pyramids and Mayan Temples telling similar stories

I stress again, unwanted behaviour of a sexual nature is an evil thing. But most of what I saw was originated by flocks of girl fans, not by the targets of their infatuation.

Not for nothing did they first apply the 'tartan army', label to wildly enthusiastic Bay City rollers fans.

The fans engineered and executed their approaches like marauding armies. A diversion here, an encounter there... and on occasions it resulted in a much planned conquest.

Conquests of course ranging from a kiss on the cheek and the gaining of an autograph, to a night of passion.

Some such conquests to be, depending on the personal choice of the conqueror ,boasted about back in school or place of work.

Some to be listed and ticked off as achieved (I observed a lot of that) and the next target selected.

Some, I suspect many years later, to be regretted, never forgiven and possibly then with the passing of time blamed on the conquered.

I also wonder if some of the wilder accusations floating around these days are not the result of opportunist thinking, ' I can make a few quid's, selling my story.'

Some, many, perhaps most , are simply the result of that regret and remorse.

The morning after effect. 'My god, did I really, eat, drink, say –DO --- that.'

Peer pressure, followed by regret, was I suspect more of a factor than girls succumbing to unwanted advances.

That regret, on occasions being a guilty secret.

Or a guilty regret that *then surfaces with a desire to blame someone*, anyone, *but yourself.*

Of course for many, the instant reaction will be: 'Well he's a bloke, of course he'd say/write that.'

When some women journalists have written bravely and honestly of their own, shall we say, opportunist experiences, in those 'liberated' years , they have been slammed as, 'We always knew she was an old slapper. Obviously a slut.' A stupid reaction to some bravely and honestly written pieces.

For the n'th time I stress any forced behaviour on anyone, by anyone, for anything, is appalling.

So no winners in this really. I am sure others will write more intelligently than I, of the reasons for such wild behaviour.

Some, just a few, a very few, of the school girl crush at Top of The Pops or pushing to get into the dressing rooms backstage at clubs, theatres, cinema's and shows, became hard core groupies.

Most retired to live with, or bury their memories. I repeat again the phrase about guilty regrets 'that then surface with a desire to blame someone, anyone, but yourself.'

Note please, I report this, I am not trying to sell you this angle on the story, although it does sound rather likely!

I just saw a survey of the readership for, Fifty Shades of Grey.

I haven't read the book, but from the survey, I guess many of those buying it were in that school girl crush outside RSG or TOTP or dreaming of the three David's , the Rollers, the Osmond's, Monkees or many others.

Living now on a pension, may be I too should have cashed in and called this book, Fifty Shades of Music that are my Only Friend.

I say again, I have no brief to either judge or justify any of that, no brief to defend or criticise the BBC, or any males or females from those long gone, but obviously in some cases, not forgotten days.

Then it was the sixties- now we are the sixties, or in my case seventies, but I think I have reported there in a fair and constructive way based on much observation at the time.

Post Script. The BBC, which generally speaking is brilliant. It-the BBC - comes in for a lot of stick.

Having spent a lifetime of observing broadcast content in almost every country of the world, I think the PWL Kylie phrase should apply again: We should be so lucky.'

Soon after the BBC started, Lord Reith, the inspiration and pretty much founding father of the organisation, was figuring out how to broadcast accurate time signals to sailors. Such information, when accurate ,aiding navigation and greatly boosting safety at sea.

Admirable stuff. The Astronomer Royal, Sir Ralph Dyson,(who had then formal responsibility for British Time keeping) lived and worked in Greenwich Observatory in East London.

As my grandparents were abroad for a long working trip, my mother and her sister lived at that time with Sir Ralph and Lady Dyson and their four daughters.

My Aunt could recall, many conversations and discussions around the Dyson family kitchen table at the Royal Observatory, on how best to give the accurate time on radio, or as she always said, 'On the wireless.'

Eventually the powers that be decided on some musical, 'pips.' Then the discussion was, long or short pips, and eventually after also involving the Navy and many others, the first broadcast, all short pips, was made on 5th of February, 1924.

 The current four short and then one long pip was started in 1972.

When BBC boss Lord Reith, came to the time keeping meetings, my Aunt told me that Lady Dyson always sent the six girls away to their rooms, as apparently Lord Reith had, as she put it, 'very active hands, where young girls were concerned'.

My Aunt always added to that by saying that she was rather slow in leaving the kitchen one time and his Lordship's hand were also very cold!.....*Not much changes at the BBC then.*

15. Myths and Leg Ends...Defenestration. Of Don Dangling and Mixing with the Mob.

A brilliant teacher at a school attended by my children, managed to attract their enthusiasm for the dry old subjects of Greek, Roman and Latin History by organising a club for them called: Myths and Leg Ends.

To keep with the scholarly tone let me say this part of my book involves : Defenestration.

Just in case you missed your Latin lesson that week it means: The the act of throwing someone out of a window.

Origin Latin. De...Ex... Fenestra... A Window.

In this case referring to a music business executive. "He grabbed him and took him over to the window and hung him out over the ledge"

In books, newspaper stories and TV documentaries, the story of music bosses dangling people from windows has been told and repeated, usually by people who weren't quite, at the event, but really knew all about it, and were 'almost there'.

Now according to those often told and much repeated, 'I was there... I saw him do it,' stories, this defenestration is apparently a much used technique, a regular habit even, in the music industry.

The aim being: for the suspender to obtain the co-operation of the suspended, in paying their debts, or for them to abstain from pursuing a course of action. Or perhaps to forget they ever knew something.

The threat being: The only way is down. I think I much prefer Yazz and 'The Only Way is Up.'

This regular exercise obviously requires some physical strength, a victim of usually less size, and of course an open window.

There are variations in the reported height of the window. Yellow cabs or black taxis below, or far below.

Or even the very same, but, way, way, below. In fact so far below, the yellow or black taxis looked like little toys.

Experienced travelers or CSI USA fans will have already deduced that yellow cabs would suggest

New York as the window's location.

Looking down on black taxi's, would suggest both London and more likely a lower storey window than would be required to produce, 'so small they looked like toys.'

Although it is I suppose possible, that one of London's tall new Shards, Gherkins or Canary Wharf buildings, could provide useful high windows.

But is this defenestration a truth, a reality or is it a modern folk tale. A Myth or even a Legend, sorry Leg End?

'I was there,' is a claim I make repeatedly throughout this book-because in most cases in I was there.

But this one... not there. Not me. Not guilty, of being either the suspender or the suspended.

I knew or know many of those apparently to have been involved in such strenuous activity. In many case they talked to me about their alleged activity.

So 'He told me himself' applies to most of the following.

I have concluded that for most of those involved, the story boosted a certain image they were happy to cultivate. So much so, that to hear certain musicians, promoters, agents, managers in the music industry talk, you'd think that the only function of a window was to provide a useful facility from which to threaten to hurl someone who has annoyed you.

Don Arden. Manager, Agent and apparently multiple suspender.

The first time I encountered the story about Don doing it, it was from Surrey's Nashville Teens. Their single, 'Tobacco Road', produced by Mickie Most reached Number 6 in the UK and 14 in the USA in the summer of 1964.

Some time later, they had been trying for months to collect monies they believed to be long overdue from their manager and agent Don Arden. As the story goes, they had a now legendary confrontation with him, in which he grabbed one of the band members and held him out of his Carnaby Street office window.

A wiser man than I would usually insert: allegedly, it is reported that, or similar words in a story like that, as making allegations such as that could produce a folio of lawyer's letters with denials and demands for damages and retractions.

But given that Mr. Arden is also alleged to have held Bee Gee's manager Robert Stigwood out of a window, and on another occasion's to have done the same to Steve Marriott of The Small Faces, window dangling would appear to have been a speciality of his. Maybe even a habit.

So possibly the lawyers letters are a 'not likely.'

Don being, incidentally, Sharon Osbourne's dad. Of course, she didn't have much choice in the matter of paternalism. On the other hand, she has been such a feisty manager, fighting on behalf of 'Her Ossie' and others, that a bit of dad-inspired, window dangling, 'Sharon the Suspendress', reputation might have boosted her image even more.

Now given that Don—the very same Mr. Arden himself—punched me to the ground, gave me a good kicking, and poured my bucket of poster paste over me in the sixties; even if the lawyer's letters arrive, I have my side of a story to tell also.

Unluckily for us, Don had gone out late one night checking that his publicity people had done a good job putting up posters for his shows. Unfortunately, he had caught 'us' putting up our own posters for some of our forthcoming shows, by sticking them on top of some of his posters, which were still wet.

Don is no longer with us, so it's neither proper nor professional to bad mouth someone who can't respond. But the point is, Don relished parts of his 'hard man' reputation. It developed in many ways over the years, and as with many show promoters, I suspect he found it a useful front when keeping control of a competitive part of the industry.

I do have to say that he also bounced cheques, which were never honoured, on us and our companies several times, so in that instance I have my own memories and opinions of him.

But back to Don-Dangling. This time the Don is as implied in the Godfather or The Soprano's. So you will have guessed we're in the land of the yellow cabs.

This time, with the apparently 'connected' New-York music man Morris Levy.

I can vouch for this one; in this instance, 'I was there,' as I visited Morris quite a few times on business.

'Connected,' in this case means associated with organised crime. I have heard it told so many times, that Morris carried out or threatened, the old hung out of the window trick, on so many people, musicians, club owners, song writers, agents, chart compilers and others that it's hard to imagine he had any time left for the 'day job'

The day job, apparently being, operating his very successful music companies and apparently, allegedly, it seems, it is reported, all the while consorting with known criminals and members or associates of organised crime gangs.

Morris was on occasions confronted with photos snatched by hidden FBI or other crime team cameras, showing him accompanied by organised crime figures; mafia men as they are usually referred to. Morris, was very proudly Jewish, and indeed a major supporter of Jewish Charities. He would, when discussing those accusations of 'consorting with crime figures, photos,' point at a picture on his office wall of himself with New York's senior Catholic Cardinal, Cardinal Spellman and growl, "Just because I'm in the photo with that guy, doesn't make me a Catholic."

Now as events showed, Morris did have some serious connections with organised crime, and eventually received a ten year sentence for, 'racketeering.' He died of cancer before serving the sentence. Several movies of his colourful life story are apparently in production.

Actually, some parts of the stories of the Music Business and its Mob connections are told wonderfully (and truthfully) in Jersey Boys: The story of Frankie Valli and The Four Seasons.

I can recommend that as being brilliant, absolutely the best. I knew and worked with many of those represented in the show, so when I say go and see it. Trust me! More to the point the songs are the best there are. Do not miss Jersey Boys. Play the songs to your children and grand children first, so that they know them a little, and then take them to see it.

Years back, 1971 or '72, I went in to see Morris as I had to collect some overdue monies or at least get a royalty statement from his Roulette record label.

The origins of some of the music on his labels and publishing companies were sometimes clouded. Of course, both ourselves and his other European representatives had no control over that. This was not, I stress, illegal copies or bootlegs, just the usual, 'who owns what?' when small companies run into problems.

So I am in New York. Tasked with collecting a debt from 'The Real Deal'.

Over the preceding days, various executives at major companies have laughed, sniggered, pointedly shaken my hand and said, 'Hope you can swim with concrete boots on', 'Have you got a head for heights,' and stuff like that. Thanks for nothing guys.

Having waited nervously in the slightly dated-looking reception to Morris' office, in all seriousness getting more nervous by the minute, in came a man called   Phil Kahl.   Brilliant music man, really brilliant, who had built Mr. Levy's various publishing companies up into multi million dollar affairs.

Having greeted me affably, he asked who I was waiting to see. I told him that I was there to try and get some money or a statement from Mr. Levy. Note: I am in his office, hence Mr. Levy not Morris, Mo or Moishe. In reality I never got to know him well enough for anything other than Mr. Levy.

Phil said, "Let me see what I can do."

Moments later he ushers me in to see Mr. Levy. That bit was good. The introduction, greeting and handshake was also good.

Phil then says, "Morris, young Rod here's a bit put out. Seems your people haven't paid him, or at least sent him statements. He's English so he's very polite, but I can read those Brits. He's really pissed with you."

Well, considering whom I am sitting across the desk from, I nearly faint. Morris looked at me and said. "So"

Now "so," can be a statement. It can be "so?" a question.

"So," right then came over to me as a threat, and cement shoes clomped into my mind. Phil Kahl, said. "Morris, he's come a long way to ask for the money."

I brighten up a bit at this,

Kahl continues, "Morris, he deserves more that just a, 'So', you can do better than that."

Morris looks over and says. "Son, you want royalties. Go to your Buckingham Palace. They got lots of Royalties." And He and Kahl collapse in heaps of laughter.

I smile wanly.

Morris, says. "We'll see to it. OK." I nod.

Then he says, "Rod, what's your plan B young man? In this business you've always got to have a plan B."

Without really engaging brain, I say. "Well I think our English company owes you more than you owe us. So I've kind of done plan B already and already deducted what you owe us from our next payment to you."

He stood up, came round the desk, and said. "Good plan. I like that. You'll do well in this business, and you can learn a lot from Phil here."

We shook hands and as I was leaving he said, *"You know it seems to have become a bit of an industry sport these day sending people to see me to collect debts."*

Phil showed me out, and about a week later we got a statement in the mail.

Just to repeat: in 1989, Morris was convicted of racketeering and consorting with organised crime and sentenced to jail for ten years. He actually died of cancer before starting the sentence. The industry mourned his passing, he was a much liked, 'character.'

Back to defenestration.

The point is, or the problem is, these legends have been around since time began. They pop up in the days of Knights in Armour, Shakespeare and Chaucer's times. I bet if the Pyramids had windows these stories would be carved in hieroglyphics on the sandstone.

I further encountered them—the defenestration stories that is—not Egyptian hieroglyphics, in Brazil, Hamburg Germany, Glasgow, and even Japan.

I found them and heard them again and again, usually in connection to concert promoters. In Hamburg they are told about Manfred Eichler and some others of Hamburg's Red Light Reeperbhan district clubs and bars, where the Beatles and a generation of beat groups learned their trade.

A German Publisher (whom I liked a lot, and was happy to work with) Rolf Bierle claimed to me that he had done the same to various people over the years. Rolf, brandy in one hand, big cigar in the other, was fine company in a late night bar after a good dinner. In his case of course it was a Vindow—not a Window.

But what's a 'double vv' between friends.

It seems to me that the schoolteacher to my children got it right for this story with his title Myths and Leg Ends...very appropriate.

Apart from Don Arden, the only other person I have spoken of rather disparagingly in this book is Richard Branson.

Not that he will notice, but if he does, at least his office is on a houseboat. So with him being a fit and active sort of guy, if he takes up window hanging, and he decides I need to be hung out, at least I'll get a soft, if wet landing.

16. A wedding invitation. From Bill Stickers...Not.

So it's early 1980's a few days before my wedding (actually my second wedding) and I am driving from the suburbs into my West London office. Usually a 30 minute journey. I am sharing a car with Sandy Sneddon our radio promotion man.
At the umpteenth set of red traffic lights, I am gazing relatively zombified at the car in front when Sned. speaks. "Terry the Pill's been busy."
Terry the Pill being London's king of the fly posting business and a mate of mine since 1965. Fly posting being pasting posters on empty shops, building site fences and other places. It was technically illegal.

I glance over at an old shop front covered in posters for London's Marquee club, The Hampstead Country Club and some shows at I think the Roundhouse in Chalk Farm also North London. All the usual suspects.
The lights having changed I am a hundred or so yards down the road before the words on the final posters sink in. ' Rod Buckle invites the World to His Wedding.'
As a string of "what the ... and who the... and 'bloody hell's' escape my lips, as at every set of Red Traffic lights I can see posters on empty shops, building sites with posters on the fences.
Now I need to bl****dy speak with Terry the Pill.
Sandy I and take the long way to our Ledbury Road Notting Hill Gate office...invites to my wedding are everywhere. We take the even longer way up through central London. Posters all over the place. In the end I give up and drive to the office.
The front of our office, in a converted shop, is covered in posters....'Rod Buckle invites the world to his wedding'
I am out of the car like a rocket, but luckily Terry has left the date and venue blank. Phew.
Business that day was a write off. Terry the Pill is not to be found, and the entire office is fielding calls from music business chums all over London and the suburbs enjoying the joke.

Simon Bates even refers to it just before 'our tune' on Radio One. Eventually, my 'wife to be,' saw the funny side of it.

Terry the Pill was a scouser, serious Liverpool wit and style. All the artists and managers, record company execs knew Terry and used him to put up their show or new music posters on all available empty shops, on those building site fences and any other place that was reasonably flat.

From the days of trad Jazz in the late fifties through to the mid sixties, a nice old guy called Vincent Stitts pretty much controlled the trade. Not , 'controlled in a strong arm way,' but those trying to do their own postering, even some strong arm types such as Don Arden, soon learned that posters they had themselves put up, tended to get stickers added saying, 'cancelled' or 'postponed' or 'sold out 'all over them.

So they all soon used Vincent's services.

Local councils were always at war with the 'fly posting boys,' but again, as it developed they had a respect for Vincent, and later Terry, because they kept their sites tidy, cleared up the litter, never put posters up on signposts, or important electrical switchgear etc. So an uneasy truce or tolerance had developed.

Eventually as Vincent tired of working with his rolls of posters and posts of paste on dark cold nights, in all weathers and Terry took over the, 'London North of the River' business. Terry also had good contacts elsewhere around the country – so business thrived.

Eventually politics intervened and local government rules, put Terry out of business. Which then left the local authorities fighting a battle with many uncontrollable and unprofessional gangs of poster stickers, littering the streets, covering up important signs and even ventilation shafts.

It cost the ratepayers thousands and the new legal controls didn't work, whereas before, in a real example of , sometimes it's better to look the other way, one quiet phone call to Terry, as before , would have fixed a lot of problems.

Now of course, I assume all you need to know about gigs in pubs and clubs is available on the internet......*not sure about the wedding invites though.*

17. Of Fixing the charts. Plugging the Playlists and Why I Can Never Enjoy Watching 'The Sopranos'

So now we come to the murky bit.

I think this call's yet again for Editor Mr. Sears, and his now famed.
1. Get 'em in the first few lines...2. Tell the truth and get it right.
3. Get it in on time.

I really rather hope that, 'One' applies as I really do want you to read this part.

Two?' Best get it exactly right in this bit, especially as the facts we are dealing with are usually rather, 'hot' items and most participants would prefer they were left unsaid.

'Three? ' Well, forty or so years on from some of the reported events, I'm not sure about being on time. So dear reader, once again you can be, the editor of the day, and have a choice:

Fixing the charts opener: Draft One.
It's summer 1965, I am in La Giaconda Cafe in London's Denmark Street, having a late breakfast with Kenny Everett. Kenny has just told a music promoter called Peter Meaden to: "Go and bung Tony 250 quid's and your problems will all be solved". Meaden had been moaning about his inability to get a certain record on the 'Big L' playlist and thus heard by millions, (at least in the South of England).

Fixing the charts opener: Draft Two. *It's spring 1966. It's lunchtime. I am in De Hems pub in Macclesfield Street London, when a smooth looking character in a well cut grey suit comes in. Seeing me, he comes over and says, nicotiney breath very close to my face, "I need a Bl***dy word with you chummy."*
He: Mr. Nicotine. Tony Martin. Advertising salesman from the all-important New Musical Express. A good job indeed. Our Tony though, has a side-line. He sells places on their music charts.
His problem, it seems, has suddenly also become my problem.
I had previously recommended two gents to do some business with 'Mr. Nicotine Breath'. The two gents? The Kray Twins. London's most notorious East End Gangsters.

Fixing the charts opener. Draft Three. It's summer 1976. Ten years on from the above, and chart fixing is still on the agenda. And it's killing my company. Many music companies are buying copies of their own records, in specific shops, those on an allegedly secret list used to calculate the charts, and their activity is pretty much controlling the lower places of the UK Pop Charts.
One of my people has just come back from the BBC with bad news. Rival producer and performer Jonathan King is just about to wipe us out. He's recorded a version of our song and is putting it out in two weeks time. We have to develop a plan—and fast—to beat him, or to stop him in his tracks...the latter seems more achievable and so....

On Fixing the Charts. Draft Four. It's 1985 and I am having a conversation on how best to economically and reliably fix the music charts in the UK and the USA with Michael Levy, the owner of London based Magnet Records. He, later to be ennobled as Lord Levy, Tony Blair's tennis partner and chief fund-raiser for Great Britain's Labour party.
In case you've only just tuned in, Paying 'Payola' to fix Radio Station playlists, and Chart Fixing to boost interest from retailers but mainly also to gain radio play is very illegal in the USA, and definitely of dubious legality or at least repute in the UK.
Michael, whose very successful Magnet Record label was having a quiet spell, was wondering if he had been wasting money. Why some of the records he really believed in hadn't succeeded in getting any exposure.... and what could be done?

Fixing the Charts Opener Draft Five. It's early evening. February 24th 1986. I am sitting in a bar in New York, waiting for a friend, thinking about dinner and casually watching the NBC TV Nightly News. Ten minutes later and I am rooted to the spot. I have gone cold. I am hyperventilating. I feel sick and my hands are shaking. I am seriously frightened.
It seems that I have apparently been doing business with the Mafia. This is not an episode of the yet to be invented Soprano's. This is, unfortunately, the real thing.

I had been in New York and/or LA every few months over the preceding few years. Mainly trying to promote similar success in the USA for Depeche Mode, Yazoo, then Erasure, that my company was having with them in the UK and the rest of the world.

That fateful evening, the big story on the evening TV news had started off in a fairly usual (For New York) style. The presenter, Brian Ross, started to speak over some pictures of fairly normal looking New York Street pictures:

"This block on First Avenue on the Lower East Side is a stronghold of the Gambino Mafia family..." By then I had pretty much lost interest, the presenter drones on. Sounds like all the usual stuff. I relaxed and started to make those plans for dinner. Until I catch the words, "As part of an investigation of corrupt practices in the rock music business."

'Rock Music Business,' woke me up a little. I paid a little more attention. Just a little. I assumed it was old stuff re-hashed. More droning on about the FBI and the like. Sounded like a hundred TV shows or movies, and even harked back for me to the books of Damon Runyon, which had partly inspired me to try and become a journalist before I moved on to start a record company.

But as I am about to discover, this is the real thing. The real deal...and I'm both real and probably in the deal.

Over pictures, some grainy from hidden cameras, some sparkly news stuff from a music industry function, Ross the presenter continues, "Among the guests, two of the most powerful and feared men in the music business. Joseph Isgro, who, authorities say, has described Mafia 'capo' Armone as his partner and Isgro's close associate Fred Di Sipio." That's when I started to shake. When I went cold and clammy.

On my office wall with along with many gold discs, charts and awards was a framed series of receipts from those very guys for work they had done for us..............Suddenly I wasn't hungry.........

So lets go back a little... "Get me a hansom cab please . I must hasten down to the Tavern and pay their pianist to introduce this new medley of songs to the happy throng."

A little background to the Charts. We're talking about: Popularity lists. Sales charts. Radio airplay listings. We're talking about "Your Fab Forty", "Our Top Twenty", "The Nifty Fifty".
 "All the hits and more...non stop"..."It's Top of the Pops." "From Beat to Be-Bop."
Then there's one that I heard in Texas: "Slow 'n Dreamy and Hot 'n Steamy: You'll hear them First on your Flirty Thirty."
I think the Flirty Thirty might have been on, "Colour Radio. Illuminating your ears from, 'Wake up to Make Up and Make up to Make Out,'" again in Texas.
Texas, generally speaking, was the original starting place of a radio programing style, most likely familiar to you from most UK stations, even if the name isn't : 'Top Forty Format Radio.' i.e. a short play list of regularly repeated records. Usually interspersed with those 'singy bits' telling you which station you are on.
It was likely in the '80's that someone first started compiling lists of popular songs, with the idea that promoting the list would result in more repeated exposure of the songs, and thus more sales of the featured items, or result in larger audiences who liked the repetition of familiar items.
Nothing to shout about there, except that the 80's I am referring to in this instance <u>are the 1880's</u>, just in case you missed that I repeat- it's the 1880's, and with radio more than a goodly few years away from being invented, 'hastening down to the tavern to pay the pianist to put a new melody on his list of songs he will play for you,' was the name of the game.
With the Model T Ford car not arriving on the scene till 1908, (and even then after all that wait, it still didn't have a radio installed), all that hastening and those early music lists were compiled and promoted when there were still horse carts and buggies on America's West 28th Street. The so-called Tin Pan Alley.
Around the same time, as horses pulling cabs and carts clip clopped by in London's Denmark Street, also nick-named Tin Pan Alley, just

off Charing Cross Road, similar lists were prepared, also referring to sale and popularity of printed sheet music.

Sheet Music being the magic dots and lines that musicians can use to learn or play the music written on them.

So the origins of our much loved, 'Hits Lists' go way back.

Lets just clarify that these are hit lists as in 'Hits Lists' as in, 'Top Music Choices,' and not, 'You're on a Hit List,' as in very bad news from the Mafia, although as we learn later, there are apparently some crossover connections between the two.

The only truly effective way of building genuine popularity for music of almost any kind is to catch the listener's ear.

Hopefully then to interest the listener, to also become, the user or the buyer.

On rare occasions , just one hearing of a song is enough to implant a melody in your brain, but more usually it takes several repetitions. Hence all the arguments around that 'home of the instant, one play only-hit or miss,' The Eurovision Song Contest, *where originally the judges only got to hear the song once.*

Indeed it was the need to try and create, 'instantly memorable songs for Eurovision', that was both blessing and bain to that now outrageous extravaganza of political one up-man ship.

Once a song is 'top of your personal memory pops', it tends to stay there for a while, but then of course, gets replaced by a new favourite. Sometimes we remain faithful to a past fave and file it in our 'golden oldies' memory section.

Favourites, come in all types of music.

Performances of certain classics, from Bach, Beethoven, Brahms can regularly fill concert halls week in week out. So much so that talented conductors and orchestra's have been known to say, 'We can't play any more of that 'B***' music again this month. It's driving us crazy.'

On hearing that, from a classical violinist, who was doing a little 'extra work,' in the recording studio for us one afternoon, I suggested he had a choice to move on from that 'B' music and try some 'M' music instead. Mozart, Mendelsohn. Mahler... He was not amused.

No surprise there...but that appalling joke does illustrate a real problem.

Rock bands, singers of all styles, usually sympathise very much with those orchestra's, as they too, like to demonstrate their varied talents and introduce their new songs, but the general public usually want to just hear the hits. Again.

Audiences tend to be somewhat unsympathetic. "We do the same job, day in day out. So they, the musicians can do the same. Play the hits we know."

Or as they said in those clip cloppy Hansom Cab days, or even earlier, "He who pays the piper calls the tune."

Sacred or religious music is not exempt from, 'The Greatest Hymns Syndrome.'

Constant requests for the same old favourite hymns at weddings, funerals, christenings and at Christmas, drive Vicars , choirs and church organists to distraction. At least for them, 'Christmas only comes, but once a year'. For the rest of us Christmas tends to start, in the shops at least, around mid September, so the relentless repetition of Jingle Bells and the like becomes a bit wearing, or the same old song syndrome.

On the subject of hymns and popularity, an old style music manager in New York, was quoted as once saying, "If there was any money in hymns, I'd be managing Moses.'

But for any song, melody, or parts of a symphony to become lodged in your mental popularity programs, you have to first hear it. A poster or an advert in a music paper is not enough. Then of course you have to like the song or the recording enough, before shelling out your pennies or dimes.

If you are a devoted fan of some performer the advert can be useful information. But in most cases, you still prefer to hear it, before buying.

Originally it was live performances, starting with our pianist jangling the ivories, and later dance bands and combo's that caught the ear. But over time, thanks to Mr. Marconi, Mr. Bell, Mr.Baird, Mr. Cat and Mr. Whisker, not forgetting Mr. Sony and anyone else who 'invented' Radio – it was plays on the new fangled wireless gadget, that became the dominant factor.

It very soon became clear that music on radio worked best when the music is repeated frequently. That is, works best, as in, keeps the radio station popular and also make's the music companies happy. I say, 'used to,' as the world of selling music has changed more than a bit over the past 15 internety years.

So back a while, by 1936 in the USA, both urban transportation and indeed printed music lists had moved on a bit since the 1880's. The 'Billboard' trade paper for radio and music had started printing it's own weekly charts. This was based on sales of discs and reports from radio airplay.

In the UK, jazz fans, then skiffle, folk and eventually pop fans had charts of their own from the fifties, compiled by a journalist calling round a few shops to check the sales. The New Music Express from '52, Record Mirror from '55 and Melody Maker from '56. Those charts were displayed wherever records were sold.

In the late fifties and early sixties, here in the UK, the British Musicians Union was still restricting music on BBC radio to mainly, 'live,' performances. Eager record buyers, might if they were lucky, get to hear a real new record once a week on the BBC Light Program's Pick of the Pops.

But, for our song-starved teenagers in the sixties, the best of the new releases were most usually to be found on just two shows, Saturday Club or Sunday morning's Easy Beat.

In fact, both of these shows were also forced by musicians' union restrictions to broadcast a serious amount of music, not from records, but played live in the studio. At the time we found the live sessions with the regular studio bands, despite their excellence, very annoying.

Then, thanks to inspired and informed BBC producers, especially, Jimmy Grant and Bernie Andrews, they added some 'live sessions,' recorded from most of our chart favourites. And thank goodness for those M.U. rules, as we can now hear live tracks by most from the era, The Beatles in particular showing that all their time playing clubs in Hamburg, had produced a brilliant and polished band. I just thought I'd mention that, as once the hits started coming and the screaming started, no one could ever hear the Beatles play. For once the tabloid stories about crazy music fans were correct.

A number of the shows mentioned earlier were hosted by the wonderful Brian Matthew.

Brian's relaxed, friendly approach and slight London accent were wildly popular, right across the UK , but got him in huge trouble with his fellow BBC announcers, who sounded as if they were still dressed in formal evening wear, and of course with a mouth full of plums.

In the Sixties and seventies, Saturdays... 'down' or even 'up' at the shops were special.

Amazingly 75% of all records and cosmetics, were sold on Saturdays. Saturdays were the key days when groups of youngsters, now becoming known as teenagers would descend on branches of Smiths, Timothy Whites or Boots. Yes they all sold records then, as did hundreds of Woolworths shops.

Some electrical retailers had record departments hidden amongst the Rental TV's and Radiograms. There were of course some 'Record Specialist's' shops.

At the shop, having studied the NME, Disc and Melody Maker chart lists pinned up, they would request, "Can we hear that one please?" Girls and boys tended to shop separately, and mostly had differing tastes in music.

So having perused the pinned up lists, and requested their selected disc from assistants, large groups of either sex would crowd into a listening booth, usually made for just three people.

The shops tried bringing in rules, 'no more than three,' As in, three choices, three plays per disc or indeed three people in listening booths, all in an attempt to control the afternoons free entertainment, and get some real sales.

But skillful rotation of the person going to the counter to request hearing something different, usually managed to keep the discs spinning for an hour or more.

Eventually, the girls, realised time was passing, and the make up counters with their 'Miners or Maybelline' mascara's and more still needed sampling. The boys needed to get down to the Motorbike or Scooter dealers to see the latest Bikes or Lambretta's and Vespa's they couldn't afford.

So record choices were made, and hard earned or saved pocket money, was handed over to the patient shop assistants, who themselves were quite likely to be friends from school with a Saturday job.

The discs they received were seven inches across. Slightly flexi plastic, not shatterable like Dad's old shellac 78's.

Mostly one song on each side. Paper bag just advertising the disc company, but with a circular hole in the paper cover through which you could read the record label.

Bags, and discs were most likely to be from : EMI, Parlophone, Pye, Colombia, Oriole, Decca, London, Deram, RCA, Coral, Phillips or fontana - with a small f.

In the '70's EMI revived an old label name of theirs from the 1930's, the wonderfully named Regal Zonophone. Many of the company names and logo's on the discs were familiar to our teenagers from the Radios, TV's and Radiograms on display in the shops, or in some cases in their parent's living rooms.

Taking a lesson from Texas, the mainly off-shore based pirate radio ships, started to repeat the hits more, and feature less new material. Top Forty Radio had arrived in the U.K.

All the hits and more.

 Then we had the classic chicken and egg situation. If your music was on a sales chart, you stood more chance of getting radio airplay....but to get on the sales chart you needed radio airplay. For the industry, plays meant sales...provided of course, as they used to say, provided the record had legs. (Presumably legs comes after the egg stage.)

Of course a big fan following, could be directed to rush out and buy their eagerly anticipated fan fave's new single as soon as it was released. In this way established popular performers could kick start a new hit.

The tabloid press, politicians and the 'aren't we clever and arty,' sniffy critics, have always likened pop fans to easily led sheep. Who will, buy anything that x, y, or z records.

I have always, back to the Jackie days, found this to be very insulting to those who in most cases have to think and choose carefully before spending their hard earned or saved cash.

For sure 'the fan club' will often want to add to their collection...but if a disc by their favourite performers is not up to scratch, then sales will die off quickly.

Too many duff discs, and it's career over.

So always lots of pressure on the whole 'P' team. Performers, producers, promoters.

Catchy, toe tapping, annoyingly memorable, maybe simple and maybe not full of meaning pop, has a rightful place in the lives of most who want it.

As do the deep and meaningful recordings for fans with different tastes. So I would suggest that the denigration of, 'a bit of fun, pop music' by mean - minded critics (on either side of the fence) take heed of Gordon Small's words and don't underestimate the average music fan.

Beatles versus Rolling Stones was the tabloid newspaper story of the Sixties, as over previous years it had been Cliff versus Elvis. For the tabloid's it was, "The Battle of the Haircuts." Again.

Most Jackie, Mirabelle, Marilyn, Romeo and Fabulous readers knew better, and understood that the differences, were simply a matter of music style and the influences that created that style.

Another reason why Jackie mattered more than the scanty and scandalous pop coverage in the national media.

Incidentally, in later years I was fortunate enough to own and live on a farm, and those who likened pop fans to, 'Flocks of easily lead sheep', have obviously never tried moving, let alone leading, sheep from one field to another.

Also in later years, sheep were needed by me, for 'counting purposes', as a music company owner, as the need and pressure to get on those charts, could cause yours truly a real lack of sleep.

So why all the pressure, the hype, the scams.

First of all blame the DJ's ,for yakking too much.

The big music news /showbiz story has always been about getting to number one.

In reality the big music business story is the vital point of a records career is when it first makes the chart list. As then, and whilst it still goes up in the charts, you've got a better chance of it being played on radio throughout the following week.

The problem is that hundreds of new music recordings are released every week. All aimed at, and needing space, on radio shows where there's only space available for say four or five new items a week.
So it's that competition that has created various strategies, some clever—others, shall we say—too clever and aimed to beat the system and be one of the few new tracks to receive multiple plays.
But why so little space for new songs.
Despite all the promises to deliver 'non stop hits', 'much more music' or 'all the hits back to back.' In every hour on music radio there's not time for music.
The DJ's cleverly entertain, inform, joke, promote other shows but quite often, just witter for a while. In days gone by they also played a lot of requests and dedications.
Usually, 'at the top of the hour', there would be a couple of minutes of news. Most shows or DJ's have a theme tune which takes up another minute or two.
Tony Blackburn's, Radio One Breakfast Show theme featured a barking dog, woofing over a tune called 'Beefeater'. The theme tune recorded incidently by someone a million miles away from plastic pop, respected Jazzman Johnny Dankworth.
Some theme tunes were brilliant. Stuart Henry's, 'Soul Finger,' set you wanting 'Much More Music,' as did Johnny Walker's, 'Time is Tight' by Booker T' or his livener, Duane Eddy's guitar twanging, 'Because they're Young.'
So, with the theme tune using that minute or so, the news, some promotions for upcoming shows, time for a few competitions, possibly some traffic news, and in non BBC stations loads of adverts, there's not much time left for music in every hour.
Even on: '100% Music Radio,' in fact music can actually take up less than thirty or forty minutes in every hour.
For quite a while, although trends changed frequently through the years, records were most likely to be just over three minutes long. So the average one hour radio show contained about 10, or if you were lucky 12 tracks.
Plus all that DJ witter and other audio clutter.
From the late fifties, crafty music companies started insisting their artists record shorter songs, or make shortened versions for the

Radio Stations. With many single A sides then coming down to just over two minutes. More exposure for more songs, good for the listeners with more songs to enjoy, and extremely good for, you guessed it, the record companies.

More plays equals more sales.

Unless of course those plays are free on demand on the Internet, often with video free to see. Then the performers, most of whom are far from being millionaires and the music companies lose out almost completely....do you the listeners win?

In the short term yes, but in the long term with no 'real' monies coming in to the music companies there's not much for them to invest in new talent.

The TV talent show can, for a fortunate few, provide an instant way to a usually short-term career.

For years, parents, knowing I was in the music industry would frantically seek advice as their teenage offspring announced they were quitting college or Uni. to become a musician. In those days there were some good long-term, reasonably sensible ways to work in music. Now with the internet that's mostly gone. But that's another story and not for here.

The real story here is about resolving the vital need to get your music heard.

So lets hark back to the early days of music radio in the UK and let's go for :

Fixing the charts opener: Draft One.

It's 1965 and I am in La Giaconda Cafe in London's Denmark Street, on Jackie Magazine duties, having breakfast with Kenny Everett. Kenny has just told a music promoter called Peter Meaden to: "Go and bung Tony 250 quid's and your problems will all be solved". Meaden had been moaning about his inability to get a certain record on the 'Big L' Radio London playlist and thus heard by millions.(at least in the South of England).

Kenny is in the early days of what turned out to be a glittering career and is at that time doing daily shows on Big L. The Pirate station based on a ship moored just outside UK waters, and thus avoiding UK Law. The 'Tony' concerned was an affable Brit with an Aussie accent and a chin like Jimmy Hill...actually this is a tale of Two Tonies:

One a Toney and the other a Tony. Both, or more correctly either, were the keys to getting your record played on the then all important 'Big L' where the original main DJ was Tony Windsor.

The other one: Was Ben Toney. A very professional experienced radio man from Texas who had been involved in the build up of the station and was then running it as Programme Controller.

Which means Ben Toney was responsible for hiring the DJ's and then controlling most of the music chosen for broadcast.

For the many of you who lived out of reach of the ships transmitter and thus Big L being a name but not a sound memory, I should mention just some of the DJ's given their big chance in the UK by Ben Toney on Big L: Kenny Everett, Dave Cash, Ed Stewart, Duncan Johnson and of course John Peel. Tony Blackburn started on Radio Caroline and then moved to Big.L.

In search of extra income, the owners of Big L had set up a music publishing company called Pall Mall Music. In exchange for this company obtaining some rights from the music companies, and thus a share of any sales earnings from a record, one could then expect a goodly amount of exposure on the station.

The problem for the station owners was, Ben Toney thought this rather a sell out. He felt that it compromised his professional mission to play only the best. So despite the 'system' working, unless the record in question fitted in with Ben's ideal, it didn't receive many plays.

But 'slipping a few quid's to Tony Windsor produced more tangible on air results. Windsor, real name Tony Withers, had been a major star in Australia where he'd been brought up, but had returned to the UK. With his deep voiced 'Big L' trademark catch phrase he was quickly a favourite for London and the South of England.

Whilst he was a great DJ, he had developed a bit of a problem with alcohol, as he discussed in some detail with me.

That problem became apparent by his consumption, but not by his demeanour, one evening when we met in a pub somewhere in Hertfordshire, where I had gone to, 'slip him an envelope full of cash'. I hoped that he'd remember what record my friends were trying to get played when he woke up the following morning.

Kenny Everett, already a creative genius, was never one to always engage brain before launching off on a (usually amusing and inspired) rant about something; in this instance about broadcasting style. Even then, despite them having way more experience than him, he rather lacked patience with 'older' DJ's radio styles.

He lectured Pater Meaden and I. "The problem with Tony, meaning Tony Windsor, is rock and roll. When he's on the ship even on a calm day the height of the aerial makes it sway from side to most of the time. When he's on land he's the same as the booze makes him unsteady and what's worse is the music he prefers is middle of the road oldies."

Luckily, Kenny wasn't on the air at that time, later in his career his usually amusing but often risky words got him sacked from a variety of radio jobs. Such sackings usually management decisions, mostly regretted by his creative radio producers and much mourned by his listening fans.

His comments about Tony were not said with any malice; indeed he was more critical of TW's music tastes than his apparent liking for alcohol. From Kenny, just a kind of speedy instant review of a factual situation, and all, as usual delivered without much thought for the consequences.

He was always absolutely as disparaging about himself.

After breakfast Kenny and I then wandered down to the basement offices of Lionel Bart's, Apollo Music at 164 Shaftesbury Avenue. Kenny was, I think waiting for the arrival of Dave Cash. For those of you who lived in Southern England within reach of the Big L broadcast signal, those Kenny and Cash breakfast shows were inspired insanity. Wonderful Big L indeed.

Not only were they the birth-place of many of Kenny's characters, revived later on his TV shows, and also by popular demand years later by Dave and Kenny in their own Kenny and Cash show on London's Capital Radio.

At Apollo we had a cuppa, with well established songwriters Ray Cane and Pete Dello, who later came to much fame with their Honeybus Hit- 'Can't Let Maggie Go.'

Fame yes, but no fortune then. Luckily a few years later they were well rewarded when 'Nimble' Bread used the recording in a series of TV adverts. Kenny was very loyal to people that he liked, and he later much supported the Honeybus with on air enthusiasm.

I still have my 'Pete Lennon Journalist' notes from those days and I note that also in the office that day was Brit. song writer Brian Potter. It took him a while to find his niche in the business. But after teaming up with American Denis Lambert and moving to LA, they had hit after hit as producers and/or writers including:

The Four Tops in '73 with, 'Keeper of the Castle,' and then the fantastic 'Ain't no Woman (like the one I've got)' and my favourite. Tavares, in '75 with 'It Only takes a Minute.'

They also re-started Glen Campbell's career in the Rhinestone Cowboy era.

I just turned the page in my notebook and note further that we were joined by Tommy Moeller and his brother Billy. Tommy was the lead singer with Unit Four Plus Two soon to top the charts with 'Concrete and Clay.'

Billy Moeller, at the time Unit 4's roadie, later went on to have a hit of his own as Whistling Jack Smith: 'I was Kaiser Bill's Batman.'

Beyond my diaries and notebooks I haven't had to do much research to write this book, but on occasions, needing to check exact dates, I have of course used the internet.

Just now, as I sit typing this, looking online to check exactly when Concrete and Clay was released, the first description I see online is this:

I copy it exactly: Unit 4 + 2's song "Concrete and Clay" became a big hit the following year, reportedly thanks to exposure on pirate radio stations, most notably Wonderful Radio London. The radio station's music director, Tony Windsor, later recalled in an interview that he had initially rejected the song for the station's playlist, but was persuaded to change his mind by DJ Kenny Everett.

Well I rest my case. Star-studded morning or what?

Fixing the charts opener: Draft two. It's Autumn 1965. It's lunchtime. I am in De Hems pub in Macclesfield Street London, when a smooth looking character in a well cut grey suit comes in. Seeing me, he comes over and says, nicotiney breath very close to my face. "I need a Bl***dy word with you chummy."

His problem, it seems has suddenly also become my problem. I had recommended two gents to do some business with 'Mr. Nicotine Breath'. 'He can help you get your project started.' The two gents? The Kray Twins. London's most notorious East End Gangsters. Soon to be convicted of appalling crimes including murder, but at that time we were only aware of the rumours and some lurid press stories but not the facts.

He: Mr. Nicotine. Tony Martin. Advertising salesman from the all important New Musical Express. A good job indeed. Our Tony though, has a side-line. He apparently sells places on their music charts....but this time for some reason the dosh has been trousered by Mr. Martin but the promised chart entry has not materialised....and so...and so....indeed.

The Krays notorious even then are not happy...and despite us then seeing them more as, 'Arfur Daley chancer' types, than killers even now, I can recall my concern. Concern?

That's an understatement to say the least...

De Hems Pub, just off Shaftsbury avenue was, one of, if not the main, watering hole and meeting place for the very much London based sixties music industry. Those being the days when a few beers at lunchtime were the norm. De Hems, with it's good bar food, quite a rarity in those days, and a restaurant with an Oyster Bar, was on the must visit at least once a week list, for musicians and performers, club owners, agents, managers, instrument and equipment suppliers.

Their presence attracting record promoters and PR people. Obviously us junior journalists settled for ploughman's or shepherd's pie rather than the pricy Oyster option.

Of course location had helped. Record Mirror, then a useful and well informed weekly paper was almost next door. The NME was just a brisk walk away in Long Acre.

The warren of offices of many agents and managers along Soho's, Gerard, Wardour, Dean and Greek Streets were just steps away. If you wanted a new guitar or needed an amp then Shaftesbury Avenue and Charing Cross Road were right there.

One can't underestimate the vital pivot that De Hems had become. So much so, that the distance from De Hems was a serious consideration when looking to set up an office. Obviously the meeting place helped, but so did the proximity to those you needed to see regularly in that pre-internet industry.

Many years later my son ran a pub for a while, and I was moaning to him about the noisy fruit machines and football tables. He explained, "Dad, when you used pubs they were the meeting place, the place to catch up on the sport, news, girls and business."

He continued, "Now everyone's got a mobile phone, and by the time my customers arrive, they've done all their catching up on that news gossip and business, so they need new stuff to entertain them."

Pre internet, De Hems pub provided the communications hub of the day . That was the point that made it work. (my spell check's at it again wanting change point to pint.) OK, it was indeed not a bad pint and pie. At that time I didn't dare try the oysters, even if someone else was paying.

On any-or almost every—given day, I would be rubbing shoulders with half the musicians from the top twenty, with their managers hovering protectively, or their PR people offering drinks or lunch in the hope that we would feature them in Jackie.

Kink's manager Ken Pitt would be chatting to Tremeloes manager Peter Walsh, The Gunnel brothers Ric and John, agents managers and club owners, talking bookings with top manager and agent Terry King.

Next to us would be ex Animal, now manager Chas Chandler and his business partner Mike Jeffrey, with their new signing Jimi Hendrix chatting with Jim Marshall of amplifier fame or indeed his rivals from Vox,WEM and Orange.

An agent would be jotting down dates for his backing singers needed by a BBC producer. Record Mirror's, Peter Jones (wanting take a lunch time break from music and talk football) would be avoiding Rolling Stones managers Andrew Oldham and Tony Calder.

Also from Record Mirror, the excellent and very musically committed, Norman Jopling would be keenly organizing to see more music, and hoping that the NME's Richard 'The Beast' Green or Keith Altham, wouldn't also get to interview the same band.
At least not in the same week.
Brian Epstein's affable assistant Tony Bramwell, would be trying to buttonhole me about Tommy Quickly or the Foremost. Over at the Oyster bar New Musical Express Advertising Manager Percy Dickens would be talking advertising with someone.
Whilst next to him sat Reggie or Ronnie Kray-deep in conversation with Laurie O'Leary. Laurie having been the music manager of the Kray's West End gambling club, Esmeraldas Barn.
And tomorrow and the following day the De Hems scene would all be repeated with a slight change of personnel and combinations of conversations, plots, intrigues and innuendo.
A few weeks earlier, before my encounter with Mr. Nicotine Breath, Laurie O'Leary, always keen to feature in demand, but appropriate, bands in clubs he was involved with, had persuaded me to come down to the Krays' new club, The El Morocco on nearby Gerrard Street, to see and hear about some new singer that "The Boys' thought was great."
In the club, one of them, Ronnie or Reggie had asked me about chart fixing, saying, "We know most of the angles, and the operators, but who do you think can really deliver."
I have wittered enough that the key reasons for chart fixing are to gain radio play and other publicity.
Once BBC Radio One started with it's 'national' coverage as opposed to the local range of most Pirate ships, the Radio One Chart was the one every one needed. It was produced *for them*, making every effort to avoid scams and manipulation, in association with the Music Week/Record Retailer trade paper. But of course, Where there's a chart, there's a scam.
The most common one being, an employee of the chart compilers, already knowing the chart positions a day or more before the chart is published...would suggest that for a few Pounds or Dollars that they could 'help a record to position X Y or Z. In reality the item in

question had already achieved that position. Money for old rope until you get caught.

When I had the conversation with the Krays in 1965, pre Radio One, the NME-New Musical Express chart was the main benchmark. Over the weeks I had observed that Tony Martin, an NME Ad salesman, could apparently deliver.

Sitting in El Morocco I passed on that info, adding; "I don't know if he can, or even if he's the best."

I then added "But for what it's worth it's probably better to pay to get your record on the Pirate ships, then if it's any good it'll do the chart job for free."

Reggie, "We're thinking of getting involved in that radio game. Every one's been banging on our door wanting our help."

Laurie, (their club manager) says "Rod, you've been out there to the radio boats and the forts. Every one we talk to has always got an angle, I told the them you probably had a good and very fair view on what's kosher."

Indeed I been out to most of the ships several times.

Jackie had run picture features on various of the DJ's. I made one trip with Simon Dee,(now there's a Sixties name to remember) and another with Tony Blackburn. He had a PR lady, who used to carry his photo's, biogs and stuff around in a wicker shopping basket. I have a strong recollection he told me he'd had a summer season singing, I think in Bournemouth, but I have never seen that referred to anywhere. Tony seems to have a very clear recall of all events, I must ask him sometime.

Someone even took a boat load of models the three miles out from Clacton and did a fashion photo feature on one of the ships.

So yes, I had some information which I passed on.

Under the circumstances, sitting in the Morocco with two, 'dodgy geezers', as Del Boy and his brother, my namesake, would have called them, I was keen to assist all I could.

My main point was, that with a good transmitter and using one of the forts and not an unstable ship, you could put up a higher aerial, and reach a lot more of the country.

The reality was I had no idea of the economics of operating a station, but I needed no prompting to keep pushing the angle that control of a radio station could create hit records for the owners.

Having enjoyed a few drinks, I grabbed a cab back to Kensington where for a while I was sharing a flat with Bryan Morrison, then manager of the Pretty Things and later very involved with Pink Floyd, and George Michael.

But it seems the Krays were indeed hooked on the idea of an involvement in Radio and our paths crossed again on radio business a few years later. Laurie , who worked with them as the very correct, talented and much liked music manager of various Kray operated establishments, went on to run the Speakeasy, and he discussed the matter many times with me over the years.

Looking back now, with all we know about the Kray's , I suggest Mr. Nicotine, the NME's, Tony Martin, had a lucky escape when he paid the Krays back their stake money and De Hems was restored to it's usual demenour; a peaceful meeting place.

I think Laurie O'Leary helped sort out the 'little misunderstanding.' The record in question was something to do with Kathy Kirby...and her manager, but I have no idea which one, either record or manager, that is.

Time to move on...and the 'move on is ten years...I have had several hits with my own music company but in that summer of 76...

Fixing the charts opener. Draft three. It's summer 1976. Ten years on from the above, and chart fixing is still on the agenda. And it's killing my company. Many music companies are buying copies of their own records, in specific shops, those on an allegedly secret list used to calculate the charts, and their activity is pretty much controlling the lower places of the UK Pop Charts.

For weeks now my music company has had a record 'bubbling under,' on the verge of breaking into the UK charts, but we're not quite strong enough to move up the few vital places that matter. Not strong enough in airplay and real demand from buyers. Not wealthy enough to buy enough extra 'ticks' in the UK's 200 or so chart shops . At the end of each week the nationwide tally of 'ticks' made for each and every sale, make up the chart.

Now, Sandy Sneddon, one of my promotion people has just come back from the BBC with bad news. Rival producer and performer Jonathan King is just about to wipe us out. He's recorded a version of our song and is putting it out in two weeks time.

Not only that, but Jonathan's deal is with Phillips/fontana means that their aggressive sales force, their equally aggressive 'in-store promotions' team and their huge financial resources will wipe out all our efforts... and we've got the 'real hit original' version of the song that's already sold millions right across Europe.

If we lose this battle, we lose not only the hit for the band, but we lose a lot of hard gained respect in the business...We have to develop a plan- and fast-to beat him, or to stop him in his tracks...the latter seems more achievable and so....

As I said, it's despite the best efforts of the Music Week trade paper, The BBC and the Record Industry Association, that the lower reaches of the chart are still being manipulated by Record Companies.

In addition to their sales reps, most of the major companies have, or hire, 'sales promotion or merchandising teams,' mostly girls, touring the particular shops that send in weekly diaries or sales information to the chart company from which the charts are compiled.

In each shop they would buy one copy of a particular record or one copy each of a few different singles if they had more than one target that week.

In later years, timed sales marked on till rolls and efforts to stop chart fixing were to become more effective (slightly) so multiple sales of more than one copy of a record was not on.

With so few records added to the Radio One playlist each week, even a low place in the top 30 or 40 increased one's chances of getting airplay; higher entries, could even get you on Top of The Pops. But the higher places in the charts, where commercial sales from the general public were significant, required thousands of extra sales to gain places...the lower places just a few hundred.

In those later years, as the retrieval by the chart compilers of the sales figures from shops became more sophisticated a variety of other manipulations were tried

We couldn't afford our own chart 'merchandising,' team or one of the growing numbers of freelance teams, now called strike forces, specialising in all this subterfuge. But we had to join in.

Over the previous weeks, with a collection of wives, office staff, girlfriends, and friends—each of them with a car full of their friends...we had set out to, 'cover,' i.e. buy discs in as many of the specific shops as we could.

The 'worker bees', as our promo girl Sonnie Rae once called them, would earn about £20 a day, plus petrol expenses and of course would be stocked up with cash from us to buy the discs.

We knew we had a hit.

Each time it got even one play on the radio, orders shot up (real sales!) The record had sold millions across Europe. (That was part of the problem, apart from a couple of producers who supported us and our efforts, Radio One wasn't too wild about 'foreign records). Abba (deservedly) fulfilled their restrictive quota.

But our workers bees were not winning. Our cash was running out. Sandy Sneddon's news from the Beeb was thus: Jonathan King who had just had a major hit with Una Paloma Blanca had now recorded a version of 'our song.'

I knew Jonathan liked the song as he had called me several times to see if I would transfer our recording to his label UK Records. (UK was also home to 10cc, First Class and many other great pop acts.) Jonathan had helped me in that way in 1972 with the distribution of our first home made British Hits 'Seaside Shuffle' by Terry Dactyl and the Dinosaurs.

I liked and admired Jonathan. One of the most creative and inventive of producers, indeed I still have him listed as being in my all time top five of the most creative and inventive of pop producers. He knew we had a hit song, and he was right...and at that moment we were not delivering the hit potential.

So our fight then, and the memory now is not-absolutely not-directed against J.K. Our fight was with the mighty distribution company he was using.

We had improved our own distribution and also grown and developed as a company but were still minnows by comparison. As you have seen elsewhere in this book, we'd even had a massive hit on our own in '74 with Yviva Espana. So when he made us the offer to take over our record some weeks before, we had said no thanks to Jonathan and ploughed on alone.

We checked the release sheets sent to dealers and the records being offered to the BBC. There it was. UK records Number 147. Release date July 30th.

I sat in the office reception area. Head in hands.

I knew that with the backing of his distributor JK had tens of thousand of pounds and a big team at his disposal to kick start his new record label with them. All looked lost.

The staff (all six of them) sat around looking at me.

Our royalties and accounting man Alan Whaley, suggests someone gets some sandwiches and he'd rustle up a cup of tea. Alan always was a wise man in a stressed situation. Some years later—rushing downstairs in the office wielding a cricket bat, "Put that gun down Mr. Ranglin, and take your foot off Rods head"...but that's another story.

I wander into my office, and start leafing through the trade paper Music Week. The pages are a blur. "How can I explain all the expenses to my partners. How can I justify to the band and its producer not accepting Jonathans offer, which they knew about."

Sandwiches arrived, and with them the irrepressible Terry the Pill-Slater, who it seemed just happened to be passing and found himself in need of a cup of tea. We thought he'd bugged the kettle as this happened a lot.

Terry, a friend of the Beatles from their Hamburg days, and now a friend to the entire UK industry— artist and business, was used by all the UK music companies and the concert promoters to do their, 'fly posting' or sticking posters up on old buildings, empty shop fronts, building sites and the like. Terry, (or Pill) as we called him, had the London, north of the River, exclusivity of this slightly borderline business.

He accepted a cup of tea (no surprise there) and I poured out my woes to him. He made pertinent and sensible comments and agreed we were likely to be crushed. As he gathered up his stuff to leave he made a comment "Mind you, they (meaning UK records and their distributor), will have to be careful, a lot of those dealers out there

not on the chart shop listings, and thus not getting free bonus
supplies and promo stuff, are getting very jealous.
Quite angry they are."

Terry particularly mentioned a well-established and respected
dealer called Paul Quirke, who was very professional and who
always had the long-term interest of both producers and retailers at
heart. I thought I recalled seeing some letters in Music Week from
him, along with others, questioning the free goods to specific
retailers as being unfair, and also questioning record-buying tactics.
 Sandy Sneddon our promo man who had brought in the bad news,
about the copy-record, agreed with Terry very clearly.

Sandy, who as an ex rally driver, quite liked escaping the office and
zooming round to loads of shops organising the 'Worker Bees,' was
very aware of the care needed to be taken not to get caught, and was
continually stressing the rules to our little team of amateurs.

'Ding'... or 'click,' if a light of inspiration coming on makes a noise in
one's head. I had an idea.

Having established from Alan what small amount of funds we had
available, I hatched an evil plot. Knowing we couldn't beat the copy-
records mighty distributor, we went another route.

We printed ten T shirts with bright yellow UK records on them. We
put the same on some folders.

I scoured Music Week and elsewhere for letters and stories of
complaint from angry or possibly, as Terry the Pill put it, 'jealous'
dealers. The following week the Worker Bees went out.

New instructions...Get caught. Make a fuss. Ask for receipts. Buy
five copies of Jonathan's record...they all called back to query this:
"Surely boss you mean buy ours?"

No, we said buy Jonathan's.

Now repeat, I liked and admired Jonathan then.

Recent publicity about his private life is not good; in fact it's
horrible. For a while both our offices had been at 37 Soho Square. I
had first met him in my Jackie offices at 185 Fleet Street when he
had his first hit with Everyone's Gone to the Moon (1965), and I had
supported his Hedgehopper Anonymous hit. Then, with his strong
promotion and better distribution than we had at the time ('72), he
had succeeded to make Seaside Shuffle a hit for us..

To clarify. I liked him then...and I like HIS MUSIC ACUMEN.
Don't believe all the various new accusations made against him.
Until proven.
Look at the attacks on Paul Gambaccini, Dr. Fox, some politicians
and a few others. Disproven and likely based on accusations made
by fantasists or fortune hunters.
Don't start me on the odious Jimmy Saville or some others. But in
the case of JK, whilst he has had some traits which are 100% not
acceptable, as I say ,do not believe all you have read.
Accusations get printed. Acquittals don't.
I have no brief from, or ongoing friendship with JK, to make me
want to stick my neck out like this. *But I am a believer in British*
Justice, so I hope those, and some other wild accusations against
others, get properly sorted out. Either way.
One fact that is clear: there have been very few people in the UK so
adept at spotting hits as Jonathan. Having said all that. There I am
in 1976. Early August and we are fighting to win, and to kill his
record.
And win we do.
Our very obvious attempts wearing fake UK Records T Shirts to, 'fix
the charts,' in all the 'Mr. Angry' shops sparks of a mass of
complaints against the copy-record to the chart compilers, and the
compilers of the chart exclude Jonathan's version from the chart.
Not only that, but a couple of Radio One Producers, having seen our
months of hard work almost lost, take pity on us as underdogs and
play our record a few extra times.
By August the 28th Mississippi by Dutch group Pussycat is a smash.
Makes the Number One spot on the 3rd of October. And stays there
for four more weeks. 21 weeks on the charts. 4.7 million single sales.
At the Music Publishers Association Christmas Lunch I bump into
Terry the Pill.
Big grin and very Scouse, "Rodney you are a very bad bad boy doing
that, and making the chart shops angry. Wicked and well done. Oh
yes, Jonathan's looking for you."
Later, I stand slightly behind Jonathan as he is addressing and
amusing a throng of industry big wigs. He turns and noticing me,
announces to all of them, all of whom are aware of the story.

"Buckle. I wish I had never taught you all you know about promoting singles..." and with a handshake and his usual lopsided grin, he added. "Well done. Happy Christmas."

And with about 5 million discs sold by my company that year. A Happy Christmas indeed it was.

On Fixing the Charts. Draft four. It's 1985 and I am having a conversation on how best to economically and reliably fix the playlists and music charts in the UK and the USA with Michael Levy, the owner of London based Magnet Records. He, later to be ennobled as Lord Levy, Tony Blair's tennis partner and chief fund-raiser for the Great Britain's Labour party.
In case you've only just tuned in, Paying 'Payola' to fix Radio Station playlists, and Chart Fixing to boost interest from retailers but mainly also to gain radio play is very illegal in the USA, and definitely of dubious legality or at least repute in the UK.
Michael, whose very successful Magnet Record label was having a quiet spell, was wondering if he had been wasting money. Why some of the records he really believed in hadn't succeeded in getting any exposure.... and what could be done?

Magnet may have been having a quiet spell, but for them it had started so well. Back in October 1973 , with a big hit for their first release, MAG 1, My Coo Ca Choo.I Actually recorded and performed by producer Pete Shelly.

My Coo Ca Choo, Mimed to at least, by a singer with a string of names, Bernard Jewry, then re-named Shane Fenton and eventually as Alvin Stardust, and then a string of hits. With Alvin really doing the singing on the follow ups.

Michael was a well-respected chartered accountant who had more than few music industry clients on his books. I don't know if the music business bug bit him, or if he had been approached to sort out funding, but in '73, with experienced writer –producer Pete Shelley, Magnet was formed.

Shelley assembled a great team to assist him, including enticing top promotion guy Steve Collier from the mighty CBS to join the all-new Magnet. Collier, eventually bought in Pete Waterman—later to hit the top spots again and again with Kylie, Jason and many more on his own PWL label. Pete was originally very negative about the Magnet releases as they weren't in the style of music that he liked. But in the end, in early 1975 Waterman joined them

I had first met Michael in 'Autumn '73 when I called by his offices to talk to him about the upcoming Midem trade fair in the South of France. Michael was non committal—as were most of the industry at that time. and said that, as with many he might drop in, as he was sure many of his clients would be there.

With 150 or so companies exhibiting I can't recall if indeed he did make the journey to Cannes.

By the time I returned to his office in in autumn '74, Magnet was on a bit of a roll. Michael, as with many others in the industry was very pleased to discover that he could again get UK government funding from the Board of Trade export department to pay towards any exhibition space for the show the following January.

At Midem, in the January of 1975, spring-like climate of the south of France, newly employed at Magnet, Pete Waterman's talent for spotting hits came to the fore.

Despite some competition, Pete signed Silver Convention to Magnet. Actually the deal took some investment faith from Michael to top other offers on the table. Helped by great promotion work, hit followed hit. In '75, 'Save Me, Fly Robin Fly,' in '76 the mighty 'Get up and Boogie,' and the lessor hit, 'Tiger Bay.'

In '77 they scored again with 'Everybody's Talking About Love.' So for Waterman, a success.

For Michael and the rest of the Magnet team a success, and for Silver Convention also, a success. As the band, producers, rights owners were all German those mega bucks in royalties were going back to the Germans. So it was more of an export success for Germany than for GB. Ltd.

For the British Board of Trade, exports division, the Silver Convention story was less than satisfactory. In fact it clearly broke the rules if the deal was made whilst receiving money to promote British exports at Midem. The Government sent a trade official, name of Joe Patanchon, to interview me about any potential frauds, i.e., misuse of Government export promotion funds.

Fortunately, with my personal deal making and trading experience, I was able to list for M. Patanchon, all the exhibitors who had received subsidy, and show him that, taking into account the imports and the exports overall, there was not a problem. Every one had to buy and sell.

Fortunately, also on that list were two companies who really did simply export finished discs. Steve Mason's Lightning Exports and Peter Lassman of Lasgo Exports. The M.D's of both companies were mates of mine, and they could and did truthfully explain to the B.O.T. man that they were exporting millions of quid's worth of product. In fact, as both were keen to be seen as the number one export company, they both happily exaggerated their already big numbers.

So Michael, myself and indeed half the rest of the UK's music entrepreneurs, escaped being locked up in the Tower of London. Her Majesty's U.K. trade representative, in France, the good M. Patanchon was a very careful and proper guy. Totally correct. Checking absolutely everything, every line, every deal. Wanting receipts where receipts should be.

As he was based in Marseilles, just a drive away from Cannes, I arranged for his English wife Sally to tour the exhibition building, where half the industry piled her high with free LP's, T Shirts and other samples.

When, early that evening, Joe found us both, sitting outside the exhibition hall taking the evening air waiting for him, he was concerned about the gifts. "I don't want people thinking the wrong thing," he said. Not unreasonably, actually.

A friend of mine, Sam Barkshire, who sold Yachts for a living, Cannes being a good place to do that, was sitting with us, and he came up with the solution. " *Sally, you keep the discs, and play the music. Joe, you don't listen.*"

For Magnet over the years, hits followed hits, as the team put together more from Alvin, Darts, Guys and Dolls, Susan Cadogan, and later Bad Manners. Less singles orientated, but no less talented, was Chris Rea. But as these things usually go, after a string of hits, by '83 only Kissing the Pink had done well, but Bad Manners and Blue Zoo had wandered around at the lower edges of the top 75.

In '84 I think their only UK hit had been, 'Summer Holiday' by Kevin the Gerbil.

Now I am as guilty as the next man for happily cashing in with a one off hit...but even by my standards, Kevin the Gerbil didn't look like a career move for a label.

Apart from Chris Rea Magnet were, to an outside view, struggling. I absolutely do not write this in any gloating way, as at one stage my own company went through such a quiet spell, that we had a nasty feeling we had made more out of the office football pools syndicate than we had from music!

Magnet also had the services of some the best promotional people the UK could offer (Originally Steve Collier, then Kim Glover). They had been able to call on marketing advice from Steve Jenkins, and the legendary Tilly Rutherford

Terry the Pill, London's poster sticking king, chart shop expert, and long time friend of the whole industry, regularly dropped into my office for a chat. By the eighties, the control of sales data and then information recovery from the shops used to compile the all-important BBC Charts had moved on a bit from the sixties and seventies. Phone calls and sales diaries in the mail were still used as a double check on occasions, but more and more with till rolls detailing the time of sale, data ports on modern tills and then couriers delivering even more details, from more shops the system was apparently more secure from manipulation.

This of course was quite testing of the ingenuity of the, 'strike forces' as they were now known. No more Worker Bee teams of wives, girlfriends and mates driving round the suburbs. Most strike forces, and the marketing departments of music companies themselves, obviously wanted to be as effective as possible.

So touring, window displays, advertising, and indeed nationwide poster sticking and other work, from Terry the Pill, were all coordinated. Indeed Terry coordinated a lot of such activity himself for smaller labels. We were in the middle of a whole string of hits with our associated label Mute, from Depeche Mode, Erasure, Assembly, and various others from our Sonet company.

So Terry's almost weekly visits to my office were a whirlwind of news and gossip.

He seemed to be very preoccupied with the affairs of Magnet. In his inimitable, but now after all his years in London, slight, Liverpool accent "That Michael Levy. He's outrageous."

I look quizzical. Terry say's, "He's maybe more outraged. He's had some good stuff out in recent years, spent a fortune on it, and almost everything is just getting to bubbling under status."

By complete coincidence a week or so later Terry and I bump into Michael Levy, just outside the Portman or Churchill Hotel (they are almost next to each other).

I hardly knew Michael, but he seemed to know Terry very well. As ever, he was dressed more as a uber-smart accountant than a music exec.

Michael and I re-acquainted ourselves. We chatted a bit. He had been very much aware of the success that Mute was having, especially in Germany and the US, but hadn't been aware that at that time I personally owned all the Mute music and the recording rights for the world.

Having discussed Germany in some detail, I mentioned the escalating costs of UK promotion, on which he agreed. He went on to question me closely about the reputations of, certain UK strike forces that helped singles climb out of the expensive-to-sustain lower chart areas.

For what it was worth I gave him my opinion, with some input from Terry, who knew more about the ins and outs of the various UK promotion teams than I.

Michael mentioned in particular Modern Talking.

They were then shuffling around the bottom of the UK charts; I explained that I had tried to sign the band from Germany, but Magnet had beaten me to them.

Looking back I guess his concern was justified as Modern Talking and Magnet failed with their singles but the band did get a UK top five single called, 'Brother Louie,' in late '86.

Sadly for Michael, they'd changed labels by then to RCA.

Michael moved on and wanted to know what I was doing about promoting our stuff in the USA.

 Given that we had been doing so well out there with Depeche Mode, Yazoo and Erasure, I had some information to give him. I explained that most US companies were allegedly cutting back on the use of independent promotion companies, mainly due to the escalating costs, as the major companies fought each other for market share. He told me something I hadn't really understood, that in many cases, US senior executives were on massive bonuses, based on, market share, not profits, so chasing market share had been crazy for a few years.

I explained to him, that I had learned a while back, that a US company with whom I was dealing, had after much pushing by me, allocated a promotional budget to one of my recordings.

I had left their offices a little triumphantly. Such monies would eventually be deducted from our royalties, but we needed to push in that huge and varied country. If we got some chart action there, the bands could then make millions touring.

Just a few weeks later I had learned the US company had actually spent, 'my money,' on another one of their artists...nothing do with me...and I was effectively paying the bill to make someone else famous! Hence us taking a more proactive role our selves.

Michael looked aghast. I joked and said, (only partly joking in fact), "That's what happens when you haven't got a great accountant on your side!"

He asked how I was handling US promotion now, and I explained that for Depeche and the others on Warner/Sire we got a video and marketing allowance, it was paid to us and we then allocated the money, just some to video and most to hiring our own radio promotion teams.

I told him about the various independent promotional and marketing teams we were using. A very cool company called Second Vision and also a considerable number of direct deals with some gents, called Fred DiSipio, Ralph Tashjian, Joe Isgro and others in their Network. They seemed to be very busy with a lot of top acts using them for radio promotion.

I gave Michael the break down of costs for the indie promo teams, and then at his request their up to date contact details. He seemed quite surprised by my daily hands-on attitude.

The answer to that could be summed up, simply by the fact that the size of the US market and the preference of US companies for their own home produced product left me not much choice.

We finished up, with some jokes and smiles on both sides about my pressuring him to attend Midem in the early days of the trade fair, and we rushed outside where Sandy Sneddon was waiting with the car.

As you will learn from the next section in the story, for the following years later, every time I saw Michael on TV with, or referred to in the press with, Tony Blair and the Labour party, I had good reason to wonder if, before he sold his Magnet company to Warner's, he had ever called on the services of the US promotion companies I had recommended to him.

He certainly had seemed very interested.

If,repeat,if, he had worked with them, now that would be another interesting twist in the tale of Lord Magnet. Lord Magnet meets the Mafia now that would be a story ,as you will find out in the next section of this book......

........Fixing the Charts Opener Draft Five. It's early evening. February 24th 1986. I am sitting in a bar in New York, waiting for a friend, thinking about dinner and casually watching the NBC TV Nightly News. Ten minutes later and I am rooted to the spot. I have gone cold. I am hyperventilating. I Feel sick and my hands are shaking. I am seriously frightened.

It seems that I may have apparently been doing business with the Mafia. This is not an episode of the yet to be invented Soprano's. This is, unfortunately, the real thing.

I had been in New York and/or LA every few months over the preceding few years. Mainly trying to promote similar success in the USA for Depeche Mode, Yazoo, then Erasure, that my company was having with them in the rest of the world.

That fateful evening the big story on the evenings TV news had started off in a fairly usual (For New York) style. The presenter,

Brian Ross, starts to speak over some pictures of fairly normal looking New York Street pictures:

" This block on First Avenue on the Lower East Side is a stronghold of the Gambino Mafia family..." By then I had pretty much lost interest; the presenter drones on. Sounds like all the usual stuff. I relaxed and started to make those plans for dinner. Until I catch the words, " As part of an investigation of corrupt practices in the rock music business."

'Rock Music business,' woke me up a little. I paid a little more attention. Just a little. I assumed it was old stuff re-hashed. More droning on about the FBI and the like. Sounded like a hundred TV shows or movies, and even harked back for me to the books of Damon Runyon, which had partly inspired me to try and become a journalist before I moved on to start a record company.

But as I am about to discover, this is the real thing. The real deal...and I'm both real and probably in the deal.

Over pictures, some grainy from hidden cameras, some sparkly news stuff from a Music Industry function, Ross the presenter continues, "Among the guests, two of the most powerful and feared men in the music business. Joseph Isgro, who, authorities say, has described Mafia 'capo' Armone as his partner and Isgro's close associate Fred de Sippio.".... That's when I started to shake. When I went cold and clammy.

On my office wall, along with many gold discs, charts and awards was a framed series of receipts from those very guys for work they had done for us..............Suddenly I wasn't hungry.........

...The following day, and for much of the following week there was no chance of making appointments at my usual round of US record companies, or if admitted, there were no discussions about anything other than the NBC News story.

Payola, illegally paying for radio plays, had been a scandal that had reared its head in the USA many times. Newspapers and TV have told and retold the stories. D.J Alan Freed, the man who coined the name ,Rock 'n Roll, for certain types of music, in the early Sixties, was accused of taking money and his brilliant career ruined.

So Payola, paying for plays in its self is not too bad, but of course when the payments are made in drugs, various other services or

cash, unreported to the tax man by payer or payee and the law has
rather more to get it's teeth into.

Also in the USA, consorting with or benefitting from Organised
Crime, knowingly or possibly unknowingly, is somewhat frowned
on to say the least!

When we, or more correctly my company, hired, what, became
referred to in lurid stories as: The Network, we of course didn't quite
realise what we were letting ourselves in for. We were definitely in
the un-knowing camp.

Promise.

With my many years experience of promoting records in almost 100
countries, I was obviously aware of dodgy-for dodgy-read, money
paid under the table, to DJ's or Radio execs in many of those
countries.

In my considered opinion, and considering all those possible
opinions has been my life in music from 1964 to 2014, there are four
key reasons why British music has been such a global success:

1. The use of the English Language.
2. The considerable talent of our writers, composers and
performers.
3. The fact that our pop music station had nationwide coverage.
4. The fact that the BBC is straight. Not just a bit straight, but
very straight.

Of course now and again there have been a few miscreants, a few get
rich quick publicity merchants, some 'favours' for mates, and the
acceptance of a lot of hospitality.

In all my years, I observed that for most BBC producers, the more
extravagant the hospitality, the better a record needed to be for it to
get played.

Given the re-hashed and re-hashed again BBC bashing (this time
about payola) you'd think I was brainwashed in my defence of them.
Far from it.

My wages and those of my staff, our musicians and many others
relied on the BBC's straightness.

So believe me, anything out of order with them, and the bloody
world would have known.

A few days after the sensational revelation on TV I am in the Brasserie restaurant in New York's Grand Central Station, I am quizzing my lawyer if we, (me or my company), are in trouble for hiring a team, a network even, that it now seems is or are associated with people, even if you were in the Soprano's, that you probably wouldn't want your daughter to marry.

Given that, at that time my, precious little girl was just about two years old, I could probably assume the matter would be resolved by the time she was of age.

Actually, thinking about that, considering the payola problems, and rumours of links to organised crime stories that had started in the sixties, (which then seemed to be peaking on a number of fronts), but rumble on still today, Regarding my daughter and sopranos style admirers, she seemed, when a little older to prefer riding horses to delivering their heads to swarthy looking gents..so I guess we're OK there.

I was concerned enough to have consulted our friendly lawyer and pay for lunch.

He was not comforting. 'Ignorance, is no excuse in the eyes of the law,' seemed to be his main point. He was a little bit more positive about my suggestion, "It all works differently at home in the UK, and America is a big place with thousands of Radio Stations, so we had to hire someone."

He questioned me, "But you are not stupid, you must have heard the stories, the rumours of, the networks, the connections?" He went on "and before you say you weren't, why did you put their receipts on the wall in your office ?"

I said, "I've heard those rumours about everything in America. About Las Vegas, about Frank Sinatra, about President Kennedy. So we put the receipts on the wall, because to the Brits the names looked a bit like the stories and the rumours. We also wanted to show our people that we were spending money to promote stuff in the USA."

As lawyers do, he just nodded, not good-not bad, just nodded, and then he spoke again, "But didn't you think?"

I gulped a bit at that one. He seemed to be suggesting we indeed did have a problem. My response was the truth. "We asked a lot of people: who was good at the promotion job. There's a lot of promo people out there who take the money and then just go to the beach."

He nodded. Again, "So I asked around. Got those names, and was told to be careful."

Now the nod was a frowny one.

"So I made a list of recent records they had promoted and when I saw they came from almost all of Warner's labels and MCA, CBS/Sony, Virgin, EMI/Capitol,BMG almost all the big companies, I figured then it must be OK. After all those companies are stuffed with lawyers keeping them safe or better, on the straight and narrow. And by the way, if the combined might of NBC and the FBI are only just now figuring it all out, what hope did I have of divining the truth."

This time the nod was accompanied with a grin. I continue, "Seems to me that right now most of the major companies are saying, 'Not us. We didn't do it. And if we did, we won't do it any more!'"

His nod this time was accompanied by a broad grin.

The US investigation continued with some considerable strength, for many many years, and eventually some people, just a few, came to trial. Over time, after many more investigations, various accusations were made, evidence delivered, accepted, then overturned.

More evidence delivered of criminal activity and violence surrounding the selling of overstocks of records.

More trials, appeals, convictions, sentences.

"You are not going to prison as you have helped the authorities." " You are going to prison for racketeering.

The story rolled on.

It's probably still rolling on today.

It's easy to be glib, amusing, off hand. But some genuinely nasty stuff was discovered. More to do with the selling of overstocked records, tax fraud, and drug-related matters than breaking, what many see as the minor law of not declaring when music was, 'pay for play.'

Having sold my music companies I am quite happy not to be any longer concerned with all that. Then before everybody had to go and work for Bugs Bunny at Warner Brothers , along came the internet and changed all the rules again.

18. On Making it to Number One.

Making it to number one in the charts is the ambition of most musicians and their music companies...I should know. I was still contributing to Jackie, when in 1968 I started my own record company: Sonet Records.
We had more enthusiasm than money.

I did however have one secret weapon (or secret skill, as it turned out): my Jackie Magazine hit- picking training. With the magazine being prepared and printed many weeks in advance, listening and choosing potential hits from all the new releases had been my life for the previous three or four years.

Our skilled professionals, Gordon, Gavin, Samantha and the girls, didn't want to have a Jackie front cover with a, 'Who is that?' or a 'One hit wonder,' on it. Neither did the readers.

Hits came from established bands, but on occasions they produced a flopperoo. The gang in Scotland could play safe, but we also had to try and pick out the new stars early in their careers.

So I listened to all the new releases... and turned out to be quite good at picking the hits. I passed on my predictions to the office in Scotland, and chased up those I was confident about for photo sessions and interviews.

As Gordon used to say to me, "Sometimes we even take some notice."

When I started my own company, having to find and predict the hits, *when investing my own very limited monies in making or choosing and then releasing new records,* was a lot more daunting. But the ears and the instinct didn't let me down. In the first few years we had quite a few *successful songs* that we looked after for the UK or some other countries.

Then in 1972, with "Seaside Shuffle" by Terry Dactyl and the Dinosaurs, we had the *first hit record* that we had produced ourselves. It reached number two. The band were really a very hip blues and boogie band called Brett Marvin and the Thunderbolts. They hated Seaside Shuffle; couldn't see it as a hit, and anyway hits were not usually their style of music. But after much pressure from me, eventually, grudgingly, they agreed to its release, but under another name: hence Terry Dactyl and the Dinosaurs.

When it came to appearing on Top of The Pops, they showed their apathy towards the glitter and dancing glitz of the show by appearing sitting in deck chairs with old age pensioners' knotted hankies on their heads!

To their surprise, and to some extent horror, the audience loved them, and put them in the same, 'off the wall band' file as The Bonzo Dog Do Da Band. The Bonzo's, a kind of musical Monty Python, had a huge hit with, 'Urban Spaceman' in 1968, and appeared in The Magical Mystery Tour with The Beatles.

The Terry Dactyls reverted back to their real name of Brett Marvin and the Thunderbolts and are still packing them in on the club and university circuit forty-odd years later. Their current audience is today's young university crowd, just as when they started all those years ago. A good boogie band is still a good night out-some styles never change.

Then in the summer of '74, my Sonet company stunned the music industry by selling millions of copies of the foot-tapping and very sing-along 'Yviva Espana' by Swedish singer Sylvia.

But again...we got stuck at number two. They even played it on Coronation Street, but we still got stuck. 'You can chat a matador' echoed around the world for '74 and much of the next few years...and the Spanish fruit marketing board even paid us, (and singer Sylvia and the songwriters), what Harry Enfield would call, 'loads 'a money,' to use the song to advertise Spania- Spanish oranges.

So a great and company saving payday, but that elusive number one had been just that: elusive. Until...against all odds, and with a recording that the music industry loved to hate (those smart arse critics again), but which my ears told me was a smash hit, we got that elusive number one.

I can still recall the celebrations (and almost feel the hangover) when we broke open the Champagne to celebrate. It was Sunday 10th October 1976.

For various reasons we hadn't received the usual list of the new chart, faxed at lunchtime on Sundays to music companies from BMRB, the chart company that researched and then provided the chart to BBC Radio One, with the top 20 also being broadcast on Radio Two.

So that Sunday, I was at home, learning the chart positions at the same time as the rest of the UK, listening as the BBC's Tom Browne slowly, agonisingly, nail-bitingly slowly, played the records.

At Number Five, Demis Roussos, 'When Forever has Gone,'—mesmerizingly memorable.

Number Four, 'Howzat,' by Sherbet—a great and fun pop song, but that afternoon it dragged on for ever in my house.

Tom Browne spoke again. "At Number Three..." we held our breath... "'Sailing' by Rod Stewart, up 11 places from 14." Surprise and relief for us. We hadn't gone down...the previous week we'd been number two. Surprise though, at Rod's massive leap up the list from 14.

As Rod and 'Sailing' faded away over the horizon, I was on the edge of my chair, holding my breath...as Tom spoke and faded up the intro sounds of 'Dancing Queen' by my friends Abba; they'd been Number One the week before.

Assuming that we had moved up from number two that vital one place to the Top Spot, my wife started to cry, and made moves towards the fridge...with its bottle of champagne. Extra well chilled, she claimed it had been waiting there since 1968, when I had started the company.

Looking back now...somewhat ridiculously... I said... "Wait—we might have dropped right out of the whole chart completely."

I think in those days they faded the end of discs going down the chart quite quickly to make more space for the risers, but the wait, the nerves, the tension seemed interminable.

Abba and the queen were dancing on and on and on and on...until... there they were... the familiar opening guitar sounds of 'Mississippi' by Pussycat came over the Radio.

We'd made it.

My son Sam, aged about two—looked baffled as Mummy explained, "Daddy's crying because he's very happy."

For us, both the family and the company, the good news continued in direct proportion to the shock and awe, (and in some quarters annoyance), of the music industry. Pussycat stayed at Number One for five weeks.

Not only that, but for most of November and December they were joined in the UK chart by another of our records: 'Spinning Rock Boogie' by Hank C. Burnette. Thank you John Peel and Paul Burnett [no relation].... "Can't stop, and keep Rockin' Kid"!

So we closed the year with one of the UK's biggest hits.

Not bad, for a little company of just five people taking on the big boys with their hundreds of staff, money, power and a lot of influence, especially when it came to fighting them for chart places ...and that guaranteed radio exposure for the following weeks. I have written earlier about the competition to get this record started, the whole affair being well worth it in the end.

Over the years, through the Eighties into the Nineties, my Sonet company and its various labels, had more than a hundred chart hits with songs we owned, published or represented, and with records that we recorded, released or looked after in one way or another. We worked with a string of artists in various capacities that included, in some cases taking care of records for the world, in other cases just for the UK and on some occasions everywhere except the UK: Depeche Mode, Erasure, Yazoo and Alison Moyet we handled for the world.

Those annoying tunes such as "Agadoo," and "The Birdie Song," were ours for most of the world *outside the UK*.

"Beach Boy Gold" and of course Danny Mirror's tribute masterpiece, "I Remember Elvis Presley" brought us back to fighting to get a hit at home.

Danny Mirror? You don't remember? Shame on you! September 17th 1977 and we hit the charts big time with...Danny Mirror's classic tribute to Presley.'

The fact that Elvis himself had only recently and sadly become—late and great—on the 16th August, was pushing our claim to likeable credibility a bit.

When we decided to release the record 'I remember,' it was already rocketing up the Dutch and German charts. I was concerned of course about us being seen to be cashing in, justifiable accusations of no taste or style and all things you could imagine.

The problem was...it was a great tune. Well sung—even if in a 'faux Elvis style'. Even the talented writer/producer/singer, one Eddy Ouwens, had been so concerned at the potentially negative reaction that he had called himself Danny Mirror for this one recording.

In a pathetic attempt to preserve my Sonet company's growing reputation, we put the record out not on our Sonet label but on a skillfully concealed anagram: *Stone*. Of course, you never would have connected them, would you? Not!

The fact that with – for once understandable, little airplay – it sold almost a million in the UK and reached Number 4 in the charts annoyed many.

Except of course Mr. Danny Mirror and my company bank manager. Silver discs were normally awarded with pomp and publicity by the trade association; ours, for 'I Remember Elvis Presley,' arrived in the post. In a brown envelope.

Of course I do, in this case, quite understand the reservations about the 'cashing in,' and it not being too good for our Sonet's reputation...but with our Stone label we went on to have the last laugh.

In 1981 we used Stone again for a single called 'Beach Boy Gold.' Which became a UK smash for Adrian Baker performing all the voices as 'Gidea Park.'.

The multi-talented musician and vocalist Adrian then toured for years with the actual Beach Boys, filling in on any needed vocal parts should any of the 'real' Beach Boys be unable to make a show. So again, despite accusations of us cashing in and copying, I think Adrian's talent, in joining the actual Beach Boys, more than answered that.

In 1991 we dug out the Stone labels again and had a Christmas hit with our re-release of 'Donald Where's' your Troosers?' by Andy Stewart. It provided a very welcome number 4 in the charts at that big-selling time of the year.

Then came the real embarrassment. Various books publish lists of the most reliably and consistently successful labels. i.e. not having very many misses between the hits.

With three hits out of three releases...Stone UK topped the list. Beating the much more deserving Island Records, Apple or Atlantic hands down. Again, for some reason the award arrived some months later with postage still to pay.

Actually, we gained another 'thank you gift' through the post for Donald's revived Christmas hit. Andy Stewart—proud resident then of his home fishing port in the North of Scotland—very kindly sent us a box of Arbroath Smokies. (Kippers, smoked fish, to you dear). Usually a real delicacy.

The only problem was, he sent them in the post just before Christmas, and as the office was closed until the New Year they were stuck in the local London Post office for almost a month. In fact it was not until about the 7th of January that Sandy Sneddon—our promo man—went and claimed the package.

By then of course, having languished for all of that month in a hot post office—the package stank. They reeked. Whenever we spoke with Andy we were never able to own up to not having enjoyed his kind thought.

Every hit we had, even those we represented worldwide, like Depeche Mode, Yazoo or Erasure—was hard work ... record by record, song by song, country by country.

Every one was a struggle, a fight, a competition.

At Sonet we used the profits from the pop hits to build a strong and interesting base for the company by recording what we hoped was the best of Blues, Jazz, Country, Folk and other genres of music. Music where the quality and artistic endeavour was the criteria of success more than a brief week's chart position.

Those pop chart positions, supposedly true representations of sales or popularity, have lost credibility over the years as they were manipulated, mostly by the major companies, or those with very deep pockets.

The reason for the vicious, cut throat, dog eat dog and sometimes violent and painful competition was simple. I say it again. A place on the charts meant radio, or even sometimes TV exposure.

But with our dedicated and committed team in the UK and our various label partners we managed to beat the 'big boys' with their staffs of thousands and millions of cash in their promotional budgets....An achievement to be proud of for our staff, the producers, our promotional crews and of course the musicians, writers, composers and performers.

Another proud moment occurred in 1988 and it came courtesy of Parliament.

Two mighty publishing companies wanted to merge, Warner Communications and Chappell and Co Inc. The House of Lords or some such demanded that under the fair competition rules there be an enquiry to make sure business opportunities remained fair for all if such a giant merger took place. For a year or so, world experts in trade, accounting, publishing and law reported to the very official sounding: Mergers and Monopolies Commission. The report, complete with Royal Crest was published by Her Majesty's Stationery Office.

The report, stated that there were 2392 publishers active in the UK. They suggested that just 13 were able to provide a full and complete international publishing service. Hardly surprisingly the names they listed included the world mightiest, Chappell's, Warners (WBM) EMI, MCA, and some others....

.......and Sonet Publishing. That was us there with the big boys. The Commission had found, that little Sonet Publishing, our company started with my three Swedish partners in 1968 we could stand with the big boys and do the job.

That was about the first time my Mother, was not able to say: " Isn't it time you got a proper job!"

Great for me, and great for Alan Whaley our loyal and skilled publishing manager.

For me, that's enough of a reason to write this book, and at least then my own children can get a real understanding of what their dad, and his team of people tried to do.

19. Chinese Ribs, by Royal Appointment.

Giving someone a lift home after they've had a bust up with, or been abandoned by their mates, the girlfriend (or boyfriend) is of course an expected obligation and no problem.
A late night Chinese. Takeaway or delivered home after an evening that includes more than a few drinks is quite normal.
Even in the mid sixties we liked our rice crackers and noodles.

When the delivery of both the Chinese and the Abandoned Someone includes a large bag of ribs and The Right Honourable Earl of Snowdon and Viscount Linley of Nymans in the County of Sussex and the home in question is Kensington Palace, it becomes memorable.

The fact that The Right Hon, Earl of Snowdon...etc etc. You get the drift...*was at the time currently married to The Queen's sister,* Princess Margaret, made the delivery, (possibly by Royal Appointment and for Royal Consumption), very memorable.
Incidentally, all that 'Earl of Snowden and Viscount Linley etc etc., doesn't mean there were two of them. He's just got a lot names.
When the delivery driver has participated in more than a few evening drinks it becomes concerning.

When the delivery driver is me!...The evening has obviously become confusing.

It's the late 60's, in fact it's very late at night in the late sixties. As we neared Kensington Palace, a tall policeman in an old-style helmet stepped out from the side of the road, raised his hand, and we slowed to a stop by him.

As I was driving my beloved, but very beaten up old red Triumph Spitfire sports car, he had to crouch down very low to see in and communicate with us. I wound down the driver's window, and I suspect he recoiled slightly as a waft of Chinese food engulfed him.

I expected a P.C. George Dixon style 'Ello Ello Ello, what's all this then?'

But my companion in the passenger seat spoke quickly and said, "It's OK Constable, he's just dropping me off."

As I recall, the slightly ridiculous vision of an almost kneeling policeman raising his hand in a salute, and saying, "Thank you Sir. That's fine," even now, makes me smile.

Many cities have their China Town, London's now is around Gerrard Street in central Soho. But London's first Chinatown was established long ago at Limehouse, quite a way out to the East end of the city, near the then busy docks.

As with most Chinatowns, it had started with Chinese laundrymen jumping ship in port cities and following their trade by opening laundries. Sounds a bit of a cliché but is broadly what happened in many port cities around the world.

The laundries, were soon joined by restaurants and before long, as with today's modern Chinatowns, the areas became a hustle and bustle with steam from both laundries and restaurants. Exotic smells, lights, windows with orangey brown-coloured ducks and and bright red pork hanging in them and more.

Late at night, after the businesses had closed, one could apparently hear the click clack of Mah-jong Tiles and the murmur of gamblers winning and losing.

In shadowy backstreets down near the then busy docks, were the mysterious opium dens, as featured in the Sherlock Holmes novels that were written around that time.

The London Limehouse Chinatown street names are still there: Pekin Street, Canton Street, Nankin Street—all of them postal district E14.

And it was in an E14 street, Salmon Lane to be precise, that I had earlier met my Abandoned Someone, who, now, outside his very large house, big enough to be a palace, was struggling to exit from my very low car.

My passenger was hardly a friend. In fact until about an hour earlier I had never really met him. I'd spent a jolly evening in the *Good Friends,* a fantastic Chinese Restaurant. Me and the Good Food Guide of the day thought it was the best in London.

Fortunately for generations of Londoners, an entrepreneurial Chinaman named Chung Koon had opened several central London restaurants in 1908 and the years that followed.

The really fortunate part was that Mr. Chung wasn't a laundryman turned restaurateur, but had been a chef on the Red Funnel steamship line. So his various restaurants did well.

More than a few years later, in 1958 his son John had opened The Lotus House in London's Edgeware Road. Very up market and much frequented for the next few decades by the rich and famous.

For some reason he had returned to the roots of Chinatown, if not his roots, but those of the Chinese community and had opened the E14 Salmon Lane, Good Friends in 1962.

Despite it being quite a way down the Commercial Road East towards Docklands, it had become renowned for great food. It had no license for alcohol, so the off licence across the street was soon stocking a range of wines along with its more usual supplies of beer (bottled).

I was in the habit of eating there once a week, usually after I had completed some deliveries or meetings in Fleet Street.

I had noticed Lord Snowdon dining there a few times, In fact we were on nodding terms as regular customers. On the evening in question, I had noticed him dining as usual with a glamorous companion. Which, considering his fame as a society photographer and design guru wasn't unexpected. Although the rumours were that he was gay (or a poof as it was referred to then), he was that night with a very attractive blonde lady.

As well as being very attractive, she was obviously also very highly strung, or highly pissed off about something, as late in the evening, the restaurant window blinds were down and there were only two tables still occupied, mine and theirs, she suddenly stood up and exited...slamming the door behind her.

The staff, tired waitresses and chefs in whites, who were as usual after a busy evening, all settling down to eat at a large round table—looked up with some concern. Mrs. Farmer, Chinese looking (but English name), eventually went over to Lord Snowdon's table and after a brief conversation returned to the little bar and was obviously calling him a taxi.

After a while she came over to my table and delivered my bill, and said, "I don't know what to do, there's no taxis to be had for hours. It's closing time and it's now raining."

As I stood to leave, I could see her daughter, Sue, trying every taxi number they knew, and Mrs. F. apologising to his Lordship.

My then girlfriend, also Sue, and I, stopped by his table, and I said, "If you don't mind cramming into my old car I can give you a lift towards the City and the West End until we see a Taxi."

With a, "Wonderful, could you?" we all exited the restaurant.

We let Sue cram into the tiny back seats first, and then having lowered the front seat, he squeezed in.

We were just about to drive off when Sue Farmer came running out with two large bags of their wonderful Chinese ribs; still hot to the touch.

"Very sorry about the Taxis. Here's some ribs for you."

It's funny but once people know you are in the music industry it's like a key to instant friendship, so before long we were chatting happily.

With a slight drizzle coming down there were not so many taxi's in sight, and by the time we reached Trafalgar Square I had agreed to drop him at home. Although it took more than a few seconds to sink in that 'home' was Kensington Palace...hence tall policemen and all the rest.

As he exited the car, he said," You really saved the day there, with this rain I'd probably still be way out at the end of the Commercial bloody Road. I'd ask you in for a drink but it's a bit tricky at the moment. Perhaps another time."

"Of course." I agreed, and clutching his bag of ribs he went off towards the house (sorry Palace), where presumably butler and footman awaited.

Sue and I had hysterics for the rest of the journey home. She had particularly tuned in to the, "Sorry can't ask you in it's a bit tricky at the moment," with her painting a picture of Princess Margaret in her curlers and brandishing a rolling pin saying, "And where have you been until this time of night."

Some weeks later I was back in The Good Friends with my own good friends, BBC DJ Mike Raven and his wife Mandy. Lord Snowden was with a group of people at another table and I was bit pissed off that he didn't even acknowledge me with a discrete wave. Not even a nod.

Mike and Mandy regaled me with a few tales of life observed in and around the society scene. We also wondered why His Lordship hadn't got a security man or a chauffeur that previous evening. "Being discrete,' was Mike's view. "Secret assignation."

Anyway, we, as usual, had a great evening. In fact, so great I didn't notice Lord Snowden and his party departing. But I was still a bit disgruntled with him. After all, Sue and I had apparently, "saved the day."

When, late as usual, with the staff sitting down to eat, Mike, Mandy and I came to settle up...Mrs. Farmer had a surprise. "The gentleman who was sitting over there has paid your bill, and said to say, 'Thank you.'"

So in the end I wasn't disgruntled any more. *"Thanks Tony. Any time my old mate."*

20. 'One more step sir', the Two Rather Large Gents, Had Their Hands on Their Rather Large Guns.

"One more step, Sir, and we will be required to take action to restrain you." William Alton Carter 111...that's as in 3rd not a mistyped ill. Not perhaps the most immediately familiar name to our readers, is it seems a guest in my hotel.

It's 1977, and I am in a hotel in Nashville Tennessee. The large gents with their large guns, have positioned themselves, sitting on chairs with their legs across the corridor leading to my room in the hotel. Mine being the last room on the left.

Now, it's around midnight. I have had more than few beers. Possibly a little wine earlier at dinner. I've had a very jolly evening with country music star Waylon Jennings and songwriter, Harlan Howard.

Harlan, writer of way too many hits songs to list here first hit the UK charts in the fifties with Heartaches by the Number with Guy Mitchell. 'Busted', immortalised by Ray Charles, and the wonderfully innuendo driven, '(I've got) A Tiger by the Tail'.

Harlan was a pretty good friend of mine, and on visits to London his deep and strong US accent - Texas I think- caused a lot of fun and confusion as he tried to navigate his way around in London's black taxis.

Waylon Jennings, a legendary fixture on the US music scene most recently then with his membership of first, 'The Outlaws' with Willie Nelson, Tompall Glaser and Jessi Colter, and more recently with 'The Highwaymen' again with Willie Nelson but this time also Kris Kristofferson and Johnny Cash.

To English ears, less accustomed to US country music, he will always be remembered as the writer and performer of the theme tune to, The Dukes of Hazzard TV series.

So two large gents in suits are barring my way to my room. So I am a tad angry. More to point, and more on my mind is the fact that I need a pee! Urgently. American beer, in quantity will do that to a guy. So I step over their legs, and walk on purposefully.

Wrong.

"Stop now sir." louder and somewhat forcefully. I wave my key and walk on. " Sir, this is your final warning."

I imagine I can hear the click of guns being readied...but with beer driven idiocy, I reach my room, open the door- fortunately it was a real key, not one of those annoying electronic things that nine times out ten send you all the way back down to reception when it doesn't work.

I rush in, and straight in to the loo.

Sorry, this is Tennessee, near Nashville USA so: I rush in, and straight into the rest room, comfort facility. Who cares, I need the loo.

I exit (having of course carefully washed my hands.) and can hear loud-ish voices in the corridor. I step out, and the door opposite mine is now open and there's a blokey standing there , in shorts and T shirt. As I step forward, one of the 'very large guys', leaps at me and chucks me on the floor.

Over the next few minutes, I answer as best I can with my face pinned to a grubby carpet, in a very English accent, with increasing bravado and indignation ,a series of questions. Fairly speedily I am hauled to my feet and checked for weapons.

The gent in the shorts, extends a hand to me and say's, in very drawly accent, " I guess we all owe you'se an apology. You a tourist here in town?"

I nod, but getting increasing pissed off, and say, "No, not a tourist, here on music business, and believe me tomorrow when I do some radio interviews this bl**dy attack on me will be first on my list, before I start telling the world what my company is doing in Europe with, Johnny Cash , Dolly Parton, and many others who are on their way to Europe next month."

At that moment, Waylon Jennings, in leather hat, and Harlan Howard appear, and say, from the end of the corridor, "Hey Rod, you OK, the bar's closed now and we'll be seeing you tomorrow."

 Well it turns out that Mr. Shorts, who it seems is named William Alton Carter 111, "call me Billy," is in town to work on some promotional stuff for his brand of beer.

It also turns out that, as Waylon and Harlan quickly realise as they come nearer to my room. *That Billy's brother, Jimmy Carter, is the then President of the United States.*

Hence him having large men with large guns, keeping an eye on his personal safety. As it happens, I learn later they were there more in a vain attempt to keep Billy under some kind of control and stop him embarrassing the President any more.

The party in Billy's room continued till sun up. I drank 'Pabst beer,' "Rodney, you've come a long way, and we don't want to harm you any more, by forcing Billy's on you in quantity."

Billy asked Waylon, about something I had never dared to mention, now known as "The day the music died."

Now, dear reader, you are way too young to recall that terrible February 3rd of 1959. After a show in Clear Lake Iowa ,three of the biggest superstars of the day, Buddy Holly, The Big Bopper (JP Richardson) and Richie Valens were killed taking an air taxi through a snow storm to the next town on the tour.

Waylon, was Buddy Holly's bass player on the tour, and had given up his seat on the small plane to JP Richardson, who was suffering from flu, and for obvious reasons was keen to avoid yet another night on a freezing tour bus.

I am sure you will be familiar with Don MacLean's song, 'American Pie,' from which that emotive line - 'The Day the Music Died' - is taken.

Many of you may have seen the musical Buddy.

It's my belief that, over the years, Buddy Holly's recordings and more to the point, his songs, inspired more persons to become musicians that any other single individual.

He scored 25 hits in the UK. Given that Paul McCartney, John Lennon, the Oasis brothers Gallagher, The Hollies, Bob Dylan, The Clash, Elton John, Eric Clapton and countless others name him- and those songs, as the transforming influence on their choice of career. So it was humbling to sit in that Nashville Hotel, as the dawn broke, and hear Waylon discussing the events.

Too many beer's and the passing of the years, have never dimmed my memories of that night, as for me also, the music of Buddy Holly was also the major reason I had become besotted with the world of music.

President Carter's, wild brother Billy, was, after our somewhat 'interesting' introduction was that night far from wild, quietly listening.

As the conversation slowed to a murmur, and personal memories took over, Billy said; "I wonder what songs we have all missed by losing him so early in his career?".... there was then a rather uncomfortable silence.

I learn now that Waylon, very understandably, did indeed have many problems with his memories of the the event. But right then he said, "Well for sure there's' not many people who, at the age of just 22 can leave behind more than fifty great recordings and a lot of them his such great songs of his."

Billy, nodded. "I'll drink to that," and we all did.

For me, 'That'll be the day...till...'

21. Radio talks: 'To you'.

That great broadcaster Sir Terry Wogan, when asked how many listeners he had, often responded with a classic and meaningful answer. "Just the one."

And that's the point, radio is you and the broadcaster. When that broadcaster is daily or at least regularly in your home, in voice at least-you start to get the connection. Their personality comes through, their likes and dislikes, musical choices, or as much as they are allowed to show on air. When their frustrations are similar to yours, waiting for the delivery or repair man. An inability to gently open those plastic blister packs in which supermarkets pack fragile items. The weather man: Wrong again!

So the listener, who these days has multiple choices of radio stations to choose from stays with the broadcaster or DJ that connects to them.

The list of favourite broadcasters for the British (and Irish) no longer with us to which Terry Wogan's name was sadly added in January 2016, is inevitably lengthening as the years roll by. Individually, millions of us felt we had lost a personal friend, when the microphones closed for the last time on John Dunn, Ed Stewart, Mike Raven, Ray Moore, John Peel and others.

They made us smile and on occasions think. The very personal connection between radio and you makes the title of this book ring true: Sometimes Music Is My Only Friend...just add to that, and the guy that delivered the music.

Alison Moyet, one of the world greatest singers, and remarkably nice person, made her first records for my Sonet company in a band from Essex called the 'Screamin' Ab Dab's.' Fortunately for her and indeed the world she had rather more success, also with us, as one half of Yazoo with Vince Clark. Following which of course her solo recordings sold mega millions.

When Sir Terry died, her tweet, I think spoke beautifully for many millions of us:

"He has now left, entirely empty, my childhood kitchen."

22. Radio Ambitions For an Opportunist Plonker.

Having set out how 'Radio' talks to you, and is also the key factor in the promotion of music sales, not to mention it's vital importance in the dissemination of news and general entertainment it's pretty obvious that owning, operating or controlling a radio station puts one in a position of considerable power.

Radio, as we have seen can be for the good, or in the wrong hands it can be a weapon of disinformation which can lead to discontent and even revolution.

So governments worldwide tend to guard and control the licensing of radio stations somewhat closely.

The sudden existence of a whole fleet of pirate pop stations broadcasting just outside UK (and Dutch) waters was of considerable interest to the authorities, although they were somewhat taken aback by the speed of the set up, and then the instant popularity of the stations.

The 'Pirate's,' we're talking about here were unlicensed music broadcasters, not real life Johnny Depp's intent on plunder and worse, originated in 1960 not in the balmy sun kissed water of the Caribbean but in the grey green seas between Sweden and Denmark. The first I think, Radio Mercure. I guess, winged messenger and all that stuff.

Between 1960 and 63 various entities called Mercure, Radio Nord, DCR (Dansk Commercial Radio) broadcast mainly pre-recorded music programs aimed at Sweden and Denmark from a variety of ships including The Cheeta, Lucky Star and the Mi Amigo.

At about the same time, the Dutch, knowing that even with a small ship board aerial that they could cover their smallish, and very flat country, got in on the act and started radio Veronica.

Over time Veronica was arguably the best run, most long lasting (14 years) and most influential of the original ships.

The Mi Amigo, with several changes of owner/operators, spent much of 1963, sailing around Europe as various plans were proposed, plotted, rejected ,or simply failed.

In a storm the Mi Amigo's mast collapsed, and eventually after two trips across the Atlantic to Florida, she ended up refitting in Greenore, Ireland, and became Radio Caroline South.

A month or so later, broadcasting from just off Felixstowe in Spring 64 Radio Caroline was a media sensation and an instant favourite with the listeners.

Following Caroline's amalgamation (takeover really) with a rival, Radio Atlanta, the Federica, Atlanta's ship, also having been fitted out as a radio station in Greenore , sailed North, or more accurately West, round the sticky out bit of Cornwall, then North, and from July '64 became, Radio Caroline North, moored between the already very musical Liverpool and Ireland.

Caroline South's dominant position in and around London and the South East was soon rivalled with the arrival of MV Galaxy. MV being 'Motor Vessel'. With considerable technical expertise, power, broadcast programming experience and DJ talent on board, Swinging Radio London, Big L had arrived.

The apparent opportunity to, make money from radio advertising and the secondary opportunity to boost music sales had not gone un-noticed, and a gaggle of some opportunist and some highly professional entrepreneurs leapt aboard the band wagon (Wayne D. Editor: surely this should be leapt aboard the boat?)

In fact the most stable place to erect tall radio transmitting masts (and gain wider coverage for the same transmitting power) was on various old war time defence forts located off the south east coast of England.

Radio Sutch, set up by music's wild man Screaming Lord Sutch, bagged a place on the Shivering Sands Forts. After a month or so, Sutch's manager, Reg Calvert took over, and brought a degree of professionalism to the station re-naming it Radio City.

I knew Reg pretty well, although he was based at first in Southampton he had returned to the north of England, near Rugby where he was based in a big old mansion. As well as taking care of Lord Sutch, he managed a considerable number of bands, including The Fortunes and Pinkertons Colours.

The Fortunes, who were lucky enough also to have a brilliant and well connected booking agent called Terry King, not only had a string of hits in the the UK and US , with, ' You've got your Troubles,' 'Here it Comes Again', 'This Golden Ring' and 'Freedom Come Freedom Go, 'but also one of their B side's titled, 'Caroline,' became the much heard theme tune for the Caroline stations.

Meanwhile another of the ring of wartime defence forts , The Red Sands, became home to radio Invicta.

A general lack of funds and a disaster when Invicta owner Tom Pepper drowned with two employees when their supply boat sank one stormy December day and Invicta closed in January.

Radio King took their place and then in September 1965 Radio 390 went on air.

Aimed at a more mature audience, it had professional business backing and, artistically ,despite somewhat dire living and working conditions on the fort, led creatively by Churton Fairman (who had previously been on Atlanta, Invicta, and King), known to listeners as Mike Raven ,they rapidly gained a huge following.

The plan and opportunity to improve quality and range further with larger aerials and better transmitters was very much on their minds.

The trials and tribulations of the other less well organised or less well funded London stations continued, as elsewhere, Radio Scotland started, on an old lightship just off Glasgow.

In the unsheltered seas off Scarborough Radio 270 was added to the fleet.

By the summer of 66, despite massive popularity with the listeners the government had almost pushed through legislation to outlaw the pirates.

Much public indignation, many petitions and considerable support, even from certain politicians either courting votes, or genuinely feeling that there was a need for the nation to embrace new technology.

The lot of the pirates was not then helped by a string of very public squabbles over, money, equipment, rights to occupy certain forts and more.

This culminated in the death of Reg Calvert, shot by another radio station entrepreneur, Major Oliver Smedley, who claimed, and indeed later proved self defence.

Knowing Reg, who was a bit of a bluffer and blusterer, and rather known for making fairly odd claims about self defence and the like, I suspect the whole episode was an unfortunate accident, with Smedley feeling very threatened as an angry Reg pushed his way into his, Smedley's, fairly isolated cottage.

One by one, with or without court cases, with in some cases major farewell broadcasts and demonstrations of support, by the summer of 1967 the airwaves in the main became silent.

I was both a listener, a fan even, of the best of the stations, and had, wearing my Jackie hat I had visited most of the southern ships several times, and clambered once onto the Red Sands fort that was Invicta (for a while).

Rather oddly I then nearly got mixed up in something, that in retrospect was very nasty.

Laurie O'Leary , who was essentially the Kray brothers music business expert and link, was very keen for them to get involved in pop radio. 'More than just investors' (protectors?) in a station but as actual operators, *as Laurie was very aware of the promotional power of a good station and the potential earnings from recordings and artists.*

Back in autumn 1965 I had gone to Holland as a journalist to see the Supremes, Unit Four Plus Two and Wayne Fontana and the Mindbenders at an awards show. Laurie was originally coming with me, but pulled out at the last minute due I think to a licensing problem with a club.

He asked me to take a meeting for him in Amsterdam that had been set up with some suppliers of radio station transmitters. I met the two gents in the Schiller Hotel and came back with all sort of technical spec about RCA radio transmitters, both new, and ex forces.

Every time I saw him, in De Hems pub, the Krays El Morocco, or later in the Speakeasy or Bag O'Nail's, Laurie was always asking me for the latest on the radio situation. He wanted all the news on the court cases, the owners of the various stations, who was likely making money and the who was not!

Towards the end of the pirate ship era, Reg Calvert's widow had somehow managed to keep Radio City going before turning off the transmitters for the last time in February 1967.

After the station had been silent for about a week, Mrs. Calvert found herself escorted by two burly gents to The Astor Club in Berkeley Square London where Reggie Kray asked her to re start the station, claiming that they had enough of an, 'in' with the government for them to stay on air. Mrs. Calvert politely refused and heard no more of the matter.

Not knowing anything of the above meeting, *but apparently just a few hours later,* I met up with Laurie O'Leary in the Guinea Pub , just off Bruton Street, just around the corner from Berkeley Square. Laurie had called me the previous day and done his usual, 'Rod I need a word, may be a few quid's in it for you,'

We had arranged to meet at the Guinea ,as Laurie had a previous meeting with agent manager Bryan Morrison nearby.

Laurie comes in, greets few people standing at the bar, buys me a pint of Young's Bitter, and starts to tell me, as usual, a host of funny stories about the great and good of the music business.

A couple of minutes later and Reggie Kray breezes in, with him were a couple of men, one Dutch and the other Swiss. Both of whom I had met on my trip to Holland.

Straight to business, and it's all about Radio. With stations closing, Laurie and apparently Reggie, sees the opportunity as being bigger than ever.

Reggie reports on his meeting with Mrs. Calvert, although with so many Reg this and Reg that's, it took me a while to figure it all out. Essentially he says,' She's out for good. It's all clear if we want, we can take the fort that City had been on, there a few other claimants but they won't be any trouble. "

I have enough concern and knowledge of whom I am sitting with to wonder if that's an arrangement or a threat.

There's then some detailed conversations with the Dutch and Swiss gents about special transmitter costs, and yet more from them, saying that with a good RCA transmitter and a proper boat, they can pretty much do all that a fort could to, and stay further out off shore. Laurie borrows my notebook and sketches out a plan.

Ship or Fort. TBC.

Transmitter supply. Agreed.

Engineers. Laurie says, ' We've got that geezer from Radio City.'
Choice of D.J.'s. : He looks at me. I say, " With stations closing
there's plenty out there right now, some good ones as well".

Reggie starts making suggestions, and Laurie holds up his hand and
says, talking to Reggie, "Look, you and me, we know a bit about
training boxers, right. But if we're going to start training horses, we
need someone who knows the pony from the trap.'"

"Let Rod, and some of my mates sort that, they know what they're
talking about. Rods got the music as well". Which I had with several
thousand singles and LP's in my collection.

We all agree to meet in a few weeks and discuss it more. Laurie did
his usual, 'don't worry Rod we'll sort you out,' and I made my way
back to my flat in East Molesey Surrey, quite chuffed with the idea of
becoming a radio station program controller.

A. Did it occur to me that I'd in effect be working for some
gangsters.

Er no. At that time we viewed the 'gangster' tag as being in the
'Arthur Daly' style, not the killers the Kray's turned out to be.

B. Did it worry me that pirate radio was very much a hot potato and
with much Parliamentary activity was becoming more illegal by the
day.

Er no. Radio was fun, radio had been illegal and very popular for a
good few years now and so it just seemed to be an acceptable and
logical move, from press pop man to radio pop man.

I talked about a new station with my mates, and even started to
study things like the number of discs played per hour, where you
got jingles, and discussed potential DJ line ups with all and sundry.
In the end nothing came of the plans, mainly according to Laurie,
because the BBC with full government support moved quicker than
anyone had forecast.

Radio One, started broadcasting on September 30th just weeks
after the Marine Offenses Act became law.

The BBC moved fast having employed almost 20 of the best known
pirates, and simply in reality re-jigged the existing ,Light Program.

They negotiated more needle time ,thus allowing more discs to be played and slightly less musicians union ruled live music.

In next to no time Tony Blackburn with fringe and Arnold the dog, fringe situation unknown, was spinning records and telling corny jokes.

I was still tap tapping away on the old typewriter, although starting to spend more and more time working creatively in recording studios, and trying to get deals for bands that I liked.

The final two twists in this tale of radio frustration, for me at least, are both rather terrible.

So much so that I pondered leaving them out of these mainly sunny pages. But such is the difficulty in separating the facts from the fiction when posted and promoted online, it's best I get the facts over , straight, as they really were.

First of all, the Krays.

They who in recent years have again become the stuff of East End legend, rather as they were when they hovered like moths to flame around the edges of the music and movie business. As I said, to many ,in the music industry and various personalities of the day, they were at that time more Arthur Daley or Del Boy than the vicious criminals they really were.

They, the Krays,not Arthur or Del Boy, were eventually arrested and charged with a variety of offenses. Not the least of which were murder (several).

As was exposed during their trial, and is still very much proudly shown on the Metropolitan Police Scotland Yard Web site and museum, their final downfall happened when a courier, working for the brothers was arrested as he boarded a plane in Glasgow *with a suitcase full of sticks of dynamite.*

No terrorist plan there, the explosive's (stolen from Scot's coal mines), were needed by the twins for various dubious uses in London.

The courier, with the explosive, was later found to also be in possession of a crossbow and a booby trapped briefcase, apparently to be utilised to eliminate someone in the very London Court, where the Krays themselves were tried.

The courier, as I, and indeed Mrs. Calvert was shocked to learn from the trial reports, was none other than Paul Elvey the ex Radio City engineer whom the Krays, and Laurie were suggesting we could work with on their proposed station.

Just a few years later, I had noticed the Swiss gents, Erwin Meister and Edwin Bollier, suppliers of radio transmitters to various stations, one of whom I had met in Amsterdam and again in the Guinea Pub, had, after an abortive attempt to buy the MV Galaxy,the Radio London ship, had eventually started Radio North Sea International.
RNI broadcast from two ships, Mebo 1 and Mebo 2 offshore from the UK and Holland under various names for a number of years from the 70's on. Mebo being a contraction of the Meister and Bollier names and used by them to identify their electronics manufacturing and supply company.
I thought no more about them or their part in the Kray's radio ambitions until a truly terrible event some years later.
 In December 1988, a Pan Am plane was blown out of the sky by a bomb over Lockerbie in Scotland.
 Investigators later alleged, and then showed in court, that Libyan agents had used a Mebo-manufactured and supplied timer to activate the bomb. Recent forensic evidence suggests there may be some doubt about all this.
Now is not the time to add to the millions of words that have been written about both that tragedy and about the apparent murky conspiracies by several governments, including the British, in establishing the truth of what happened.
I must stress that neither Meister or Bollier have ever been held responsible for the crime, as apparently for perfectly legitimate reasons they sold timers and other electronics to customers around the world.
Although it did turn out that they had some pretty murky customers, naturally the rumours and the story put them out of business.
 Certainly, they were talking to the Krays about transmitters—were they also talking to them about timers for their explosives.?
For me, a near miss.

It shows of course that old adage you can choose your friends but not your enemies is very true.

Some years later, sitting in the bar of a very famous hotel in St Paul de Vence in the South of France I discussed the amiable Arthur Daley /Del Boy image of London's East End villains with actor Dennis Waterman.

He of course so-star of Minder with George Cole.

Waterman's view then, was that the writers of the series, had, as others had before Minder and others since, picked up on an interesting London characteristic of, cheerful cockney geezers, "duckin' and divin' to make an honest living".

A great phrase.

The style had partly started with Steptoe and Sons, Alf Garnett was in there somewhere with, 'Till Death us Do Part '(with a dash of Scouse mixed in there also).

Then or course came only Fools and Horses.

This not only immortalised David Jason's Del Boy role, but also Nicolas Lyndhurst as his younger brother Rodney.

Perhaps considering both my naivety, acceptable at the time, but still stupid, and my full name, Rodney, Del's much used phrase could apply to yours's truly. 'Rodney you Plonker.'

Narrow escape though!

23. More Radio Adventures, or Psst!

It's not every day that you wake up by, or rather are woken up by, a blonde police woman, white blouse with stripy epaulettes, very short black skirt, and a rugged looking belt from which hangs a variety of items including a torch, baton, a mysterious pouch, and a gun in holster, (with a chain attached to both the gun and the belt).
"You want to steal my gun, you have to take me with it."

Now when I say woken up, one could imagine: a tap on the door, an enquiring, "Are you awake in there?" Or perhaps a push on the shoulder, nudge on the leg, or even a vigorous shake.
Possibly worse is the old Army wake up routine of a loud yell, various words optional but including the polite suggestion to stop what you are doing, and get your arse into some clothes and on parade. Now. Or sooner.
Now as it happens I am already fully dressed, even with shoes. My personal early morning call is more of a, porcine, squealing, snorty snore. The police lady is curled up in large chair, face relaxed with lips trembling as she makes secondary sounds like a chainsaw.
I am rather instantly alert, despite my arrival in the room just a few hours earlier being accompanied by two police ladies, with myself doing a lot of swaying, whirling and holding onto walls.
For safety you understand.
So I wake up fairly quickly, and not very hungover. Matching the intake of alcohol of any kind with glasses of water does help ward off the old thumping head. A little.
I am aware where I am. It is the morning of the 31st March, 1993. I am in Lithuania, about 18 months or so after the Russian occupying powers, with their armed forces, had, for good this time the Lithuanians hoped, withdrawn.
There'd been a couple of false starts, but according to various ministers I had dined, (and drunk with) a couple of days earlier in capital city Vilnius, the Russians were gone for good.

Twenty years later, with global politics provoking the Russian Bear to start growling again, I hope the ministerial opinion in Vilnius remains as positive.

By Ministers, I am not referring to men of the cloth, admirable though they may be. I am speaking of ministers as in government types. Elected, even if true free fair and fully elected power had then been a work in progress for some years in Lithuania. Actually the ministers in question may well have had their faiths but... I have given up on comparative religion and focus on the 'now,' rather than the 'then.'

Why, how, where and when?

First of all it wasn't my idea to be there. It was Radio man's.

Now Radio man is a genius with the techie stuff. Such a whizz that back in the sixties his crazy ideas, such as installing high radio transmission aerials on ships or even on offshore forts in the Thames Estuary seemed to be actually not crazy. Radio man created lots of that, ... and more.

I have to stress here very very clearly that Radio man is not in any way the same radio engineer that I had met with some shady gangsters in London back in '67.

Radio man's enthusiasm for the business potential of radio can on occasions be mistaken for him being one valve short of a transistor. But that is absolutely not the case.

Not only does he know his AM from his FM, but he also knows the commercial economics of potential new stations. I mean he really knows that stuff...and he can discourse in non-techie speak as well. A good man. In fact more than that; actually straightforward and sincere. Quite why I have allowed him to persuade me to go to a meeting in Lithuania with him is a mystery to me.

The fact that he has chosen to traverse the country by car in mid winter would suggest that whilst he is a genius with the dosh and the diodes, maybe he needs to pay more attention to 'our man with the meteo for your weather.'

But, I'm not stupid. I have stout shoes, and warm coat and gloves, although at dinner in Vilnius I had removed them(the gloves that is) before tucking into herring, beetroot, sour cream and strong bread—both in taste and texture. There were also rather a lot of fire water toasts, red wine from Hungary, more fire water and then tinned peaches from Angola.

It said so on the tin, and I happen to understand a little Portuguese; Portuguese had obviously been much used for Peach tin labelling in Angola. However, the picture and the map on the tin helped.

Dinner in Vilnius had also involved speeches and more toasts —with more fire-water.

The ministers, all very pleasant even if their names sounded to the ignorant—such as I—a bit like throat-clearing: Algirdas Brasauskas, Algimantas Cekuolis.

But they were very welcoming and patient with the need for translations for some of the others present.

I recalled the minister (of communications I think), explaining that they really wanted inward investment to build a pop radio station.

I then rather rudely observed, over-fueled slightly by fire water number five, that this suggestion seemed a slightly unusual concept given the rather obvious aura around us of "failed communist state."

I breezed on in full firewater flow:

"If I can see crumbling buildings, decrepit buses, streets full of potholes, then one would assume that vital services such as hospitals might also be in need of a lick of paint—even a new syringe or two."

The minister agreed, politely ignoring my slurred slurs on the ancient traditions of this centuries old Baltic state.

"Of course and we are expecting, or rather hoping for much more help for all those things and more, from the USA, Scandinavia and the EEC."

He continued, having generously splashed fire water all around, "Indeed, with the priority of a pop station being so very questionable for those countries and their governments, *it was exactly the reason they were talking to a private company such as us. We had money and we had expertise.*"

I nodded wisely. Actually, in mid-nod I was thinking: Thanks to radio man we have the radio transmission and studio expertise for sure. He had over many years advised on the set up of more radio stations than we had had fire waters: i.e. lots.

I had plenty of radio content expertise. I knew what worked on radio in the west, and even had a very good understanding of, and good contacts for, what worked well in the East of the West. i.e. just across the Baltic Sea in Sweden, where I had been in the music business for many years.

The minister's point that we had the money, as well as all this fab expertise, worried me a little. But for once I kept my mouth shut. A good plan as we were honoured guests, and also a good plan because every time my mouth was open some buffoon, namely me, poured firewater into it.

I did ask, quite a smart question really, even looking back 30 or so years .... "And the reason you have serious priority need for a pop radio station is?"

The answer surprised me then, and even those 30 years on it surprises me now—the surprise, was its brilliance.

First a slurp of firewater, and several Lithuanians around the table tell me that their president has an idea. They all agree actually that the President's big idea can fix a big problem that they have.

"As a country recovering after years of difficulty behind the iron curtain and under the thumb from Moscow, we need to get business and trade moving, both in and out.

We need to build stuff, make things and sell stuff. Grow land and air transport—maybe tourism. We need to upgrade our schools, medical colleges, universities."

"We need to be in the world of the west."

I nod. Their sincerity is absolute. Not a time for jokes now.

They continue, falling over each other's words to get their point over.

Their big problem is that all the above needs English. It seems that those vital English language skills amongst young (and old) Lithuanians are almost zero. Virtually no-one in the country spoke English. Being dominated for years by the red Russkies will do that. They push their plan.

To get the country up to say German or Swedish levels of English will, they fear, take more than ten, maybe fifteen years. "They say it will happen as, 'The new babies come through the schools.'"

Now my business discussions are usually about rock n roll, songs and sales, concerts, T shirt prices, music marketing and more—not deep long term planning like this. But I am fascinated and in respect of their sincerity.

I venture, "But pop radio, where does this come into all this."

It seems their view is that an English language pop radio station, "Can be very free, not boring government controlled lessons, must really be the dream of young people to listen and keep listening. They will listen all day, every day."

With English DJ's, English music, English News and Sport, they will be pushing English into receptive minds, 24/7.

And not in the style of daily or even weekly lessons about verbs, grammar, tenses or sentence structure in a dusty old classroom.

With an English pop radio station, they will, they think, get a reasonable level of English established right across Lithuania in just a couple of years.

Although this newly found English will for sure not be great spelling, or formal verby stuff, (that can come next), it will be a cross-generational seed that can grow very fast.

They sit back, as do we, a couple of them glassy eyed.

This time it is me who grabs the bottle and splashes the firewater around...I am totally convinced that it is a great plan. "It is simple genius. I have seen the effect radio can have, in fact I have even recently observed changes in speech styles and accents as MTV has spread slowly across the USA."

We toast. I say, "Your project is so important to you. I am not sure if we have all or enough resources to make it 100% for you; but anything and everything we can do to help we will.' and I meant it.

Radio man, who knows all this, (he's on his 'nth trip to the land of herring and beetroot), has, as is his way, a cunning plan.

He knows that if the radio signal is transmitted from the right place, that advertising from many other countries, who can also receive the new station, will cover the costs for the Lithuanians. And us.

Like I said, Radio man is a genius, and he's got all the excel sheets to prove it. I've looked at them and even in the worst case scenario— he's on to a good project. As usual.

The following day, English Radio man and I take a five-hour drive through roads deep in snow, to the coast. We are at an old Lithuanian Hanseatic trading town called Palanga. Just across the sea from Sweden. It was a horrible and frankly dangerous drive, but we arrive OK. Slightly shaken and still stirred by the previous night's speeches.

Radio man as ever knows people everywhere. It seems that on the coast there is an area that would be brilliant on which to site radio transmitters. Apparently, from this unique place with a big stick up into the sky, one can send signals of various kinds, all over Lithuania, across to much of Scandinavia, into Russia, if I recall, even as far as Moscow. Oh yes and down to many of the big cities of Germany.

Again, if I recall all the technical stuff correctly, it seems that even the BBC had a desire to build transmitters in that very place to provide extra coverage to their world service.

It is surprising that I that recall anything of this as I learned it whilst standing in a field, by a frozen looking Baltic sea, as a minus something wind whipped across the white frosty grass dispatching stinging ice to sandpaper our faces.

But the Mayor of Palanga, his translator, the local police chief, his translator, my chum Mr. Radio, and several bored looking sheep don't seem troubled by the cold. There is much discussion of windows of opportunity when the permafrosted ground will be defrosted enough to be excavated to put in transmitter-tower foundations.

I am freezing. I try holding my gloved hands over my ears and start wondering about the onset of frost-bite. Through my mittens I start to hear discussions, with much waiting for translations in and out, about foundations and guying supports of 1000, no 2000 radio towers.

As terminal shuddering sets in (me not the towers), I start to wonder if they are talking of feet or meters. Then I try to recall how high the Empire State Building and the Eiffel Tower are...

Eventually we get back to the mayor's office. Hot black tea and firewater are much appreciated. Medicinal purposes indeed.

Lots more talk of surveys and steel. Facilities and finance. I just sit and thaw, dripping slightly on the lino floor. I am after all, there for the 'much music aspect', rather than the techie stuff.

Eventually Brit Radio man has to leave for the dreaded five-hour journey back to Vilnius. The snow is falling harder. I don't envy his drive. I feel a tad smug, as I am staying in Palanga that night and taking an air taxi to Sweden the next morning.

The smugness evaporates somewhat when I see my hotel room. Unoccupied, and undusted I think since Khrushchev stayed there, twenty years before, or possibly Stalin or Lenin before that.

Any remaining smugness definitely disappeared when I surveyed my dinner: watery soup with yellow cabbage and salted and stored fish heads. The fish heads having made the soup look like a puddle in which engine oil has been spilled.

But yippee there were boiled potatoes. On second inspection the parts of the spud that weren't black spots, were clear and translucent. Frost damage I learn. But hey there's pudding.

Two slices of white bread with Angolan peaches on them.

As I enjoy my lonely feast I start to consider Radio. Governments are always nervous of radio. It can destabilise the stable, (and I don't mean panic the horses). Radio speaks to, 'you' and is a powerful propaganda tool.

In fact therefore, very few governments have allowed the creation of nationwide radio for pop fans. The fact that the UK had done just that, I believed, helped UK pop music dominate the world. Holland had national coverage also, albeit it outside the control of their government; although it is hard to imagine in flat and tiny Holland radio being limited by area.

Of course the English language helped, but with the BBC being so straight and honest, it allowed the best of pop, to float naturally to the top. That's defining best as 'most liked', 'popular', and thus, big selling.

Having genuinely proven popular items at the top, kick-started the UK music industry on its path to global success.

Until MTV started, the US music fans had to rely on a million or so local stations. Access to those local stations tended to be reserved to

those with big money legally (or often illegally) promoting them.
Thus making the USA a follower of trends and rarely a creator.
In France they had a big AM station in the North and another in the
South. When FM came in it was very localised, until the Paris NRG
FM station engineered a series of local franchises, providing
national coverage   but bit by bit, licence by license.
It was very much the same story in Germany with Munich, Stuttgart,
Frankfurt, Hamburg, Koln (Cologne) and eventually Berlin
entertaining locally but not usually with the same song nationwide
at the same time.
So the UK with Radio One and Holland, with a little stick on a ship
giving Radio Veronica nationwide coverage across the low-
countries, were doing well with music sales of their local hits, which
were now also popular worldwide.
Whilst ignoring my cabbage, fish-heads, and transparent spotty
spuds, I ponder the Lithuanian, 'Teach the people English' plan.
Seemed good. Of course a bit propaganda-ish, but I had seen and
believed the sincerity of those ministers the night before.
As it happens, for little Lithuania, the power of Radio and TV had
been demonstrated in the country just 18 months earlier.
As had been occurring right across Europe in preceding years, in
1990 and '91, the Russians in Lithuania were faced with massive
street demonstrations from citizens sensing the wind of change
blowing across the old Communist Block.
The Russians were leaving and fact and rumour swirled around. On
January the 11th a form of independent and national salvation
government was declared. The Russians had made big military
noises.
They closed the railway station—they reopened the railway station.
Overnight the new 'Government' tries to contact Gorbachov in
Moscow. The Russians make military noises and a new General
takes command. Thousands of peaceful Lithuanians converge on the
Parliament buildings, the telephone exchange, The Radio Tower and
the TV studios.
On the 12th, rumour and action are on the agenda. The Russians are
regrouping. There are some accidents and some bullets start to fly.

Some civilians die. Rumours and fact are mixed but it doesn't look too good from the Lithuanian perspective.

Overnight by the 13th there are 20,000 people around the buildings, and the nation is gripped by pictures from their TV tower. The Russians arrive and their tanks fire over the heads of the crowd. In the last pictures the anxious nation sees a Russian soldier running toward the TV camera, and the screen goes blank.

By the morning, there are 50,000 or more brave citizens defiantly on the streets. But no one knows this is happening because there is no TV and very little radio.

Then by chance a techie at a local TV station, still with some facilities and electric power, starts to broadcast calls for international help, or at least support.

Within hours the TV Techie is backed up by Professors, teachers and the like, broadcasting the same appeals. Eventually, a Swedish TV channel sees what's happening and sends the story to the world.

Within a few days, despite not much more than encouraging words arriving from the West, the Russians pull back and eventually leave. The power of radio.

Maybe that's why the men from the Ministry in Vilnius have such faith in their pop radio plan.

I am finishing my beer, bread and peaches and some kind of local police chief arrives, with an escort of smartly uniformed police ladies. Some English is spoken.

Police Chief wants to show me something. Outside. We get into a car. I get a coat and damp gloves. Before we leave the bar/hotel restaurant, the ladies go and arrest and handcuff a gent quietly sitting drinking beer with firewater chasers.

They explain, "We take him, to police station on way to where we go in the forest." Having deposited the man at the cop-shop, I am quietly asking what he had done, not wanting to cross some invisible local line and end up handcuffed and locked like the mild-looking blokey.

They explain. "Old Fred" or whatever his name was, "-he's the local snow plough driver, and he has to clear the airport runway for your plane in the morning. But if he drinks too much tonight he cannot do the job."

I feel sorry for Fred, but moving on, I enquire about their very sprauncy four door pick up truck. A Ford-lots of lights and stuff. As far as I can make out it was a gift from Lithuanian expats in the USA. Aiming to help the old country.

We are now it seems, driving across the ice on a lake. " Making shorter travel." I nod and start thinking about spring thaws and the weight of big Ford pick up trucks.

With blondie-politie-ladie translating, I also learn that the boss has been on a training course at an American Police Academy. It seems she has been there with him, as translator she assures me.

I ask if it was interesting and she says not so interesting as Disney World.

And from one of the many pouches strung round her webbing belt she producers a folder of photos. Lots of Mickey Mouse and the usual stuff, mostly with Police lady in very short shorts. None of him—but in the best Colombo fashion I guess he had the camera.

I point at the picture of her in very short shorts, and say, "Next time I visit Palanga in the summer." She smiles, and moves a little closer in the backseat.

I panic somewhat when Police Chief obviously asks. "what is he talking about ". But maybe fortuitously, we scramble up a bank, back on to road or track, I can't tell under the snow, and are driving through a forest.

Ahead I can see some lights, and we stop in front of what looks like some big old barns. We exit and bloody hell! It's cold after the Miami Vice-like warm of the car. With some effort a big door is slid open, and we exit the icy wind.

Having de-misted my glasses I realise it's even colder in the building, or at least it seems that way.

An old bloke appears, bit frosty, bobble hat, gloves with no fingers and a very red nose. Red, despite the snow, not in a 'Santa or Rudolf way,' but red as in, my only anti-freeze and fuel is the local firewater. As I notice that the snow is fluttering down from the roof, and we are inside, Miss Palanga is explaining to me that, "The chief has some stuff for sale. Left behind as unwanted by the Russians."

Red nose and the chief lever open the hinged lid of a long box. They all shine their torches inside.

Bloody hell! Sorry dear reader, but when someone offers you a box of ground-to-air missiles, neatly folded and semi wrapped, it's a bit of shock. Especially when one's usual stock in trade is discs (various) with music on.

Before I can speak, they pull the covers off what looks like a quad bike with a bloody great missile on the top. Military grey green colour. Rather bizarrely, there's a knitted sock thingy covering the pointy bit at the front end.

I point at it. After some words between chiefy and Rudolf, I learn from Miss Palanga Police that the pointy bit tells the rocket where to go, and it "Mustn't freeze."

Red nose proudly lifts a flap on the vehicle and there are some red lights flashing. I step back, and learn, via my translator that the red lights mean the system is warm, against frost. It seems 'red nose' charges the red lights as needed.

The sales tour goes on for ages. Box after box, what looks like guns, more rocketry things, boxes of radios. Lots of stuff. I do a lot of nodding and thinking.

I am thinking, this is not good. This not a clever situation to be in.

I am thinking. This is not funny. If I say I can do nothing about any of this, then maybe I know too much, and maybe I won't ever make it out of the forest.

I am thinking...I don't know anymore what I am thinking. So much fear that I start to shiver. I have often read the words, frozen with fear, but have rarely experienced the fear factor full on.

The Chief is obviously asking Miss P. to ask me what I think. Fortunately for me she says, or I think she says. "Look he shaking cold; let's get in the car."

Which we do, and we start a three-point turn to find the exit to the road.

Using, or maybe not using my brain I say, "I don't know much about all that sort of thing. BUT I do know some press guys who know all sorts of people who could be interested."

"Wrong...no not wrong. But WRONG."

" No publicity, no publicity!" The Chief is so busy looking round and making his point that his smart US Cop car slides into some deep snow.

As he is cursing, and struggling to open his door, which is in snow up to the window, I have to raise my voice to explain, via Miss Palanga, "Of course publicity not allow. Only secret friends with me. Maybe can help. Can do maybe I hope,"

I notice I have again slid into abbreviated speak-speech.

The next thirty minutes or so made me wonder if it was Police Academy, 'The Movie', they had been to in the USA, not a genuine Police Academy.

Despite the combined efforts of two strong police-women, the chief, red nose and my self, we couldn't budge the car.

Much radio use is made of radios. The essence of the calls is, I learn later:

"Send Fred-the snow plough with his machine to dig us out, and make sure he goes round the lake not over it."

" Err, Fred's locked up in the cop-shop." " Bloody unlock him then." "Sorry chief, you've got the keys in your car." "Use the spare keys you buffoon."

" Err, Britt's got the spare keys." Long silence.

Britt, with a sweet smile holds them up...and later tells me that the Chief told her to keep the keys, so that she could unlock Fred in time to clear the runway in the morning.

Another long silence, broken only by the sound of the wind in the frozen trees and the odd loud snap that I am reliably informed is the snap of branches bursting in the frost.

With some politeness, and in an attempt to lighten the situation, I say. "What we need is a drop of warming firewater to keep away the cold." As I have made shot-type drinking gestures whilst saying that, the Chief and Miss Sweetness respond together.

"We are very modern. We learn the American way at academy. No booze on duty. So never have alcohol in the car."

I reach into my pocket and produce a full half bottle, and say. "But I do." Big smiles, even from the Chief; and the winter warmer is indeed just that.

As we stand there, waiting I think for a plan to materialise, the silence is broken by huge diesel engine sounds, lots of revving, and around the corner comes a very large tracked vehicle.

On the top, covered in snowy canvas, a rocket-shaped thing.

It is the work of moments for Red nose to tow us out of the snow and at the same time to demolish the only working street lamp and to nick my bottle of firewater.

The chief drives us, carefully, back into town.

At the only gas station in town we eat hot dogs—several for me. They are Swedish I notice.

Back at the hotel, many more drinks are consumed. I learn that Red Nose was a Red Army store man, who went AWOL. I enquire, if surely the Red Russians might not one day wake up to their missing kit and return for it.

The Chief stands proud and says. "We thought of that. Last summer we moved it all from the army store. Those sheds are where we keep the snow ploughs in the summer."

I look suitably impressed at my new best friend's advanced planning. And soon after as the world starts to revolve, I retire to bed.

Miss Sweetness is ordered to take me and Fred to the Airport at 7 O'clock, which indeed she does. There as my plane circles low, I learn later that the pilot, is as usual, first checking that Fred is not snoozing on the runway. I promise the chief to do my best and find people who know about arms dealing. No publicity.

Of course, I promise, no publicity.

And I have kept my promise. Until now. ends...except not quite.

Sadly, Radio Man and the others failed to raise the money to proceed with the Lithuanian English language radio dream. I believe that an Irish company eventually opened an FM station. I hope our endeavours helped.

I notice that Algirdas Brasauskas, one of those who entertained me so well in Vilnius on the 29th March 1993, later became their Prime Minister from 2001- 2006.

What happened to the Chief and the Police ladies I have no idea. Palanga is once again a favoured Baltic coast holiday spot for Europeans; if you go there and see Fred or a blokey with a very red nose, buy them a beer from me.

24. It'll never last.

It's November 1979 and I am sitting in the stalls of the London Palladium, tears streaming uncontrollably down my face. I am not prone to such emotional outpourings but I have just witnessed the usually somewhat stuffy, staid and well behaved audience at The Royal Command performance standing and cheering.
Stamping their feet, clapping in time and even yelling for more.
The cause of the excitement?

A chubby, almost sixty year old ex country musician whose original band, The Saddlemen, recorded such 1950's classics as, 'Rose of My Heart' and 'Yodel Your Blues Away.'
A fortunate name change, style and a little luck explains why our be-suited crowd have gone crazy man crazy and are yelling, "Bill, Bill."
For it is indeed Bill. Bill Haley and his Comets. His worldwide hit 'Rock Around the Clock,' almost brings the house down.
An hour later I am in tears again backstage as Bills wife Martha hugs me and says ,"Thank you, thank you. Thank you." I had persuaded Louis Benjamin (later Sir Louis) and his Boss, Lord Grade, owners of the Palladium and organisers of the charity show, to book Bill.
Bill had been signed to our Sonet records company for ten years by then and I knew him pretty well. In fact, I had spent some time in Alabama with Bill and Martha earlier in '79, due to the fact that Kenny Denton, a genius producer of ours, had recorded a new LP for us with Bill. ('Every One Can Rock n' Roll.')
We all knew, except possibly Bill, that all really was not so good with his health, but it was still a considerable shock when on February 9th.1981, less than 15 months after his Palladium triumph he was dead.
That was a doubly sad day for both my wife and I, as we had both had extensive telephone conversations with him the night before his death. He had called us and was discussing some future recording plans. As ever he was blowing hot and then cold on the idea.
In that case, with us only just having finished one set of recordings, we wanted more but were in no particular hurry, so no pressure from us.

But when Bill wanted to chat-we listened. Although he didn't really 'get' the fact that for us in England it was 3 am!

With style old-charm, he always politely called my wife, 'Ma-am;' as she said then. "It sounded so wonderful in his American accent."

Later that sad February day in '81, as I raised a glass to salute an unlikely musical hero, I remembered Bill telling me with scarcely controlled excitement that the Queen, yes our Queen Elizabeth, had said to him, "My sister and I did so love dancing to your music in the fifties."

Just today, I watched his Royal Variety performance on line and I must say I felt very proud. It had taken some effort to get the show arranged, as Bill's reputation was not, at that time one of being too reliable. But we persevered and Bill delivered.

Mind you I did wonder how Her Majesty could jive. I mean surely her crown would fall off?!

How could an avuncular, never seeming-too-young guy, in a plaid jacket and with a kiss curl seemingly stuck on his broad forehead, for ten years in the fifties have had the most recognisable face in the world?

The answer lies in his incredible nine hit singles between '54 and '56 in almost every country of the globe. Including the UK and US charts. He was by far the biggest selling, most played, most recognisable record artist of the period.

OK dear reader. All of that is before your time I know. But those classics are rarely off the radio even these days for one reason or another.

With Bill's music much admired by,' The Fonz', Richie and the Happy Days gang, between 74-84 , Haley's 'Rock around the Clock', 'Crazy Men Crazy,' 'See you Later Alligator,' and 'Shake Rattle and Roll' all had hit the spot again-just as they had woken up the world in the fifties.

His face originally became familiar, thanks to repeated global TV exposure of those then revolutionary Rock n' Roll songs, and his musical performances in some major movies including Blackboard Jungle, Rock around the Clock and Don't Knock the Rock.

In the UK, in February '57 his face was all over the UK newspapers for not such good reasons. Haley had just arrived by ocean liner at

Southampton on England's South Coast. He had then taken the usual 'boat' train to London's Waterloo Station. For most passengers a fairly standard home-coming, and indeed the standard route for tourists on arrival for a visit to see, 'quaint little ole London Town.' There may have been some tourists on the train. There may well have been some families waiting to greet their relatives at the station in the usual way.

But for Bill there were 20,000 people waiting.

All yelling, screaming, pushing, shoving and climbing high into the station roof to get a sight of 'Mr. Rock Around the Clock.'

Eventually, as the police struggled to regain order, tempers flared amongst the thousands of rockers. Tempers were their only flared item as drainpipe trousers were 100% in vogue at the time. As were drape jackets, bootlace ties and a choice of two shoe styles: thick crepe sole shoes or winkle picker pointed style.

The press had a field day reporting, 'The Second Battle of Waterloo.' Trouble flared again at many of the theatre shows that followed, where uniformed and often quite elderly commissionaires, attempted to restrain patrons from ripping up the seats to make space to dance or from jiving in the aisles.

But of course what goes up must come down, or in the pop popularity business, trends change and styles move on. So by the mid sixties' Bill was not so much in demand. I am not speaking badly of some one I liked a lot, when I say that in later years Bill had some problems with alcohol, I think we can understand.

Can you imagine going from being the most recognisable face in the world, to twenty years later standing in line at MacDonald's with people nudging each other, whispering and eventually saying,' "Didn't you used to be Bill Haley?"

It must have been unimaginably difficult. In reality it must have been horrible. Ad it happened at every gas station, airport or hotel check in. Everywhere. Every time. And of course, for Bill, a glimmer of recognition of his achievements, but in the main a reminder of long gone and better times.

Over the years there had been the usual show biz troubles with tax and tours and the usual politics of running a band of talented individual musicians.

And every day an audience who only wanted to hear the, same old hit songs. Again and again and again. A Rock and Roller coaster. Many music critics have dismissed Bills career as just darn lucky. In fact he was a lot more talented than his style and later modest demeanour suggested.

In the sixties with the iconic Rock Around the Clock then winding down, he had completely reinvented himself again. In Mexican. In Spanish as a Twist sensation.

Chubby Checker's, Lets Twist (Again) may have been the global dance sensation of the decade after Rock N Roll. But for Mexicans it was Bill's, 'Twist Espanol,' that echoed around the nation at fiestas and festivals.

The already referred to pressure on Bill just to 'play the hits' yet again, meant that in later years, motivating him for the recording studio was not easy. Renowned and respected American producer, Sam Charters, for Sonet Sweden, with very understated skill had made some excellent recordings with Bill that sold in their millions; classic stuff and properly done—good business for Bill.

But in 1979, in the UK, I wanted more than a remake, even if the remakes had been great. And in my personal, repeat, personal view (and I guess hearing), I think we did it.

The record Bill made for our Sonet UK company in the legendary Fame studios in Alabama was and should be part of his legacy. Obviously, in second place to the original hits, but it absolutely stands up with the best and will stand the test of time.

I say personal because it was my dream that Bill could do it again. I make no claims to have produced it. I partly chose the songs. The most important person, sometimes, in a studio recording session is the producer. I knew that there was only one guy who maybe, just maybe, could motivate Bill and get him back on track. The one guy, who had partly inspired my dream.

His name was Kenny Denton—an Englishman. With a lifetime of studio experience, Kenny was both engineer and producer and, also as I called him, 'a sneaky studio psychologist.' He was a genius at easing and teasing great performances out of musicians. Then just as importantly, at capturing on the recording tape, that elusive 'something' that makes the difference between a nice recording and a memorable one; one that crashes out of your speakers and into your heart and into your life. From experience, Kenny and I knew Bill would do his darndest to wander in, do a professional job on the songs, and escape back to his home in Harlingen Texas as soon as he could. But Kenny got it. He understood. We both wanted more. We wanted the vibrancy, the sparkle, the power and the magic of those 1954 - 56 recordings.

Keeping me, 'Mr. business,' well out of the way, Kenny and the Fame Studios team assembled a band of young rock roll musicians that only the Southern States of America could produce.

The culture in those Southern States of live music, on the road, playing long hours in bars and honky tonks, often with the stage behind chicken wire to avoid enthusiastically thrown bottles.

Don't stop and keep the joint rockin'—Or else!

It's dinner in Muscle Shoals, hometown of Fame studios.

No alcohol (an edict of local law) and helpful in this case. There was me, Kenny, Bill and Martha.

It had indeed been a very long and arduous first days' rehearsals and Bill was a little quiet.

Every now and again he murmurs. 'My my' or 'Well well,' and it's clear he's not talking about the steak.

We mention the band.

Bill just says, 'My goodness.' and then 'I'm not sure.'

Kenny, the experienced studio man senses of course, what Bill is not sure about is. Can he keep up with the verve, vibrancy pace and pure rock n' roll of the new backing band in the studio?

Kenny signals me to 'shut up.'

He, Kenny, has a plan, a masterstroke of long experience.

"Tomorrow," he says casually to Bill, "I thought we'd try," note, "try," "-some country flavoured stuff." 'Jim Dandy', 'Heartaches by the Number,' those sort of things.

Bill brightens. He obviously feels that a little excursion back to his roots will work just fine, Just dandy in fact.

The following evening, Bill is shattered, and not surprisingly a little wheezy even. But standing proud, Kenny has helped him meet the hopes, dreams and expectations of the young band.

That next evening the, "My My's," "well, well's" and "my goodness'",
have turned into "Well, my goodness Kenny, we really hit it today."
Enough of me, me, me. Here's what respected music critic and
author David Sandison wrote at the time:

*The idea was simple enough: put Bill Haley, the father of Rock 'n'
Roll into one of the worlds best recording studios with some of
America's best young Southern rock musicians and cut an album to
prove that true rock 'n' roll was alive, well and kicking like hell,
twenty five years after Bill started it all with his classic, Rock
around the Clock.*

*So it was on June 25, 1979, at Fame Studios Muscle Shoals,
Alabama, that a bunch of Jackson Mississippi crazies called 'The
Fame Gang,' along with legendary Memphis Horns sax man, Ed
Logan, awaited the arrival of 'The Man.'*

*The next week, the team worked harder than any of them could
remember. The musicians worked hard because they were knocked
out by the inspiration Bill gave them. Bill worked hard (harder
than he's worked since the early days) because as he said one night.
"When you got people as good as this giving as good as these guys,
you've got to deliver too!"*

*The result is an album as potent, dynamic and exciting as any
recordings that Bill Haley cut in the fifties, when they told him;
'Rock n. Roll will never last. "Twenty five years later we say:
"Happy Birthday Rock n Roll."*

A further thirty or so years on from those sessions and when those
words were written I echo those words and the sentiments
expressed.

Bill's wife Martha was his rock, his strength, easing the doubts,
encouraging and on occasions, demanding. She was his lifeline and
life support.

Although she had never let us see, I assume that taking care of Bill
was not easy. I did see and admired her in action in Muscle Shoals.
She persevered and with her Mexican wit, charm and sparkle, eased
over many a problem.

Whilst typing this, and watching and listening to Noel Edmonds
introducing Bill at the Royal Variety Show in the London Palladium

that November evening of 1979, I have just noticed, under the 'You Tube' screen, someone has written the following words:

In November 1979, Haley and the Comets performed for Her Majesty Queen Elizabeth II, at the Royal Command performance at London's Palladium Theatre. A moment Haley considered, the proudest of his career. It was also the last time he performed in Europe and the last time most fans saw him perform "Rock Around the Clock."

Thank you Martha and thank you Kenny Denton, for delivering on our dreams.
Check out that last LP. "Everyone Can Rock n' Roll."
The title track pops up on you tube, but whilst a great name for a record, it's quite relaxed.
Find the country with 'Jim Dandy', find Bill's humour with, 'The Battle of New Orleans,' but above all, find and play, 'God Bless Rock n' Roll.' Loud...
...and every day on the radio somewhere...everywhere, you cannot but fail to smile as you hear the intro:
'One, two, three o'clock, four o'clock rock, Five, six seven o'clock, eight o'clock rock'... and sixty years ago they said it would never last!
At the 1979 Fame Sessions, whilst recording 'God Bless Rock n Roll,' we told Kenny Denton, "This will last," as he got the best performances out of Bill for many years.
And indeed almost 40 years on, Bill's last recordings still sound as good as his first ones to me.
Thank you Bill..."Hasta Luego Cocodrilo."

25. Of Song Festivals, Contests, Secrets, Spooks and Spies: and...Goodbye.

The Beatles recorded a wonderful track called, 'The Long and Winding Road.' This part of my narrative is both long and winding. Quite frankly it's quite rambling as well, but I think the tales therein, all true by the way, are worth telling. I hope you agree.

Still all these years later, minding those wise words about getting the attention of readers, delivered in 1962 by my first editor Mr. Sears and so as is the way of this book I have considered a couple of 'grab ems' for this part of the story. You may remember this from the opening chapters of the book.

Opener. Draft 1. The steely eyed and very unsmiling gent, leaned back in his chair, and fixing me with those cold grey eyes said, in quite good English for a Moscow Russian in 1980, "Is it not possible that you are engaged by the English authorities for some purpose to look at us here? You will tell me now please, my chief is on his way here, and we must know the answers."

Given that I had been approached quite early that morning in my Moscow hotel, and rather firmly instructed to follow some gloomy looking men in overcoats to, "Come to office. Boss want to speak you." Their words actually translated by a nubile Cuban student girl, who just happened to be planning breakfasting with me. (More of her to follow.)

In his office, I gulped, gasped, floundered and tried to breath normally, with images of Greville Wynne, the British spy held, tried and then released across that Berlin bridge by the Russians, and other worse things crossing my mind. Thank you for nothing, Len Deighton, John Le Carre, Ian Fleming.

Even though their espionage and spying characters were fictional, at that moment in the blur of nerves and fear, fiction met reality. Big time.

Even though the Greville Wynne event had been in 1964, I was in Fleet Street then and it was a huge story, and was constantly updated with books and films.... so palpitations, cold sweat and dry mouth ruled.

I gulped again, and then almost fainted as, without a glimmer of emotion, *Mr. Steely Eyes, tossed across the desk a black and white photo that clearly showed me entering the door of No 10 Downing Street...........*

Harking back to today. Actually as me and Mr. Microsoft type this I am wondering if you can 'hark back', to come forward almost forty years. Anyway, as of this minute I am again considering the choice of intro to use for this part of my life.

The previous paragraph, set in a stern looking office building in Central Moscow is no exaggeration. It's 100% factual, if anything though, the years have dimmed the fears.

Interesting then, that even now, the adrenaline gasp and pounding heart that hit me then have surfaced again, softened a little, but real enough. But today, having harked back or forth, per Editor Mr. Sears. "Keep it brief, make it interesting to as many readers as you can."

Given that it's men who mostly buy espionage books, maybe the potential plight of a nervously innocent 35 year old music producer and ex-journalist, being interrogated in a threatening building in a gloomy Moscow dawn is, perhaps not the stuff for mainly female ex-Jackie readers.

So I'll try again, maybe this one is more, 'grab you'.

Opener. Draft 2. Moscow. Autumn 1974. The very blonde blonde, and obviously very KGB lady (we had been warned before we travelled about Russia's KGB Secret Service.) That's blonde except for black smudgy eyelashes, leaned over in the candle lit bar, and started to nuzzle my left ear.... now the beer had been strong, and very stupidly I had then moved on to local Vodka.

It suddenly seemed remarkably hot for a Moscow winters evening. Bars in exotic locations, I was used to. With British pop still exploding in popularity globally I had been travelling widely for some years in the very business of pop music...

Having moved on from full time employment at Jackie, I had by 1968, as has been overly detailed elsewhere, started my own music company. Still, trying to pay my rent by contributing stories to Jackie and also to some other magazines, as a freelance.

I started my 'Record Company' as we called them then, and over the years notched up those already mentioned hits.

By the eighties, with my Swedish business partners, the whole group of companies had around a 100 people employed in various countries.

The group turnover had usually climbed over the years, but my problem was, that my UK part particularly, was in roller coaster fashion. Alarmingly up and down. Eventually we reached many millions of turnover in a mix of Dollars, Pounds, Swedish Crowns, Japanese Yen, and soon to be Euro's. Whatever, wherever we earned it, it was lot.

Note. That's *millions of dosh turnover*. That's the money that goes through the business. Of course, what stays behind after you've paid all the bills is way less, and what then stays behind for the owners is even less.

Sadly, but realistically, what stayed behind for me in the very early years was often less than less. Or to put that another way: nothing. Not only that but it had taken years of work, to get that far with my share still being nothing.

So Herman's Hermits '66 hit of 'No Milk Today', was starting to look a bit like the story of my life, although, in the song's instance, it's referring to the loss of a girlfriend. In my case I needed to eat cornflakes at least. And have milk in my coffee.

Freelance writing was a help, and ironically DC Thomson's, the very Scot's owners of Jackie paid me rather well, but other payments were starting to look like a Scot's Tartan when viewed from a long way away: very small cheques.

Then I had a bit of luck; in summer of 1972 I was offered quite good and regular money to take on the representation of a Music Industry Trade Fair. Not only that but I would still have time to build up my own music company,

My task? To explain the trade fair's benefits to music companies that may wish to attend the Midem, as the Marche International du Music was called. At first, most of the potential participating companies would be mainly from the UK, but as my own little music company, the trade fair and indeed I, became more established and known, I was also called upon to try and rustle up some business across the USSR and a few other exotic locations...

That all sounds a bit, 'normal but with business suits needed '.

But remember, as it says on the label of some of the old Immediate Records releases, 'We are Happy to be Part of the Industry of Human Happiness'.

So even wearing a tie for a trade fair, this was still the music business. Yes, that's The music business, which as we have seen is not, (despite the headline writers), always all Sex, Drugs and Rock n' Roll.

So it's 1974, in the doubtlessly balmy warm late November weather of always sunny Dundee, in the editorial offices of DC Thomson's, and the deservedly soon-to-be famous, Nina Myskow, fragrant and lovely in a summer frock, is earnestly and diligently planning content updates to keep your Jackie Magazine ahead in style and content. You, the readers, were in your young teens but were rapidly becoming more worldly-wise.

I meanwhile, I am in freezing, snowy and icy Russia.

Stay with me through this bit readers...as I just said, you Jackie readers were in your teens, and whilst becoming more worldly-wise, that wisdom learned was usually more about personal teenage matters.

Quite understandably, as research at the time showed, for most teenagers, of either sex, news was something you only noticed now and again on TV, mainly when your Mum, Dad or you watched or were waiting for Coronation Street.

Most News wasn't usually of interest to the majority of you.

Especially as the stories, as they usually were then, were featuring Men in Suits, being interviewed by Men in Suits, the story being presented by Men in Suits. All Old men at that. The first woman National News reader was Angela Rippon and she didn't really get started until 1975.

So old blokies, droning on, and on, and on. Not a sign of a smile. Boring, boring boring. Before you all accuse me of being the same, or making assumptions about your then lack of interest in current affairs, I have not forgotten Gordon Small's important words, 'Don't talk down to your readers.'

But facts are facts...as all the research showed, most teenagers then, were simply not very informed or concerned about current affairs. *So as I say, bear with me dear reader...it's a still bloody freezing night in early November 1974, and I am still in Russia.... and I guess Nina Myskow , despite her name being only two letters away from Moscow, is still in always sunny Dundee, making Jackie even better than better.*

Not so many businessmen got visas to visit Russia back then. Visas took a lot of queuing and questions, mainly, and not only because the Moscow weather was cold, but East-West relations were usually described as The Cold War.

At that time though, apparently, according to the Politicians and the Press, and oh yes, those un- smilers on BBC and ITN, "There was a thaw in East-West relations taking place."

I can assure you, and them, that as we travelled around the East Bloc, no one seemed to have told the border guards or policemen about this thaw.

Every one, West to East, East to West, was still regarding every one else with grave suspicion. Despite the hand of friendship, the Red Menace, of Evil Communism was firmly being resisted by the USA in many locations across the globe, sometimes with full on wars, as in Korea and then Vietnam.

Just ten years before, there had been a very near brush with a total Nuclear War. This was almost triggered when the Russians started to set up missile bases in Cuba: As Cuba was, and unsurprisingly still is, just over 75 miles across the sea from Miami, the Americans were not best pleased.

In the White House and Congress, not to mention the media, many promoted scare stories and then urgently demanded a warlike response from the US. Where have we heard all that again in recent years?

American President John F Kennedy indeed took a tough line, but with a more realistic approach. Fortunately for the world, the Russians both calmed down and backed down. A deserved triumph for soon-to-be-assassinated Kennedy.

No wonder then, even ten years later in '74, that the world was still reeling with rumours about the assassination of JFK in Nov. '63.

Rumours suggested it had all been a US plot by those same warlike elements from their own country wishing to rid themselves of their 'weak' President.

Others suggested plots that involved the Mafia and Marilyn Monroe and still more suggested a KGB plot. That seemed the most likely, as after all, Lee Harvey Oswald, the apparent assassin had spent a lot of time in Russia, home of the Russia's security service, The KGB.

It seemed that British businessmen (me apparently included) were still regarded with suspicion by the Russians.

Partly because, some few years before, Greville Wynne had been taken to lunch *(at the Ivy)* in London by the head of the UK security service and asked to 'Keep an eye open for useful Russkies, and run a few errands for us.'

As I have referred to earlier, Wynne obliged and was eventually arrested by the Soviets in 1963, and convicted of spying and then exchanged over the Glenicke bridge..

(Incidentally, I was recently shocked to learn that spy exchanges were still being made over that bridge until Feb 15th 1986).

But by my November '74 visit to Moscow things were supposed to be normalising, and we were supposed to be trying to become the best of chums.

I am there, in Moscow on both music and trade fair business talking about the benefits of the Midem music market, and trying sell to Melodia, the Russian State Record Company, some of my own record company's new productions.

My record company had earlier that summer scored big time with 'Yviva Espana,' Sung by a remarkably talented Swedish singer called Sylvia Vrethammar. Or the slightly easier to say, 'Sylvia,' as I put on the record label.

I was quite sure the Russians or some others of the sprawling USSR needed a version of our hit song recorded in one of their many languages.

It had not occurred to me that most Soviet Citizens were forbidden foreign travel, even to 'Chat to a Matador in Sunny Spain, la la la...'

I didn't really think, as I sipped my Vodka (of course) in that late night Moscow Hotel bar, that Miss Ear Nibbler was considering auditioning as a Rock n' Roll singer.

I suspected that other words in the Sex Drugs and Rock n' Roll mantra were in her repertoire. I rather hoped it wasn't the drugs bit! After all drugs are not good.

Then she asked me a question.

Miss Ear Nibbler, *"I really like to know what the young peoples in England are thinking today."* So suddenly, as well as an increasingly soggy ear, I had another problem.

A real problem. I mean a really real Problem with a capital P, and it did not involve sex, drugs, or rock n' roll.

A year or so before, I too had been taken to lunch in London also by a very military type, (*at the Spaghetti House Knightsbridge, not the Ivy*) and asked to "Keep your ears and eyes open on your travels around the Soviet bloc. We really want to get a grip on what their young people are thinking."

Except for an East to West to West to East difference, very much the same words that Miss Ear Nibbler had just uttered.

The lunch in London had followed a visit made to my office by the military type blokey, by the name of Neville, having explained to me that my travels had rung some kind of bell with them.

He said he was from the Passport Office in Petty France London. It was the frequency of my regular Eastern Bloc travels that had really alerted them.

I can't recall why, but at first I nervously assumed he was a tax inspector. I think it was because, at that time for all foreign trips we had to get permission from our local bank, complete with stamp in the back of our passport to take even £10 out of the U.K. Whilst most people had just two or three of those stamps, reflecting the trend to package hols. abroad, I had hundreds.

In my case, in addition to the usual entry and exit stamps at the front and eventually filling the passport, the back pages were filled (as also were loads of extra pages inserted by the bank), all with stamps that confirmed my constant travelling.

No mention in the office, or the Spaghetti House, of MI5, MI6 or M anything. In fact eventually the only 'M' I met was Bony, singing about Brown Girls and Rasputin.

Still assuming I was dealing with a taxman wanting to know why I was taking money out of the UK, I explained that I was travelling frequently to sell the idea of a trade fair to foreign music companies. I was also desperately trying to sell music from my own company to anyone who would work on it in their part of the world, and on occasions finding and buying stuff to sell in the UK.

Oh yes, and as foreign song contests liked having me as a judge or advisor, although they didn't pay much more than hotel expenses, they did on occasions provide paid-for return air tickets.

As I was short of cash to build my company, those free tickets were very useful for meeting potentially useful music business people. And here dear reader we take a brief pause. Not, for once in my rambling style a diversion but some background to the above and what comes next, in this thrilling (not) tale.

Of Song Contests and Heroes of the State.

'I lof him so, he drives tractor so good.'

'I hope he will lof me too, if I work so hard.'

'I really dream to share my quota of lof with him'

'Lof, Lof me Do.' This one at least ,words and music: Lennon/P. McCartney. Really!

I am studying the translated lyric sheets that have just been handed to me. It's 1967 or possibly early 1968, (this stuff happened to me a lot in those days) and I'm sitting outside at a cafe table in a pleasant town square somewhere near Ljubljana, then nominally part of Yugoslavia and now after much regional upheaval, part of Slovenia. All around me in the square, preparations are being made for a televised song festival. Noisily, steel crowd barriers are clunked into place, big chunky TV cameras (in raincoats) are focused on their focusing and lighting.

Big clicky sounds are coming from the amplifiers on the stage. Brit-made Marshall amps I notice, usually in the years to come, sharing the stage with hard to miss very orange, Orange Guitar amps. Also British.

This is the third festival of it's type I have been to recently, the others being in San Remo Italy, and one in Poland.

Here in Yugoslavia, this time I am no less than: an adviser. They wanted English expertise both in music and in language.

In fact the musicians of Ljubljana are very well up do date with Western Music and their English is pretty good also. As is their

Slivovitz Plum Brandy, although it is not usually what I would have with my Wheaties Flakes for breakfast.

The English language assistance, given that I don't speak even one of the many dialects and languages in evidence around Eastern Europe, is more one of correcting obvious mistakes in song titles and lyrics.

And mistakes are what I have been requested to check for in the lyrics given to me by a Romanian TV executive. He is planning to develop one of their local song festivals into a TV show. And he has an eye on the western market.

I delay my response by reading more: *"I have much lof for him, he works so well."* It goes on, and on, for pages—all very patriotic, symbolic, and morale-boosting, to jolly along the workers. But teaching, encouraging, and more to the point controlling—the workers is what it is still, officially at least, supposed to be all about in the countries of Eastern Europe, just a few days drive by army tank from Moscow.

Back then during the cold war, the Berlin Wall had gone up in 1961, the divisions between The West with Nato and The East with the Warsaw Pact were clear. The West had a growing Common Market, the East a struggling Comecon.

Rather more relevant to my advisory role at that moment was the fact that, The West had Eurovision with its song contest, and The East had InterVision with its song contest.

InterVision was equally a feast of sequins and sparkles, and that was just the boys, and songs that had to try to be instantly catchy.

Although to be fair, Eurovision, unless I missed something, has never been very orientated towards pushing and praising the achievements of factory, farming or fishing output.

Actually, to be sure on that point, I just checked the list of the sixty years of winning Eurovision song titles and *they seem very free of propaganda, except for a lot of promotion for 'Lof'. Usually pronounced, 'Amour.'*

The rest are very satisfactorily all, boom banga ding a dong save your kisses for me on a string in Waterloo.

The 2015 Swedish winner could look a little suspect with its title *Heroes*. But thankfully, I hear you cry, no time to check here whether that song has not reverted to old style and is about Swedish farming co-operatives and their tractor operators.

Incidentally we usually blame the French for *'Le Grand-Prix Eurovision de la Chanson Europeenne.'* Love it. Loath it. Or secretly get sucked into its kitch awesomeness. It's been on our screens annually since 1956, and has become a cultural and somewhat OTT nationalistic extravaganza.

Conceived before the days of cross country satellite communication , Eurovision (itself conceived at a broadcasters' convention in Devon), was a get to know your neighbours idea from European Broadcasting Union employee Marcel Bezencon; and he got his inspiration from the San Remo Song Contest in Italy.

So it's the Italians we should really blame.

For critics firmly in the clichéd style of 'I must become more famous and show myself (the critic) to be much cleverer than the real world.' Eurovision is the peak of their yea.

Sorry critique clique cabal, the real world has voted, and you are the ones with Null Points. Eurovision Song Contest TV audience figures are some of the biggest ever, and are growing again.

For sure it makes you crazy, the whole point of Eurovision, is for them to show and you to see, and be amazed or dismayed at local styles of music, fashion, dance and the rest, from right across the region. We can't all be Abba—although for a long time many wanted to be.

I should just point out that of course singers and bands don't always perform and record songs <u>*they have written or composed themselves.*</u>

So song contests, with a mix of local and international stars is a fine way help celebrate a country's talent, <u>*and to sell or promote it's songs*</u>.

They soon discovered that if the show is televised from a potential tourist hot spot, then the publicity from that was a real bonus.

Hence all those bizarre little films that they show between the songs, whilst they change the setting for the various Eurovision performers, and hence also, some of the odd places I have been to out of season.

These festivals are not big concerts, like Glastonbury in fabulous massive and muddy style. They are more urban competitions of songs and music, usually in Theatres, Parks or Arenas.

The first country to really understand the potential of a song festival was Italy.

Back in the early fifties, and wanting more visitors in the not so busy season, the Mayor and town council of San Remo, an Italian cliff top town overlooking the Mediterranean, just along from Monaco, thought that a Song Contest could be a smart idea.

Then they also figured out, 'we should add in some superstar performers as special guests to bring in the crowds and interest the TV.' Quite how smart their 1950's idea was, they possibly didn't imagine, even in their wildest dreams.

The San Remo Song Contest became a huge local, (and thanks to those guest stars and TV), a major international event, and it still runs today. From the mid-Sixties, it was widely imitated, especially in Eastern Europe.

Not only that but, as a 'Song Contest' or to give it its proper name, 'Festival della canzone italiana di Sanremo,' many, of those San Remo events introduced Italian songs, with added English words that became huge hits for Dusty Springfield, Cilla Black, The Tremeloes, Englebert, Tom Jones, Gene Pitney, Elvis and many more. So San Remo even had an effect on the content of Jackie's picture pages. Who'd have thought?

Those Italian songs?

We are not talking obvious Italian as in, Cornetto's or Cara Mia Mine.

We all knew and know those songs as, 'Softly as I leave you,' 'You're my World,' 'A Man without Love,' 'You Don't Have to Say you Love me,' ' If Paradise was Half as Nice' and many more...all originally Italian.

Mind you it's not always obvious where a song comes from. 'Y Viva Espana' was composed by two Belgians!

Oh yes, and before you start to get picky about my typing or Italian... *Festival della canzone italiana di Sanremo*. Is it seems correct, no caps on italiana, and Sanremo as one word...so there.

So... to Eastern Europe song festivals.

For Eastern: read Communist Bloc. Behind the Iron Curtain. Those Eastern European countries and their individual TV companies had indeed all noted the success of San Remo and of course, Western Europe's Eurovision.

They had the resources of InterVision to call on. Broadcasting to most parts of the USSR, Albania, Bulgaria, Czechoslovakia, Hungary, Poland, Romania and Bulgaria. For some reason Finland was in both 'Inter', and 'Euro,' as was Yugoslavia.

You get the picture....well actually, they got the pictures, and the music, and mostly received them in fuzzy black and white.

But of course, only in many cases if they had permission to have a TV set allocated to them by the local worker's council.

So thinking about TV light entertainment for the people, which to them was mostly 'mind improving' culture for the masses, more and more of those East Bloc countries started Song Contests.

Of course 'Culture' for the masses was in the instruction book. Culture was good. Ballet was culture. Art (controlled) was Culture. Classical Music was culture. Opera was Culture.

Eventually, inexorably, in an unstoppable tide, 'Pop music', communist style, became culture. Fat ladies in shiny dresses, and very sweaty looking ex-waiters with shiny black hair, all giving bad operatic treatments to 'modern songs' was obviously (for the TV execs) the way forward.

But their audience, rapidly becoming more and more aware of Western music, leaking through the extended Iron Curtain and the Berlin Wall, were somewhat less than enthusiastic about the songs. Throughout their region, their most accessible source of music was from smuggled discs, and radio broadcasts from the west, which were then copied onto and played somehow on X-ray films, pinched from hospitals. Cassettes weren't invented until the mid seventies, by the way.

Meanwhile, back in a town square in Ljubljana:

"I lof him so much as he works so hard."

"I lof her so much because she drives the tractor so well."

"I want to share my quota of lof with him."

O.K.- O.K. I know we've been there.

And increasingly none of that worked very well at the time either. It was derided (privately) by the mass of young people across the USSR, in isolated Romania, Bulgaria and Hungary, and Moldova, slightly less isolated Poland and Georgia, and definitely not in isolated Albania.

Mind you in a more, bizarre and 'off the wall,' than behind the wall, situation in Albania, their biggest, and as it happened, smallest star, was British. Eponymous hero of many black and white films: Norman Wisdom.

It seems, Norman, the little, clearly working class chap, in a cloth cap, falling over and generally creating mayhem as he tried to survive evil bosses in factories and shops, was very much approved in Albania, in fact admired, promoted and welcomed.

Struggle of the working-man and all that.

By the way that is 100% true, and there are small, but life-size, statues of Norman to be found,in various parts of Albania.

So at those early Song Contests, the producers rapidly discovered that more and more western pop and style was leaking in, despite the censorship and that Iron Curtain. And young people wanted more of it.

In fact, *'lofing' tractor drivers, was not 'lofed' at all.*

They wanted Cliff with '*Fall in lof with you,*' or the Beatles with their *'Lof me do.'*

So in various InterVision countries, ambitious and trendy TV producers struggled to get permission to get their song festivals and song contests up to date.

In 1967/68 some brave TV execs in Romania, pulled the wool over the eyes of President Ceausescu, their appalling and much feared ruler and his equally feared evil wife, and got permission, and the funding, to stage a local song festival with some special guests from the west.

The 1968 show having been a big success they then hosted a bigger one the following year.

Thus it was, that in the second week of March 1969, in a town called Brasov, Romanian TV staged the second Golden Stag Festival.

I was there. So were special guests, Cliff Richard and Julio Iglesias, (The's father of Enrique I think for our younger readers.) and a lot of rather miffed fat ladies in sparkly dresses, who had to watch their daughters, in modern clothes, getting a better audience reaction than they ever had.

Not singing about '*loving*', sorry, '*lofing*' tractors and factory production targets probably helped a bit.

When we, the non-superstars, but invited guests, arrived for the Golden Stag Festival, we were somewhat disconcerted to find that the hotels in Brasov were all over full, and we were assigned to hotels in a town about an hour's drive away.

Seemed like a nice place, name of Bran.

Big castle overlooking the town.

Slight problem was, that all the streetlights were out, as all available local electric generating power was being directed to the TV crew and the festival in Brasov.

Hey, no problem, it's cold, but dry, we'll walk back in the dark to our isolated hotel from the very nice, candle-lit, pizzeria in town. The jovial chef, who had given us much local liquor, pointed us in the right direction. "Walk along, up the hill a bit. When you get near Castle Dracula keep left and you'll find your hotel."

We stepped off into the dark, and as what he said sunk in, we just as quickly stepped back again. "Did you say, Dracula Castle?"

The off-hand response, "Sure, this is Transylvania you know. That's always been the Dracula Family castle. For many hundreds of years. But it's not a problem, they are a bit odd, but keep themselves to themselves. We don't see much of them for most of the month. With a cheery wave, he stepped back into his restaurant and closed the door.

We stood there for a while.

My girlfriend at the time, said, usefully, "and it was a full moon yesterday." Such a comfort, that girl.

But hey ho, we made it, and the following day, exhausted after a sleepless night nervously listening to the creaky buildings around our room, we saw the ever young Cliff Richard, earnestly and very genuinely affable as ever, rapturously received as he earned his fee of $2500 (a lot then).

A (reasonably) jolly time was had by all. I think all the free local plum brandy helped.

Although local liquors usually remove memory cells somewhat, surprisingly I remember the names on the bottles there. Tuica, Palinca and the final-worst one, Horinca. Apt name.

On the Tarom, Romanian Airlines flight back to Heathrow, Jackie, for that was coincidently my girlfriend of the time's name, of course read Jackie Magazine.

I only travelled on Tarom Air one other time. That was from Amsterdam to London. I don't remember the exact date, it was sometime in the early eighties. But I recall the flight for three reasons.

One: the lights by the seats, which had little lampshades on them, like an old-style train.

Two: the windows had curtains.

Three: initially I seemed to be about the only passenger on the plane, until the last moment when the entire Romanian Girls Gymnastics team got on.

It had been on July 18 1976 that Nadia Comaneci won her first of three Olympic Gold medals with the first and only score of a perfect 10. I note that Little Miss Comaneci, as well as her Olympic medals, deservedly also won the Romanian Hammer and Sickle gold medal, and extra deservedly a Hero of the Socialist Labourers award.

No one else will equal her achievement at 14 years old as the youngest ever Olympic Athletics Gold Medal winner, as now 16 is the minimum age for gymnastic entries.

I don't want to give you the wrong idea, but on that, my only other Tarom flight, almost the entire contingent of girl athletes, with giggly enthusiasm did cartwheels in the aisles, vaulted over the seats, or, with an arm on the seat backs either side of the aisle did those swingy up and over with the legs thingy's.

I stress, I was in my thirties then, and I am sure Olympic Reg's. being as they are, that they were definitely all over 16, but quite frankly regardless of that, trying to eat your airline meal with a fast moving series of nubile smiley leotards about an inch from your face is enough to make anyone reach for the Plum Brandy.

Even if it's the bottle of Horinca.

But back to English days and Moscow nights, and my left ear has just been asked a leading question, very much the same targeted question I had been requested to investigate by the military-style chap in London some months before. No Horinca in Moscow, vodka there, and over an Italian style lunch in London it had been a bottle of Chianti, in it's little straw coat.

Mr. Brit Military style Neville, who seemed very keen on his Spaghetti House Italian food, and who was by now quite friendly, enquired, "How did you get in this music business game then"?

I explained that prior to starting my own music company with some great partners but little cash, I had been a full time music journalist.

His response was, "So you can write and report then?"

Without waiting for an answer he said, "I might have a bit of freelance writing work for you.

That would be paid work of course." And he invited me to lunch again the following week.

Now it still hadn't dawned on me that this Mr. Taxman wasn't the walking embodiment of the George Harrison song of the same name; on reflection, quite why a UK tax man would want some freelance writing done I don't know.

But a free lunch was a free lunch, and the bloke seemed O.K. Even if he was, as my mother said, "A bit Kensington and Chelsea."

(It later turned out that Neville had visited her making some kind of background check on yours truly. He had claimed to be from a bank making some credit checks.)

After another rather jolly lunch in the same place, which seemed mainly to be answering questions, "Have you ever met the Beatles?" and the very usual, "How many of those singers are gay?" In those days of course, as previously reported , the question was, "Are they all queers or poofs?"

So, after considerable friendly but wine-fueled discussions, we parted on the pavement outside the Spaghetti House, just down from Harrods.

The Brit gave me a business card with his phone number on it and said. "Don't forget, any thing you learn about young people and their attitudes around the East Bloc let us know, no matter how trivial. It's feelings and background we want to get a grip on."

He went on, "Write it all up as a magazine style news story and I'll make sure you get some extra cash expenses for doing so,"

As he walked off he added "-let us know if the Russkies approach you as well," and with a "toodle pip old chap." he was gone.

Incidentally, that's the only time I ever heard anyone say ' toodle pip' in my life, apart of course from any TV adaptation of Jeeves and Wooster.

As you know from elsewhere in this book I had lunched with Ian Fleming, had an Aunt who had been in the Secret Service during the war, and I was a keen reader of spy novels. But did it occur to me that Neville, my Spaghetti House, Chianti and Carbonara chum, was anything other than a taxman?

For some reason it did not.

Truthfully. I was only focused on the fact that a hundred quid's or more so added to my income for a simple bit of freelance reporting could be very helpful.

So over the months I wrote quite a few general pieces for him about song contests and festivals in Romania, Poland and even the Italian San Remo Festival. He tucked the papers in his inside pocket as he tucked away his spaghetti.

Now I was, as he put it, "on the firm," he took me to the rather more up- market, Mario and Franco's Trattoria Terrazzo in Soho.

During each lunch he discretely paid me £150 in ten pound notes. So getting paid by the Taxman or whoever he really worked for, instead of paying them, was a comfortable and innocent thought, that remained firmly in place until that Moscow evening a few months later when The Nibbler says, 'I really like to know what the young peoples in England are thinking today."

Now despite me imbibing a barrel of beer, a vat of vodka and indeed having been totally confused by Miss nibbly nuzzly, the alarm bells and flashing lights of illumination suddenly sunk into Mr. Thicko. That's me, as you have obviously deduced.

Maybe Neville wasn't a Taxman after all. Maybe Eva wasn't a real student. Maybe this is the Russkies approaching me. Maybe I am in deep doo doo...

Well, 'bugger what the young people were thinking in England, or bloody Moscow.' Suddenly all I'm thinking about is Greville Wynne again, and being locked up as a double agent.

I have an instant flashback to the conversation in London and Neville's leaving comment all those months back after that first lunch "Let us know if the Russkies contact you." I am suddenly wondering if I am going to get home very soon.

The pavement outside the Knightsbridge Spaghetti House seemed a long way off. I was, apart from my Cuban ear-washing specialist, alone in Moscow...(*My spell check is at it again, it does not like 'ear-washing' and is insisting on 'car washing.'*)

Like Wynne, I had been travelling extensively around the region. Unlike Wynne I haven't to the best of my knowledge been meeting spies or even having secret message microdots stuck on me or my luggage. At least I didn't think I had seen any.

We've already established that I was Mr. Innocent Thicko in this world of spies...so on reflection that: 'haven't seen any microdots,' was really a bit of a Dad's Army moment, "Stupid boy Pike," that's the idea behind secret message microdots.

You don't see them."

I really had, either on music trade fair business, or whilst attending Song Festivals, been to almost all the Soviet Block countries. Russia, Hungary, Czechoslovakia, Poland, Bulgaria, Romania and more. There were rumours of an upcoming trip to the then Soviet occupied Baltic States of Latvia, Lithuania, Estonia- but that seemed to be Visa impossible at that time.

Way to the East of Moscow, the state of Georgia, with it's abundance of good weather, and, as always somewhat jealously mentioned by the Russians, wine and good food, was on the next visiting list. Subject apparently to the not so minor matter of, who actually ran the country.

Trade fairs never really caught on generally in the music industry, with the exception of the already referred to, Midem.

It had been set up as a multinational gathering in Cannes France. And every January it was a growing success, since it had started in 1967. More of a meeting point for the creative and business sides of the music world, than traditional trade fair exhibits.

It also provided a useful showcase for talent from various countries to hopefully find music companies who could exploit their work in other countries.

For example, at Midem, a French music producer played a cassette of a new and unknown artist to one of my Swedish music company partners.

He instantly recognised the commercial potential of the recording. So our Swedish company released the records.

Result: Richard Clayderman (for it was his then first recording of Ballade Pour Adeline on the cassette) sold millions of LPs, Cassettes, then CD's through our company in Scandinavia.

For me, with well paid Midem music trade fair stuff, not so well paid trying to find and sell music around the world, and multiple visits to those song festivals across most of Eastern Europe, my passport looked like it would be full again long before it expired.

In yet another meander in this long and winding road tale, as I write this in January 2016, I am 70 years old.

I notice that Peter Ustinov (As it happens Russian, but a good and jolly one) the actor raconteur, when reaching 70 announced his ambition was to live longer than his passport.

Seems like a good idea that. My passport expires in 2021 so we will see.

As I said, no Horinca Plum Brandy, but equally strong Vodka was what was all happening in Moscow 1974. Miss Cuban Ear Nibbler, now known to be called Eva, has just asked her 'bombshell question'. *"I really like to know what the young peoples in England are thinking today."*

My brain is racing. Was this an innocent student question?

Or was this, as Neville had put it, "an approach from those Russkies?" Ironically asking the exact same question he had asked me to investigate around Eastern Europe.

My head was spinning, at that stage with confusion, the alcoholic spin cycle would start up later, helped I suppose by the fact that I've just stupidly ordered "another one please."

 I really couldn't say, Stolichnaya Vodka before I had started that evening, and certainly wasn't going try and pronounce it now, after the number I'd had; hence the presumably very slurred 'another one please.'

My ear is now somewhat over nuzzled.

I learn that Miss Nuzzle being Cuban, Speaks Spanish and can sing Yviva Espana! Her familiarity with my repertoire, rings more alarm bells, as my Greville Wynne complex cuts in again and I then start to seriously wonder if her knowledge of Yviva Espana is a coincidence or are the KGB very well informed.

I order yet another Vodka to steady my nerves. After all I've only been going to song festivals. Rather a lot of them, yes, but always invited.

Eva, is keen we talk, she leans forward and breathes into my clean ear, 'You know, we talk, privado.' Five or seven vodka's and a few beers earlier that whispered invitation might, regardless of the standard warnings issued to businessmen against meeting very friendly ladies in bars, particularly in Russia, have been an attractive idea.

Right then, I was starting to suspect that shortly the bar, in fact the whole room was going start revolving. And it wasn't a revolving bar. So I pay my bill, and hers, and rushing off, promise, *"Same time, same place, tomorrow,"* and stumble off, tipping the old lady on the bedroom floor.

Let's try that one again. All Soviet-style hotels had an old lady 'A Babushka', stationed outside the lifts, or stairs, who managed the access and affairs of each and every level of hotel bedrooms.

So the key lady wasn't actually on the floor of my bedroom when I tipped her the customary few roubles cash to receive my room key. The following day, ETN, Eva the Nibbler, is not only planning to be there in the evening for 'same time same place,' but she's turned up there at breakfast. In the hotel dining room, all brown velvet tablecloths.

Even if Eva was, breakfast was no surprise. Yet again we were thrust portions of tired dry black bread. Squidgy, watery looking cream cheese, salty ham or cold herring. All with amazing fluorescent pink jam. (Sweetened with beetroot I am told. Of course I should have known that.) Oh yes and tinned pineapple so astringent it turns the serving spoon black.

Tea arrives with nasty yellow tinned milk! Ugh.

With a smile and torrent of Russki from Eva, a fresh new and rather good tea, and real milk arrives. With some biscuits and then a solitary fried egg. Now she is proving to be useful.

Too cold to go out, we talk in a kind of indoor/outdoor covered terrace, with wood burning stoves.

She is, she says. 'A student.' Her scholarship, from Cuba is to enable her to write a thesis on international young people and sociology. Her professor, "He ask many questions".

I ask "Her professor?" Apparently he knows all about me and that I am in the, "The Music Showbiz." Seems he has seen me at various song festivals as a judge, guest or journalist. In answer to my innocent question, she says, he was at the festivals as an observer and translator.

Can she ask me some questions?

I make another excuse. At that moment for no reason other than I am suddenly feeling more than a little queasy. Feeding a killer hangover with pineapple and runny ricotta style cheese dressed with pink jam can do that.

I say, "Sure, but maybe later."

She says, "OK I bring me, and some questions to you, in you room at 4.0'clock. Then we go to a Cuban Restaurant. We can get real good food there." Despite my queasies, real food sounds good to me, and Cuban sounds very good. She leans forward and seriously quietly, and quietly serious, says, ' You now understand, in your room, I am not one of those girls. I am student. OK.'

I agree "OK," and retire to my room, and try to sleep. No chance. All around me the Babushka's are apparently maintaining, racing or trying to park aeroplanes or trucks in the adjoining rooms and corridors.

Eventually, at about lunchtime, with no knock, my door opens and a jolly lady appears, with one of the noise-generating machines. It's a Russian industrial floor cleaner. 'You stay in bed,' she gestures, (which I do, as I have no clothes on) and about an hour later she leaves. Pissed off I think, as no tip was forthcoming for her. Unfortunately, the potential tip money was in my clothes in the wardrobe.

The next thing I know, it's dark outside the windows, and I am being shaken awake by ETN, who has a tray of tea in the other hand.

"I need tip, money for she," she says, gesturing at the Babushka who is glaring at us from the doorway."

I start to say "But why?" but Eva is hearing none of this...so I get her to chuck me my jackct and ask her how much is needed. "To bring girl to your room is 100 Roubles tip."

I try again and say, "But you're not a girl," but in the end just observe as Eva, who is very obviously a girl, but not apparently one of 'those girls', very clearly shows me that she has taken exactly a 100 roubles from my wallet, gives it to the old bird who glares at me, and shuts the door.

"Harry", (the first name on my passport) she says, "The only way I can get in here to wake you up, is to tell Babushka I am one of those girls... and before you start thinking that you said something really stupid, I can tell you, but not show you, I am a girl, and as it is now 5 o'clock, and you had said, 4 o'clock it is late and I am very hungry."

Big non-stop speech, but hunger can lead to big speeches.

The evening went better and better.

Not only relaxing good fun, so much so I largely forgot about the potential, 'problem'. The Cuban students restaurant was the best food I ever had in Moscow, as was the rum, although it was mixed with black coffee and lemonade as Coke wasn't available.

I gave Eva, and a gaggle of equally friendly and very beautiful ladies, some very general answers about British youth, music, clothes and suchlike. There was nothing, she could not have read in the UK daily press, or found in Jackie or any of the other girl's magazines of the day. But of course most were banned in Russia.

Later, much later, I learned that, tips paid to Babushkas had a 24-hour validity.

Eva turned out to be great fun, and after eventually meeting with Melodia I was sorry to say goodbye to her, and the source of Cuban food. Melodia did book to come to Midem again, but they said that they didn't really want to buy Y Viva Espana from me, as it had already been quite a hit in Russia. A rather nasty and first hand lesson in early music copying piracy for me. As ever, it was the writers and singers of the songs that were hurt more than the music companies by such music copying theft.

Back in the UK, I called Neville, he who had requested me to keep an eye on 'Youth feelings' in Eastern Europe. Having told him that "I thought I had been approached by the Russkies," this time we met in an office, somewhere quite near Waterloo Station.

There, he and several others poured scorn on Eva likely being a student. But they were keen for me to, "Keep up the good work, and tell us anything that seems good from there."

Looking back, I can't think why, but I didn't have the nerve then to confront him about who they, the Brits, sitting around the table were, and exactly what they wanted.

Perhaps a lack of resolve on my part?

Or was it just, 'left unsaid' in a very British way. For some reason, I also didn't really make it clear that I wasn't intending to do any more reports for them.

Sitting on the BEA flight back from Moscow, just being relieved to be away from the city, and the USSR in general, I had decided to stop writing reports for Neville and his team. I would just claim to be too busy.

George Harrison could keep his 'Back in the USSR,' it wasn't going to be me that was going back, and if I was, I was only dealing with music. Having, as I said, reported on the Moscow trip in some detail, and despite having been paid another £150 cash, I stopped communicating with them. Who ever 'them' were!

But about six months later in the spring of '75 I needed to renew my passport, and eventually found myself being summoned to Petty France at the London passport office HQ.

Much to my surprise, or possibly not so surprisingly, I meet Neville who was keen to talk.

He had a fairly extensive list of song festivals taking place right across Europe. I can't recall the list but, Split, Brasov, Dubrovnik, Sopot, Skopje, Gibraltar, Malta were probably on it. Not only that but also festivals in Cuba and Mexico.

His question, asked in a backroom at Petty France passport office, "Which was I intending to visit?"

Still feeling somewhat pissed off with him / them/whoever/ and indeed whoever them were/ and really wanting to extricate my self from anything that wasn't music business, I muttered that my business was now struggling, so no festivals were on my plan. Except Midem in Cannes, and I was getting paid to be there.

To my complete shock, several weeks later, having been persuaded that, "What they wanted wasn't risky," I agreed to continue.

They said, they wanted my help because other sources they had were not so in touch with 'young people and their views.'

I guess that indeed most foreign based mainstream News and TV reporters seemed quite old so maybe my 'pop era' based stuff really could help their general understanding of life and feelings in the East.

Having agreed, ten days later I walked out of a flat at 15 Hay Hill, Berkley Square, with a brown envelope and also two new passports. (One of them wasn't English). Neville saying "Just in case you have a spot of difficulty old chap."

After further questions from me, this was explained as, "We occasionally give two passports to some business men who need to visit both Israel and the Middle Eastern Arab countries for their business. Makes the exporter's life easier as border crossings between the two are not very easy."

To this day I really I don't know if I am proud to have done my bit for Queen and Country. Or even if I did do my bit.

I also am not sure if I am ashamed that I was encouraged to do so by that brown envelope that contained $4000 dollars in American Express traveler's cheques. $4000 is a huge amount of money now, and then it was incredible. Then it was almost £3500.

Weekly wages were about £40. So as I said—a lot of dosh.

Neville wanted me to use $2000 for expenses. The traveler's cheques were a big wodge, as they were all $20's.

Neville: "Helps us know where you are when you cash 'em, old chap."

Blimey, I hadn't even seen that one in my James Bond books.

I asked him about the other $1000 and he said $1000 was for emergencies, and with the other he might need me to pay some travel agents' bills with them, and he'd let me know later.

With them all being twenties it took me an hour to sign the bloody things !

Possibly of more potential help to my business was the account they gave me at a travel agency in Holland from whom I could buy any and all travel tickets as needed.

 I had to report 'cash' and travel expenses, but they didn't need receipts, and the travel agents didn't send me bills.

I asked what to do if I was approached by Eva, her boss, or another ear-nuzzler looking for information about the west.

Neville and his bosses' response: "Jolly good show. Give 'em what stories are easy for you. There won't be much they can't read in the Guardian Newspaper, and tell them that you need paying as a journalist for writing freelance stuff. That way it can just be a journalistic assignment, if there's ever any problems."

Before I could splutter, "Problems? What do you mean by problems?" Neville quickly continued, "When and if they do pay you, then good luck to you. Keep the money. But do let us know what you tell them."

So at that moment, it seemed I was engaged by an M—MI 5 or MI 6—or whoever the hell Neville and his senior manager actually represented. I was also being encouraged to take money when offered from the Russians.

All I needed was the Americans and I'd have a full house. As it happens some years later, thanks to US President Carter's brother Billy, I did have a brush with the US secret service...but that's yet another winding road altogether that I've already related.

So over the following year I went to a whole flock of Festivals. But, needing to focus on building my company, I went strictly only when I had a need to attend for my own business reasons.

Neville and the Brits had said, you can even go to non East Block ones, as there's always loads of Eastern observers at them, from many East Bloc TV, Radio and other media. He suggested that, "Outside their own territory, such observers, might confide in you more."

I took them at their word and went to a festival in South America and another one in Acapulco. Didn't meet any Russians there though. At least I don't think so, and no microdot secret messages, at least I didn't think...("Careful Pike, not again!")

That was all fine. 'Help' was now more than a Beatles album. I seemed to be helping my country. The cash was helping me, especially as I had a small son by then, with another on the way. The air tickets helped the most.

But best of all, at one of the festivals, I met a German guy called Reiner Etzrodt, and re-met a Dutchman called Ton Van den Bremmer.

On just about the first cassette tape machine I had ever seen and heard, they played me a Dutch recording and said, "You have to get this Rodney, to put out on your Sonet label in England.

It belongs to EMI, but EMI England don't believe in recordings made in Holland, not only that but as they are very busy they won't promote it well enough."

After some crafty maneuvering, assisted by EMI Holland, I got the rights for the UK and Eire (thanks again to EMI Holland's Theo Roos) and "Mississippi" by Pussycat gave me my first ever UK Number One on my own Sonet Record label.

The band were happy.

I was happy....and so was our company bank manager.

EMI Holland were very happy.

But EMI England, who around that time had a Dutch MD, name of Gerry Oord, were very embarrassed and pissed off at missing a hit that really belonged to them.

For the second time, some of my own recording artists were now being featured in Jackie and the other music magazines.

If I have the dates right, Tim Smit, also Dutch, who went on to restore the wonderful Cornish Gardens of Heligan, and then devised and built the Eden Project, worked at EMI then. Now the Eden project is great and good for jobs in Cornwall, *but what I also like is his palindromic name.*

Tim Smit: Reads the same from back or front.

I had realised very quickly through '75 and '76,' that what young people across the East block were listening too was now pretty much the same as young people in the west were enjoying.

Tastes and styles had moved on from the protest and anti war songs of the sixties.

Even in musically starved Eastern Europe.

Disco was in. In a big way. Gloria Gaynor, Chic, The Bee Gees, Ottowan, ('Hands Up' if you remember them). Also, non-disco, but very big, The Eagles, John Denver, Gilbert O'Sullivan, Thin Lizzie, Diana Ross, Simon and Garfunkel's Greatest Hits.

None of which were very likely to ignite the flames of revolution. There or in the West.

Our good friend and many times Jackie cover star, and I can assure you from personal experience, all round good bloke, Cliff Richard, was even doing concerts in Leningrad. (Now called St Petersburg). I know because I was there, actually talking to the promoters of the show. Cliff's visit to do a show in Russia had picked up a lot of publicity in the UK.

Neville came to our offices in Notting Hill Gate.

Was I going to the Cliff show? As it happens I was, and I wasn't.

I was busy in the UK trying to make a hit with that Dutch band Pussycat in the UK. But I had a quick trip to Moscow planned on trade fair business.

But having booked the flights and sorted the visa, it now seemed that most of the people I wanted to see out were away on holiday, or would be in Leningrad for Cliff's show.

I wasn't sure if the plans could be changed...things like that were not easy in Russia. But changed they were. So I was in Leningrad. And I have $1000 in cash, and the $1000 in traveler's checks Neville had given me some months before.

In my London office he has said that a 'Grigor' will contact me and ask if I need a driver. Use him as a taxi and pay him the $1000. Not too tricky really.

Leaving one's hotel in Moscow you were always pestered by Taxis, touts, and money-changers. The first two were OK...the money changers dodgy as it was illegal.

I assumed it would be the same in Leningrad and it was; Grigor the taxi driver drove me around. I saw the people I needed about the trade fair and left after three days.

When I paid him the money, he said. "You very stupid guy.," which made my heart jolt...but he went on, laughing at his own wit. "If anyone ask you about this $1000, you just say you get ripped off. Say I promise bring you girl tonight to your hotel."

So I kept writing and delivering my increasingly bland reports to Neville. But all the time I was thinking that they had missed the boat. They really needed this job doing in the Sixties when there really was, 'Something in the Air.' And I don't mean Thunderclap Newman. I mean Revolution.

The sixties had seen cities alive with demos. The streets with marchers with banners and more. A fast developing underground press. All noisily alive and vibrant with usually well meaning, and sometimes wise, but often inflammatory words.

Admirable, anti war, anti nuclear, anti racist—causes were of course very widely supported... Much of the sixties 'revolution in attitude, if not in government, was focused and fermented at Universities world-wide.

From the Sorbonne in Paris to the sunnier climes of the campuses of California. Radical messages were the thing.

Protest expressed in poetry, paintings, print and of course music. Messages of peace and love so eloquently delivered by Bob Dylan, Joan Baez, John and Yoko, Pete Seeger and many more.

Not forgetting the somewhat milder protest songs for the UK's Peaceful and Lovely, from Donovan.

Also *laid back man*, but somewhat more commercially, *The Flower Pot Men,* telling us in 1967, *Let's go to San Francisco,* 'With flowers in our hair.'

With the mild, drug innuendo of Flower Pot Men doubtless shocking BBC TV's dear old 'Bill and Ben,' the talents concealed behind the Flower Pot Men and their huge San Francisco hit were Brits. John Carter and Ken Lewis.

Otherwise known as the The Ivy League, sometimes as Carter Lewis and the Southerners. They were well known BBC, Saturday Club and Easy Beat favourites.

The same team, with on occasions, Perry Ford or Tony Burrows, and several others were the voices behind many other hits.

In fact Tony Burrows, was so busy working as a session singer in various recording studios that in one short period he popped up on Top of the Pops, as the lead vocalist of Edison Lighthouse, (Love grows, where my Rosemary Goes.) White Plains, (My baby loves Lovin,) The Pipkins, (Gimme dat Ding) and The Brotherhood of Man, (Save your Kisses for me.)

Quite how Tony also found time to also record backing vocals with Cliff Richard, Elton John, James Last and others I don't know.

Back in 1974.

The Flower Pot men had morphed again into the John Carter-led 'First Class' and the sounds of, "Beach Baby, Beach Baby," were everywhere, including the USA, where it reached number 4 in the Billboard charts.

So by the seventies, the 'Times they are a Changing', had, at least musically, changed.

After several East bloc festival visits, all I had to tell Neville was that, as well as "Beach Baby, Beach Baby," and later my company's' hit "Mississippi," it was the sounds and beat of Boogie Nights, Village People, Abba and even Boney M singing about Rasputin, that were resounding round the Red Squares and echoing off the Lenin statues across the whole region.

Didn't seem to me to be much that was newsworthy in my reports. But the traveler's cheque supply was topped up with new ones, and the travel agents in Holland knew me by my first name, and never billed us.

Notwithstanding, the fine service from the Dutch travel company, travel then was not without its nervous moments.

There had been a spate of terrorist aircraft hi-jacks. In 1970, various TWA, Pan Am, Swiss Air, El AL and BOAC planes were hi jacked and mostly blown up in a deserted airstrip in Jordan called Dawson's Field. In the middle of all this we also had the horrible affair of the massacre at the Munich Olympics.

Then in '76 and '77, despite increased security measures at airports it all kicked off again. In July '76 an Air France plane was seized after take off from Athens, En route to Paris. It ended up in Entebbe Uganda. As was dramatized later in a movie, Israeli commandos seized the plane and rescued many passengers. But the casualty count was high. In Sept '76, TWA suffered a hi-jack as did Japan Airlines. In October '77 a Lufthansa Flight from the holiday Island of Majorca scheduled for Frankfurt ended in Mogadishu, having been in Cyprus and Rome. German commandos moved in and 87 passengers and crew were saved.

Talking to Neville about all of this, over yet more Chianti and pasta, he said "Keep both of your passports handy. You never know when showing one, other than the British one, might save your life."

I mention all this only because constant business travel—involving flights anywhere, became more than a little nerve-wracking.

But the odd thing was that in the UK, for one's family and friends, life went on as normal, even during the anxiety period between a hi-jacking and its resolution in one-way or another.

Hi-jacking, as with IRA bombs, (and with a shocked acceptance even the massacre in Munich), had become a fact of life.

Life must go on. *Don't let the bad guys see that you are rattled.*

Back in April '76, The Brotherhood of Man had won Eurovision, with "Save Your Kisses for Me."

Jackie magazine of October 22 1977, Issue 720, was featuring Paul Michel Glaser, David Essex, The Alessi Bros' and had some 'Free Fruity Coloured Rings for you to wear.'

I point this out—not to be crass or disrespectful—but just as examples of how life went on. Just an hour or so away from terrible and evil events.

As I said, *Don't let the bad guys see that you are rattled.* Again, maybe that's why music, with its ability to relax and entertain, across so many borders, remains so popular, and very much needed in stressed times...

On the subject of relaxing and entertaining, Eva surfaced again...

At a festival, this time at the Sopot festival, in Poland in 1978. I still didn't know if she was a student, but this time she introduced me to her boss; the alleged Professor.

He was happy to buy the beers, but wanted to know all about the UK, "You must tell me about youth politic feeling in England".

Of course I was suspicious, but if he was actually teaching sociology, the questions were not unreasonable.

But he then concerned me by asking if songs by *Bob* Lennon and *Joan* Dylan could start a revolution on the streets, and if the Rolling Stones', "Street Fighting Man" had coded messages for the youth of the world.

Bob Lennon and Joan Dylan were a bit of a clue.

He was obviously either stuck in a time warp from the sixties. Badly remembered at that , or he was tasked to make 'meaningful conversations.'

He then asked me if, "In your country, I believe there is very truly strong resentment at the inequality of the classes. Can this be enough to bring people to the streets."

He seemed very keen on streets.

Having had a few too many boring beers, and taking into account his '60's mania, purely as a joke, I started to tell him that actually the most influential messengers for young people in the West had been The Flower Pot Men with their coded drug messages.

Another beer (strong) and I ploughed on...telling him that the re-incarnation of the same Flower Pot Men as a band called First Class, was again a strong message to the youth of Western Europe.

I then realised, he was not taking this as the joke it was intended to be, but was seriously writing notes as fast as he could. Oops. But too late then for me to stop, and too many beers to engage brain or find the brakes.

So I expounded about First Class, indeed being references to the potential for troubles in our divided British society.

Another beer, and I launched off on descriptions of commuting into London on over-crowded trains, standing room only for the masses. Whilst just a the other side of a piece of glass in First Class, our rulers stretched out in spacious luxury, being served fresh coffee and bacon rolls by servants as they read the London Times.

Professor Longhair—as I had obviously called him—as he was completely bald—tut-tutted, and could hardly write his notes fast enough. I couldn't judge whether Eva could tell it was a wind up, but she kept ordering the beers.

But a good half an hour later, I think even Eva realised I had consumed too many beers, as I then launched into an explanatory

tirade telling the Prof. that many years ago in his part of the world that songs about tractors and production targets were the big thing.
I explained that only just recently, at last, in England top of our charts we had just had a song called. "'I've got a Brand new Combine Harvester.'
Having both spelled and explained the Wurzels name to him, and told him this was just the tip of a revolutionary iceberg.
The British revolution when it came would be led of course by the farmers.
The song carried the messages, carefully concealed to enable its important messages to get space on BBC Radio.
I also told him that both Beach Baby and The Wurzels record were on a label called UK records. The name was very meaningful.
He said he would study their releases for other messages.
As an afterthought, I then remembered that, back in '66, the anti nuclear weapons song, 'It's Good News Week,' by Hedgehoppers Anonymous, had also been on UK records.
At this point, I think that I had better apologise to Hedgehoppers, J.K., John Carter and his songwriter wife, Gillian Shakespeare, and those Somerset reprobates, The Wurzels; if they detected any surveillance or suffered any visa problems around this time. It was just the beer speaking. *Honestly.*
Back in Poland at the festival Eva was now kicking me under the table, and so I decided that maybe I had had enough of both beer and invention.
A couple of days, later I had a last coffee with Eva. She handed me an envelope from the Prof. Inside was $1000 US. In 100 dollar bills. Also in there, a small shopping list. *'Could I get a Frower PooT Men's LP and also Coombined Harvesters LP's from the Whorsels. '*
With the lyrics if I could.
This made me start to consider if my English diction was up to much, at least after a few too many beers. I did notice the Prof. spelt Combine Harvester correctly. Almost.
 I told Eva I would indeed get all of the discs and would post them forthwith. The address was a Moscow University one.
I also gave her, discretely, $500 of the dollars, which almost made her weep.

A week later, standing in Barclays Bank Knightsbridge Branch, I was almost weeping as our bank manager, a Mr. Bardell said: "These dollars, I don't know where you got them from Rod, but they didn't come from the US Treasury."

Not only were they forgeries, but I didn't even get to keep them, as the rules were apparently that they had to be sent off for further examination, or returned to the US. There was some kind of system to try for payment from America but I don't think we ever got it sorted.

Luckily, we had been banking with Barclays for years, or I could have been in big trouble for passing on forged notes. As I write this now, it occurs to me that maybe Eva knew they were hooky notes, and that's why she wept.

I had returned to the UK with a photo of the three of us talking in a bar, glam Eva now with dark hair, and very beautiful, and the totally bald, Professor Long Hair. My Brit. chums in their cavalry twills and chukka boots, seemed very pleased with my scornful report, and the photo, which didn't seem to surprise them.

But they loved my Wurzels and Flower Pot Men story and called in some others so I could repeat them.

This time, however, I pulled no punches and firmly told them that I had had enough. And that was pretty much that for my apparent secret service career. I never heard any more, no more traveler's cheques, the Dutch travel company started to send us invoices for tickets.

That was it.

Except it wasn't.

Around a year or so later in late 1980, I was again in Moscow.

Same dreadful hotel. Same Barman. Same black bread. No nibbling lady, but a new flock of rather overly made up blondes eager to catch one's eye. (*My spell check's at it again, now it keeps suggesting a new frock of girls...not flock!*)

I was back there in Moscow to try, yet again, to sell something to their state record company, Melodia. In the UK and the rest of Europe, my music company was well on the way to selling more than a million LP's by a great non-stop rockin' boogie and blues band called, George Thorogood and the Destroyers.

When the band had earlier played sold out shows in various countries, some Russians had approached me, saying the record should be released in Russia.

So there I was back in Moscow.

And then suddenly shock, there *she* was, Eva.

In an attempt at a jokcy greeting I covered my ears and said, 'No Free dinner.' She completely blanked, ignored and obviously didn't want to understand what I had said. Not surprising really.

But as Gilbert O'Sullivan, Ray to his friends, sang in his evocative and seriously wonderful song, 'Alone again, Naturally.'

With no agenda to entice a lady upstairs, 'Hello Babushka,' Moscow is a very lonely place on a series of cold and gloomy winters evenings. Waiting and waiting for a business meeting to be confirmed.

A friendly face to share a chat and joke, and maybe some food, is really what's needed. To see a 'lady friend' even if a slightly dodgy one, was good, and a lot better than talking yet more double glazing with the German salesman standing next to me in the bar.

So seeing Eva again was great.

And there was dinner, not Cuban, but with African students at the University this time, which was my first introduction to Ethiopian food, now so fashionable, particularly in the USA.

I guess, as I paid, for Eva it was free. But that wasn't the point; it was a fun evening, and no Babushka tips were needed.

As she gathered up her coat and gloves from the bar to go out in the chill of the night, she said her boss wanted to see me.

I said (politely) that I had nothing to say to him, and anyway I was very busy. I thought that was the end of that.

But at seven the following morning I am sitting squashed in the back of a black car between two big blokes in rather damp blue coats.

Eva is sitting in the front seat turning and saying in answer to my annoyed questions. "No worry Harry. There's really no problems. I just think my boss he not understand properly why you not have any time for him."

So dear reader. It's been as promised a long and winding road to get to this part. But here we are: *Remember this: Opener. Draft 1. The steely eyed and very unsmiling gent, leaned back in his chair, and*

fixing me with those steely eyes said, in quite good English for a
Moscow Russian in 1980 "Is it not possible that you are engaged by
the English authorities for some purpose to look at us here."
Given that I had been awoken quite early, and instructed to follow
some gloomy looking men in overcoats to, "Come to office. Boss
want to speak you."
Their words actually translated by a nubile Cuban student girl,
who just happened to be breakfasting with me.
As I gulped, gasped, floundered and tried to breath normally with
images of Greville Wynne, and other worse things crossing my
mind. Thank you for nothing, Len Deighton, John Le Carre, Ian
Fleming. Even though their espionage and spying characters were
fictional, at that moment in the blur of nerves and fear, fiction met
reality. Big time.
I gulped again, and then almost fainted as, without a glimmer of
emotion, <u>Mr. Steely Eyes, tossed across the desk a black and white</u>
<u>photo that clearly showed me entering the door of No 10 Downing</u>
<u>Street...</u>
The Prof, who was obviously not Eva's boss, who had said not a
word, but had nodded when I entered the room, leaned forward to
look.
The two blue-coated heavies leaned forward to look.
Eva leaned forward to look.
I leaned forward to look, but could see very little as there seemed to
be a red mist floating around in my eyes.
Steely Eyes again: *"It is you? Yes ? It is there where I think? Yes?"*
After several attempts to speak, words eventually came out of my
mouth. "Yes sir"....looking back, what the hell was that 'Sir' word
doing in there? Anyway...
"Yes, sir, that's me. It's a very old photo.
I have been there, to No 10, twice in fact; both times on music
business. That time you can see the man I am with, a Mr. Geoffrey
Bridge. He was the director of the UK's record companies
association. The BPI. That's the British Phonographic Industry
Association.

We had gone to Downing Street together, to make a briefing to Mr. James Callaghan the Prime Minister, to explain the importance and value of British Music Exports to our balance of trade.

Mr. Bridge speaking for the music companies and me representing the Midem Music Trade Fair.

Mr. Bridge was keen, as the BPI rep.to keep getting UK Government help to keep British music exports rolling.

At Midem, we were very keen to keep that Government money coming into those music industry members, as they spent most of it with us, using it to subsidise the cost of attending the Midem show. Steely Eyes didn't blink.

I started to witter on.

"The meeting was originally scheduled to be with Harold Wilson. He was the British Prime Minister before Mr. Callaghan but the meeting had been postponed several times. The rumours were that Mr. Wilson was out to 'get even,' with an industry that had embarrassed him twice."

" The fear was that he would stop the UK trade ministers from supporting the music industry's export efforts."

Steely Eyes: "So you haf been making problems for your government ministries?"

It took me a while to figure out what he had asked.

I blurted out a garbled answer, "No, no. Mr. Bridge and I were trying to make sure there was no problem."

" You see, Mr. Wilson, the last Prime Minister, before Mr. Callaghan, had some years ago arranged for the Beatles to get MBE's...very special awards from our Queen. Then John Lennon in 1969 sent his award back saying he didn't want it for various reasons. This embarrassed Mr. Wilson."

" Also a band of musicians called the Move, had put out a postcard advertising their new music with a naked picture of Prime Minister Wilson on it."

At my words "naked pictures of Prime Minister Wilson," Steely Eyes had flinched and removed his glasses.

 Probably, on later thought, a bad sign, but I was in mid flow, no brain engaged. I went on.

"Also Mr. Wilson was seen as being the one that closed down many popular music radio stations on ships around the country. Young people were not happy with that."

I paused. Somewhat breathless.

Long pause. Long silence. Then Steely Eyes: "If I have this right, you went with an official of your industry, to create an atmosphere where the new first minister of your country would help you sell your songs ."

I nod.

He continued: "That is because your previous efforts to gain power by threatening with naked pictures of Mr. Wilson have failed. So you have influence in high quarters I think."

It was not said as a question. Before I could splutter a reply, he went on, "We have learned that there are people in your press who write that this Prime Minister Wilson is a closely friend of USSR, and they make him resign the job. Maybe you are in that gang of trouble-makers?" Long pause.............At all this, particularly the menace in the word, 'gang', I think I started to hyperventilate on the verge of hysterics.

Behind me, I could hear, but not see, the door open.

Eva, the Prof, and Steely Eyes all stood up, as presumably their chief came into the room.

He came round the desk, reached over and shook my hand. At that exact moment, the heart pounding and rushing sounds in my ears stopped me almost hearing anything...it was Grigor. My Leningrad Taxi driver of four years before.

He spoke with Steely in Russian.

Steely then, with no change of facial expression, said, "OK you may go. Do not try and make any influence here with our young people. Enjoy the rest of your trip."

He nodded at the Professor and Eva, and spoke in Russian, saying, as she later explained to me, "I assume you will be showing Mr. Buckle the way to the airport when he leaves."

I stood up, shakily, and as we stepped out of the door, Grigor said: "Take care now. Enjoy the rest of your time in Moscow."

A couple of days later, sometime-Eva did indeed 'show me to the airport'.

My meeting with Melodia, confirmed many times previously, and scheduled to be with people I knew quite well, was delayed and delayed and then cancelled. I never asked Eva about the dollars, or the Wurzels. As far as I know, Melodia never released the George Thorogood record. Maybe they feared our influence on their young people.

I wrote it all up, and this time despite having said, "Never, never again" to Neville, I think they could see that now I really meant it.

He told me I could keep the last few traveler's cheques that had been sitting in my desk drawer. He reminded me that all we had done was confidential.

And thank god he walked out of my life...almost.

In May of '82 I was having dinner with a promotion lady from Vogue, a French record company in La Coupole, a large and busy restaurant on 'the Left Bank' in Paris.

As I returned from the loo I suddenly noticed, 'Neville', seated, with his back to us but just a few tables away from mine.

I almost went and spoke but thought better of it, until I had had another few glasses of wine.

At that time in '82—as well as our international hits with Depeche Mode and Yazoo my Swedish partners and I, with our Sonet company and *I had a huge series of million selling hit records in almost all countries of the world (but excluding the UK and US) by a Swedish band called, 'Secret Service'.*

As the wine, on our table, and most probably his, went down, I suddenly had an idea. The promotion lady from Vogue, with whom I was dining, had brought me to the restaurant in her car. The back seat of which was piled up with a heap of promotional materials.

So she nipped out to her car, which was parked nearby, in very French fashion, and returned with a large poster and some records of Secret Service.

As we left the restaurant, I walked up behind Neville and tapped him on the shoulder. As he started to rise in his seat, very surprised, but hand out in greeting, I gave him the records and the poster, which we had rolled into a tube. I told him that we had named the band after him and his mates...

It's taken a long time to get to these final paragraphs of, Of Song Festivals, Contests, Secrets, Spooks and Spies: and...*the Goodbye bit has yet to come.*

Actually somewhere, I signed a bit of paper with Neville and the Brits, in Hay Hill and again in my office in Notting Hill Gate, promising not to reveal anything about my dealings with them.

But that was 50 years ago—well 45 years anyway. What's five years between 'friends'...as according to John Le Carre, the spooks are known as.

Oh yes, between '79 to '83, we really tried like crazy to succeed with Secret Service and their records in the UK but the attitude of the all important Radio One was, "One Swedish band on the playlist is enough, thanks." That band of course being Abba.

Try and take a look on the internet for music by them: Secret Service. Good songs: "Oh Susie," "Ten O'clock Postman," "Flash in the Night" and many more.

As I said we sold millions in almost all countries of the world except the UK and the US...so take a look on You Tube and see what the UK missed.

In fact, I just did exactly that whilst writing this, and even all those years later. Those were damn good records.

As for the other Secret Service, the real one...keep up the good work guys. It would appear not to be an easy job. I cannot say I know *anything* of the reality of your job, but perhaps, I understand just a little.

The fear on occasions for me was real enough. It would have been fun though to know if, in Neville's office I had a file number. I guess 007 was already taken. Maybe, considering the music I could have been 0045 or 0033.

It's taken years for the details of my aunt's really vital, wartime SOE service career to emerge. Maybe one day one of my children will find out the details and figure out what it was all about...

All that Neville stuff. Was it nonsense?

My business benefited from the travel tickets.

But was I, did I, waste, my time?

Was there an agenda I had missed or didn't understand? I didn't know then and almost don't know now.

*But then almost ten years later.....***In the weeks following the 9th November 1989, as I watched the Berlin Wall come down,** *it turned out that as the thousands of East Berlin kids poured in to the west for the first time in their lives, through the holes they had cut in the wall, they knew of, and enjoyed, and needed western music, as much as we did.*

My ex-wife, but still good friend, and I will never forget then; standing in the gloom of a Berlin evening, listening to the chip chip chip of hammers as thousands of East and West Berliners demolished the wall that had divided a city and a world since 1961. To keep the worlds apart, it was more than a wall.

The East side was patrolled by armed guards, the ground laid with a network of lethal explosive mines, strong searchlights meaning that along the many, many kilometers of the wall, there was never night. Many died trying desperately to escape the authoritarian regime. November 9, 10, 11 day by day, we came back, haunted and fascinated, by the still constant, chip chip chip sounds: bit by bit, concrete block by concrete block opening up the way to a freer, and hopefully better life.

We watched as returning east siders squeezed back through the wall carrying huge packs of oranges for their families. Oranges were apparently like gold dust in the impoverished regime on the other side of the wall.

My wife and I wandered through the now almost un-guarded 'Checkpoint Charlie' crossing place into the East, (better to use the existing controlled gate way as land mines were still a threat elsewhere).

We changed a little money. There was little to buy. I think that all we found to buy were a couple of cheap looking china mugs as souvenirs. I still have some of the money we changed.

But despite the vile barrier, as I had observed at the various song contests, and even reported on to Neville, *the music of the West had got through somehow.*

So much so, that with the chip chip chipping still being heard across the city ten days later on the 19th November 1989, Erasure, one of the bands my company had looked after around the world from the day they had started, gave one of the first concerts in the city since the wall was opened up.

With the initiative and encouragement of Erasure's Andy Bell and Vince Clarke, and the promoters of the show, free entry was encouraged for kids who could show their East Berlin ID cards. Thousands came.

As the hall filled, thousands more stood outside.

They knew the words. They knew the tunes. They had cheap nylon tracksuits and cheap trainers, no 'Nikes,' so they stood out amongst the fashionistas of the wealthy West...but they danced, they sang, they cried...they embraced us with thanks and we cried as well. A lot.

I guess if in Branson Missouri, USA, a tired and rather sad eyed, breakfast waitress could say to me and Kenny Denton, "Sometimes Music is my only Friend." I guess that music effect could be as, or even more, powerful in the depressed, repressed and mostly deprived states of Eastern Europe.

As they offer in those annoying little screens on your computer, always at the exact moment when you are busy:

An update is available.

With my Swedish partners in 1968 I had started my London-based music company as I eased out of full time typewriter tapping for Jackie and other magazines. We survived and over the years did very well with records on the UK, and then other charts around the world.

By the late 'eighties, with big money earnings from CDs, as the world updated their music collections, big multinational music companies, especially those with CD factories were doing very well. Their hunger for increased market share encouraged them to make some huge, and it turned out irresistible offers to the owners of the best independent labels to sell out.

Magnet went to Warner's who already owned Atlantic, Electra and Sire, all once major independents.

 Sony had already absorbed CBS.Then over an 18 month period, Virgin and Chrysalis were sold to EMI.

Island and A&M to Universal, and then Jive/Zomba to mega German media giants, BMG.

If you had lived in England, those many and independent, often rival, companies, had likely accounted for a major part of your music collections between 1960 and 1985.

If you lived in Scandinavia: Denmark, Norway, Finland and Sweden; much of the music from many of the above mentioned labels was delivered to you, not by a collection of rivals but by one local representative company.

That company was. Sonet.

Or rather the Sonet of my three Swedish partners.

Started in 1955 by Gunnar Bergstrom and Sven Lindholm, lead over time by Dag Haegggqvist, they had, with their artistic skills, and financial probity provided unwavering support, and also huge earnings for those companies and many more.

So when the big guys snapped up *Virgin, Chrysalis, Island, Jive, A&M* at such mega millions, (that we could never blame the owners for selling), we lost, just from those labels, almost overnight, a major part of our Scandinavian business.

With fewer and fewer up and coming labels available,no amount of work locally by the loyal and talented Scandinavian Sonet team, could replace such a sudden and dramatic loss of business.

So Sonet Sweden, including its very much-respected name, was also sold to Polygram, one of those very global multinational companies we had competed against, and generally beaten—for many years.

A sad day for us.

The world's press viewed it as a sad day for Music.

Journalists and former critics alike, united to shower praise on Sonet—Particularly on Mr. Haeggqvist's' style and taste.

What they liked was that we, under his guidance, had used the money that we made from the catalogues, or in the case in England from the pop hits, to make hundreds of mostly brilliant, often award winning, recordings of Jazz, Blues, Folk, Brazilian, World Music, Cajun, Zydeco and more.

Many recalled a very good review in London's Observer Newspaper praising some of those special recordings, and the headline to that review: '*Sonet records are brave and possibly slightly mad*'.

We liked that.

John Peel called it: *'The day the music really died.'* We liked that too, but it reduced many to slightly tearful hysterics.

For my little English company, started in 1968, thanks to the faith of the Swedes in my hearing and ability to predict hits and also apparently, they told me later, in my furious enthusiasm for music and promotion, it was also the end and we had to close.

Between Sweden, or more accurately Scandinavia and the UK we made or supplied the soundtracks to a lot of lives, in those countries and around the world, from 1955 and 1990.

But in England, there were mouths to feed, family of course, and a somewhat reduced, but loyal staff.

I started a new company. We called it Habana.

Habana is the Spanish way of writing and saying what we Brits, call Havana, capital of Cuba.

As told all those pages back, there being an all important stopping point for those old sailing ships, with their various styles of music on board . So Habana, for a record label, apart from people thinking we were going to only make Cuban music, was a cool name.

So with just a few UK staff, and no money, we had a go.

Rather quickly we sold several million records in Germany and France, by an outrageous band—from Sweden of course, called The Army of Lovers.

Then we had a big hit in Holland with a song called, "Oh Diana," by the very dreadlocked, and remarkably nice, The Man Ezeke.

But my heart wasn't in it.

Internet piracy loomed and marketing budgets meant more to big company distributors than music making.

I called the remaining staff, and together over the next few years, we wound down the company.

Our old musician friends and many at other music companies were sad.

My whole family were shocked.

My son Joe, very entrepreneurial, as much as his brother Sam is artistically inclined, said, "After all the history, all the hits, all the stories you can't go out with a whimper. You've got to go out with a bang at least."

And so it was, that in June 1995, Habana UK released the last record, either found, made, invented, chosen, produced or published or handled in any way by yours truly.
The Artist's name was by the way: Gompie.

As ever there were problems. It was such a great idea that others were lining up to copy it, and some already had recorded it, possibly even before our version hit the street.

Our version had started well, was already a huge hit in Holland, Germany was looking interesting, and I was getting reports of it being popular in Rugby Clubs in Australia and South Africa.

Rugby Clubs?

Well one of the problems was that the chorus had some, 'naughty,' words in it.

But after a few beers, the chorus was much sung in Rugby clubs, and the word, or rather the chorus, was spreading worldwide...

Naturally, the BBC were never going to play a record for which a major part of the chorus was a 'naughty word.'

The F*** word in fact.

So of course we called in Mr. Bleep.

He made his trademark noise over all the naughty bits.

 Actually, editing in that beep sound on top of the F*** word, is a little more difficult than you could imagine, as it has to be on the beat, not too long, and in tune!

But we delivered the bleeped version to Radio Stations across the UK (all 600 of them) and started to pick up some interest. It's now July 1995.

School summer holidays loomed, and Katy and Tom, my two, then very much younger children, blissfully unaware of the real reason for bleeps, had happily given away a few of the radio's bleeped version of the CD to their chums in the junior school.

 Every one was happy, and many a parent from the school heard their nippers cheerfully singing along: "Alice, who the *'bleep'* is Alice."

In the first week of September the new school term started,and it seemed the parents were not happy with me.

Not happy at all..quite understandably. Oops!.

In Spain and Portugal, belting out of sound systems around hotel pools, echoing across campsites in France and Italy, around the Tavernas of Greece, was our Gompie record.

The problem being the Europeans were all playing the un-bleeped version! F word and all.

"Mummy, what does...what does....F*** mean?"

I went and hid in the office, but did emerge a few days later, on Sept.9th, with a wide and stupid grin on my face.

Gompie's 'Who the F*** is Alice?' had shot into the UK charts at number 29.

Habana had a UK hit with it's last release.

With the BBC and other stations now playing it, (in it's bleeped format) the tension in the school car park eased a little.

Over the next month the record climbed the UK chart: 29, then 19 and peaked at 17.

So as Joe had suggested, we went out with a bang...or possibly with a bl**p.

"When my son Sam was about five, and in class at a new school (the same one, as mentioned above actually), the teacher had asked; "And what does your dad or mum do?"

The answers ranged from: "My dad's got the village garage," "My mum's the doctor," "My dad's got the shop.".

When it came to Sam's turn he said:

"My dad takes people out to dinner.".

.... So now you know.

A life after Music : I spent the next few years travelling the Far East advising companies on music copyright and intellectual property.

In the UK, my company, *now only doing video production and graphic designs,* had a wonderful five or more years working with legendary craft person Joanna Sheen. Joanna was riding high with regular appearances on various TV Home Shopping Channels.

The card making and paper craft CD roms that my designer Emma and son Sam made for her were selling in pop record quantities.

But eventually I called it a day, with big plans to,' do things I'd always wanted to' but never had the time.

And one morning on his Radio 2 breakfast show, I heard Terry Wogan saying, "Retirement day" 'With a modicum of good health should be a happy occasion."

Not for me: that's when the problems started.

I had been working, mainly pretty much for myself, or at least working with others on stories, schemes, songs, plans, mostly originated by me since summer, 1962.

Doing nothing didn't work. For me anyway.

I read a lot of books.

For someone who had roamed the world 100 or more days a year for 40 years, sadly, a severely reduced pension pot didn't allow for much travel. I read a lot of travel books.

The ever loyal and very wise Joanna called to see how I was getting along, and recoiled somewhat from my litany of fed-up-ness.

She advised, by email, with her trademark smiles,

"You need a project Rodney. You only work well when you have a project. Why don't you write a book?"

Well, of course she was right.. a project, that's a plan.
So I started again.
Possibly at 70 years old slightly less agile than in my Pete Lennon days, but no less ambitious. I will go back to being a writer and reporter.
      And dear reader you just read the first book.
 Rather autobiographical I fear, but I hope some fun stories along the road. Thank you for reading it.

If you happened to have enjoyed it then on the following pages you'll find some details of the next one.

'Just in Time'.
A thrilling new novel from Harry Buckle.

A clear and sunny morning on the Canal du Midi in South Western France.

'No Milk Today', is a song. 'No Food Today,' in your supermarket or local store is a family threatening situation, likely leading to a rapid breakdown of law and order.

Delighting, after a years hard work in waking on their now completed barge, in fact so complete and luxurious that, 'barge' seemed a bit of a misnomer, Andy and Faye-Lin had a leisurely start to the day.

Eventually Faye-Lin unloaded a bicycle from the davits on the back of the boat and set off along the – *flat* - towpath to buy fresh morning bread.

Andy relaxed in the shade with his first coffee of the day and considered the situation.

He had, by his early forties settled down somewhat. After what many would call a misspent youth-surfing and travelling- usually with a gaggle of girlfriends enjoying his good fun company. He was one of those guys who men generally didn't view as threat, except perhaps to their daughters.

Settled down with the plan to become the owner skipper of a 'péniche'. A luxury hotel barge that, for much of the year, hopefully fully booked with guests, would make it's way in stately fashion along the gentle sun kissed waterways of The Canal du Midi in southern France.

The Canal, winding its way between the vineyards of the Languedoc or Aquitaine basically joins The Atlantic Ocean with the Mediterranean.

Shaded by tall trees along most banks, the passage of huge old converted wine or general cargo barges through sun baked villages is an idyllic and peaceful journey interrupted now and again by the bustle of an 'écluse' or lock.

The plan had come to him in 2009. He had been working long hours, often offshore, as a surveyor in the oil industry. One evening had been flipping channels on his TV, when he saw a now familiar sight.

It was a boat on the Canal Du Midi. He watched on, and observed a famous and much liked British chef, Rick Stein, on a very luxury 'péniche' cooking and extolling the virtues of local produce, markets, restaurants and of course the wines, as the boat with its luxury cabins, and ambiance to match, made its leisurely way from Bordeaux down to the Med.

There and then, as he viewed the program he announced, to the shock of his work mates, friends and family, "I'm going to go and live on a boat."

After quite some weeks of searching he had stumbled up on an old boatyard baking in the hot sun. The faded and rusted old sign had seen better days, it probably read, *'Bateaux Construits et pour les Vendre, ou a Louer'*, and the yard with rotting and rusting old boats of all kinds wasn't much better.

Even the dog and the owner looked like they had seen better days, although over time Andy would discover that was a bit of a hasty judgement of both dog and owner, and not a considered evaluation as a professional surveyor like him should make.

Even the tumbledown buildings turned out to be a treasure trove of old fittings and hard to find spare parts.

There amongst some sad looking rental boats, there were two barges. One was on a slipway half out of the water, half way through a serious maintenance attack on it. An attack, he learned later, beaten back by the sad demise of the original owner. The other floating low in the water rather surrounded by tall reeds and grasses.

The boatyard owner, a wily old gent called Jean-Baptiste was keen to see the back of the boats. But he was also keen to get paid for work and rent already in hand. So he greeted Andy amiably.

Despite some hesitation by the owner's widow , the fact that the boats had failed to sell for more than three years, and with a threat from the boatyard to re-possess one in lieu of outstanding fees, she accepted Andy's basic offer.

Within 8 weeks, quick by French standards, Andy became the owner of the two rusting hulks at pre Rick Stein prices. Chef Stein's globally successful TV series having set off similar lifestyle dreams for many others as well as Andy and had also revitalised the tourist business along the whole length of the canal.

The boatyard owner, on seeing the years rent in cash, said, "Mai Oui, Andy could install a shipping container on the quayside and convert it to live in, at no extra charge, but he would have to feed the guard dog."

Within a few months Andy, now with shower and toilet installed in the container, and gas barbecue outside under an awning was learning new skills as a boat builder. Or more strictly a boat converter.

He employed two carpenters, Carlos and Joao, both Portuguese, who it turned out did have boat building skills and were delighted to work with Andy. A boss who didn't mind getting his hands dirty- and as it happened who spoke good Portuguese.

Within one month more, as spring approached a small flower garden and a veggie patch appeared around the converted trailer. A tablecloth graced the outside table.

When some remarkable underwear appeared on the washing line it became clear to the boat yard owner, who only came in occasionally, that either Andy had feminine side to him or a ladies influence was at hand.

Even the rough, tough and generally red wine coloured and fueled Jean-Baptiste was surprised and then entranced when a diminutive and extremely beautiful Asian lady appeared from the bowels of the Peniche with tools in hand and a smudge of dirt on her face.

"Bonjour Monsieur," she smiled.

It transpired that Faye-Lin was a second generation Vietnamese. Her parents lived in Paris and had a small café near Place Pigalle. She had followed some 'university romance to Narbonne', and after that failed she had got a job working on the cash checkout of a hypermarket near Montpellier.

Several shopping trips by Andy, 'do you really need more fromage, sir, that's the third lot this week.' and eventually, discretely, as invitations from customers were somewhat frowned on by management, she had enjoyed a laughing and wine filled evening in a nearby Pizzeria.

A few more evening pizzas, and some Vietnamese food in Narbonne and suddenly Andy's trailer was home to two.

Now a year on, and after the combined efforts of his Portuguese boat builders, with much input from Faye-Lin, friends, family and his long suffering bank manager, he had the urge to stay relaxed on deck, soaking up the sun and enjoying the morning..

But duty called and he decided that he should try and connect up the satellite TV system that they had installed for the use of guests who perhaps , despite the promise of, 'a vacation away from it all,' couldn't quite disconnect from the real world.

Much to his relief it connected very simply, and the first pictures that flashed and then steadied on the screen were from a 24 hour news channel showing huge container ships, tug boats, harbours, cranes and all the world that he hoped he had left behind.

Never the less, he couldn't resist turning up the audio and listening as well as watching. The sincere and, *very serious*, news presenter, of course these days, wearing a regulation life jacket, was balancing on a smallish boat with a selection of huge container ships in the background.

The choice of words and pictures shown on screen now varied to fit with the sincere, *very serious* and now also *uber dramatic* voiceover:

'*Just in Time.*' You go out to buy something. In a market, a stall, a store, a village shop, a massive hyper-supermarket , a gas station. Whatever. Wherever. " You pick up what you want, need, must have or can afford...Food, a phone, clothes, medicines, furniture or a furry toy."

The presenter steadied himself and continued: "You take delivery of manufacturing parts, equipment, spares, chemicals that purify the nation's drinking water, fuel to keep us warm or different fuel to deliver unto us what we need, want or can afford."

With extra uber dramatic emphasis the presenter-now looking a little wind blown, continued:

"These days almost all of what you buy, need, or covet is imported or relying on imports in some vital way. Even if locally produced, it's probably manufactured, harvested or processed and then delivered, using *imported* machinery or parts."

"You wander the malls or high streets of the world gazing at the well stocked window's, or look at online shopping catalogues. Make comparisons and choices, your goods are instantly available."

Dramatic pause. Presenter looking as serious as he can, despite trying to keep balanced on a small boat.

"But find a gap, something out of stock and not on the shelf or in the catalogue, a missing display, a rack with one item not there, not your size, the empty space is like a missing tooth. Very annoying."

"Unlike your missing tooth ,the space in the store, the gap on the shelf, out of stock items are mysteriously filled or replaced overnight. As if by magic. Someone's boat has come in."

Andy started to consider it lucky that they hadn't shown missing teeth-but then listened carefully as the presenter, even more earnestly continued:

" In some cases, the now available goods are vital to, or even save, lives. Drugs, surgeon's tools, hospital equipment, fire trucks, phones, they all arrive. Just in time. Life continues. Just in time."

"The old and new worlds all now live by, *'Just in Time'*."

"As many have wisely observed and oft been quoted, it's almost like magic. A cargo cult of consumerism, it just works, it happens. Always."

"And 85% of everything, everywhere, to fulfil that magic, travels by ship across the oceans and then by train or truck in containers. With 20,000 'boxes,' containers on some ships, that's a lot of trucks ."

" Most of our daily essential foods, fruits, fish, meats and more, everything, all arrive in those big boxes.

Very few reserves are held in stock by your local supermarket or corner store.

" **Note this**. *Again.* Even if we grow it or harvest it locally, it's very likely that the machines needed to plant and then reap that harvest, process, transport, sell and deliver our vital foodstuffs all rely on imported parts."

"Stop the flow of goods : and it's like turning off the life support of a nation or nations."

"Most nations, as with the retailers are so confident of this regular supply miracle that they also hold few or no reserves, or emergency stocks. There's no votes in planning for the unthinkable."

" But as has been shown many times, there is nothing more likely to produce *an instant break down in law and order* than empty supermarket shelves."

The presenter stood, even more unsteadily, and now looking a little off colour, delivered, what Andy assumed was his closing lines:

'No milk today,' is a song. No food today with empty supermarket shelves , is a riot."........but there was more, and by now Andy, who had been somewhat converted by the facts presented, listened carefully:

"If Just in Time isn't.

If for some reason the boat doesn't come in.

Then very quickly, spreading like wildfire, with both the reality and the rumour of empty shelves in the food shops, the unthinkable will happen.

Our peaceful society, as we in most western countries have known it for many years of plenty since the 1950's will break down. Very quickly."

The camera cut away to fairly recent dark and blurred shots, complete with dramatic music, of street riots and looting in North London and parts of the USA ....and after a few moments the voiceover came back, in slightly ironic tones:

"But hey, relax. When we need more, of anything and everything, it's on the way, from somewhere, it always is. It'll all be here tomorrow. Surely, **'Just in Time'**, the last minute magic will happen."

" **Won't it?"**.....*long silence, and the TV screen cut to logo's and credits*........ **In Andy's case, he was still sitting, somewhat concerned by what he had seen, when Faye returned with bread and chocolate croissants. Just in time.**

Read on.....

Friday June 17th. 4.00 pm. On the Bund. Shanghai. China.
"It took more than one man to change my name to Shanghai Lily."
Marlene Dietrich in the 1932 film, 'Shanghai Express'.

'Shanghai.' Just the name is an exotic cliché for most Westerners, conjuring up images of a bygone era of dimly lit, misty riverside wharves, secret agents and smugglers ,intrigues and espionage, slinky ladies, bars and dens (various).

One's thoughts almost revert to flickery black and white with a slightly crackly soundtrack. All, as I said, clichés, but I suppose my thoughts these days should be more cell phone than celluloid.

I have been in the security business for around twenty years.

In U.K. Government service for the first ten with M.I.6, and the latest ten with my own company, mainly based in Asia and the South of France..

With most of my clients now being in the ships and shipping business, I deal daily with a varied repertoire of threats, some real, many angry, amateur and opportunist. With my researchers we try to head off, the modern world of smuggling, terrorist and extortion threats, and old style piracy, not to mention scams and fraud.

Information is key to what we do and it was a suggestion that I could learn something of use that had taken me to Shanghai.

Security relies on the securer having a good reputation. Thanks to my predecessor and my current team we are both well respected and also well connected. But even I was surprised when, at the appointed time I responded to the tap on my hotel room to admit my visitor.

Not the once predictable slinky oriental cliché in slit skirt, cigarette smouldering in a long holder and husky voice, but a damned close descendant.

I suspect I stammered, as I greeted and shook the proffered hand of Liu Qiang the chief of China's MSSS. Their all powerful Ministry of State Security organisation.

The Chinese equivalent of the CIA / MI5 / Homeland Security / NSA all rolled into one.

He spoke, perfect English, English. No US inflection. "Daniel, good to meet you, thanks for coming over."

That's when I suspect the stammer crept in. "No problem, only a short hop from Singapore."

"Oh yes of course, I was thinking London, how stupid."

I offered, "Coffee, tea, something stronger?"

In almost BBC English tones he refused all, with thanks, and said, "No, I've got a meeting with some of my political masters in Beijing later, so just a quick word."

He glanced around the room and said, "I suppose we are reasonably secure here."

I started to say, " Well, if," and then thought better of it, then again what the hell, so I continued, "Well if anyone knows if this room is clean of listening bugs I have a feeling it should be you."

He laughed, not a knowing chuckle or conspiratorial smile, a real laugh. "Good point."

"Actually no one knows I am here officially, and even if they do unofficially, then what I have to say will very soon become State business for the general benefit of both the Western nations and ourselves. So it needs to be said, and then sorted.".......*The story continues in a somewhat deceptively relaxed, but increasingly urgent and somewhat nail-biting manner as we visit: ......*

The Philippines: *'Beware of gringo's bearing gifts'.*

New Zealand: *'No one expects trouble to come from New Zealand unless they are an opposing rugby team'.*

England: *'The only problem with having children is eventually they aren't. 'But mum, everyone's going to Glastonbury, I'll be fine.'*

US Naval Airbase. Fallon Nevada : *'It's not every day that one's barbecue chef is the President of the United States'.*

Germany: *'Surprise and sudden fear can re-design your life plan in seconds'.*

Singapore :*'Save the World. Sure, but after last nights excesses, breakfast first'.*

Taipei: *'One of those long frustrating getting nowhere days, where even the hum of the aircon drives you crazy'.*

On A Gulfstream Executive Jet. GS650. *'En route to Europe, Flying at almost the speed of sound. And we are discussing the alleged fact that at any one time 10,037,021 people are waiting for a pizza .*

We are perhaps more occupied with the thought that we are now tasked with collecting and then delivering what is by far the largest ransom of any kind ever demanded. 9920 kilo's of gold. At more than $40,000 per kilo that's a lot.In fact it's around $400 million dollars.

But for the four families paying, it's a small price to pay....'

Tokyo. City center : *'Is an expensive place to keep a horse'.*

Nice. France :*'All a bit of a 'Montagne Russe ', which I am hopefully reliably informed is French slang for 'roller coaster'.'*

Morocco/Western Sahara : *'Terror stopped sleep but eventually exhaustion won.'*

A somewhat irascible Swede in Geneva: *'We may well be traditionally neutral but we sure as hell aren't neutered.'*

Castelnaudary. South Western France. *Home of both Cassoulet and the French Foreign Legion and currently where the accidental millionaire has currently moored his old converted wine barges and is awaiting the arrival of his booked guests.*

****

Just in Time. Harry Buckle. Published by MarosaJokato Media.
Paperback...... ISBN: 987-0-9935576-3-7
Kindle.ebook.. ISBN: 987-0-9935576-4-4
www.MarosaJokato.com   Contact: MarosaJokatoMail@Yahoo.com

Harry on Just in Time. " *I love to read. Particularly John Grisham, Lee Child. Also early Clive Cussler and David Baldacci and some of the Scandinavian writers.(Particularly Jonas Jonasson)*
But I do find many of today's new books are rather overly dark or require the readers brain to be fully functioning in movie style computer graphics to keep up!
So, Just in Time' is somewhat sunnier, but no less thrilling I hope.

If I had an ambition it would be to bring together just some of the style of Provence's descriptive champion, Peter Mayle who captures the essence of the sun and the land so well, and Ian Fleming's 'can't put it down,' story telling.
Of course as I was advised, all those years ago to take up typewriter tapping by Fleming, I guess that's an OK -ambition to have.
But those who have read, 'Just in Time,' seem to think I am on the right road- with the story at least. I hope you enjoy it.

By the way. Despite this novel being an exciting easy read, the lingering reality is that, any threat to our total reliance on 'Just in Time' for all that we need for the comfortable and safe life we are mostly used to, is a much needed and considerable wake up call." May 2016.

Dr Wayne Deakin did a skilled and much appreciated editing job on my rambling manuscript. Any and all errors existing have likely been added by me fidgeting with the book-after he had completed his work.

Recommended Reads about Music.

I guess you bought or were given this book because of your nostalgic memories of Jackie magazine or of the lifestyle of that era. Or perhaps you are keen to know more about music and those who make or made it.

Others will be more informed than I about the lifestyle books, but I can recommend some books about the music and those who made it. These by their very nature also tick lot of those life style boxes.

Simon Napier Bell has been delivering excellent, I mean seriously good books for a number of years now. SNB managed Johns Children, Marc Bolan, Japan, Wham and then George Michael.. so he has a lot to tell. More than that though, he is an acute observer of the overall scene. Our paths never really crossed in business or socially, so he is not a mate of mine in any way, but his books are of the best.

Find both: Black Vinyl White Powder and his more recent one: Ta Ra Boom De Ay.

For ten years I had a lot to do with Depeche Mode, having represented for the world both their recordings, made for the wonderful Mute UK label, and also all their songs. *Just Can't Get Enough by Simon Spence is in my informed opinion a fine and very accurate book about one of the most interesting and important bands of the past few decades.* He charts their progress, from pretty new romantics to stadium fillers in readable style. Too many music books are written from the 'I'm a fan they can do no wrong angle' but Spence posts a constructive and interesting account of their formation and development.

Norman Jopling's recently published, Shake it Up Baby, is really well written, factually correct, (I was there for much of it) and a great read. He covers so many pivotal and key points of the British music scene in brilliant fashion.

Be Stiff, by Richard Balls, as the name suggests covers the life and times of the Stiff label: Home to Elvis Costello, Jona Lewie, Madness, Tracy Ullman, Nick Lowe and the very special Ian Dury and many more. Good stuff.

Also great is Cowboys and Indies by Gareth Malone, which covers much of the same era but focuses on a varied selection of labels.

Although most books, about various labels miss one vital point.

Most of the English Independent labels- Island, Chrysalis, Virgin, Mute, PWL, Jive, Charisma, Stiff and indeed my own Sonet label relied on the UK to create and promote our recordings. But we all needed the rest of the world to provide us with the earnings to survive.

One of the most influential and important figures in the global music business world over the past twenty years has been Sire Records founder Seymour Stein.

I understand that at last a book about him is in progress. Keep your eye open for that, it should be, with luck, the real deal.

In the meantime, see if you can find online the details of a CD box set called, 'Just Say Sire'. Check out the track listing and you will see why any story of Seymour Stein's unique contribution to the soundtrack of the world is worth learning about.

Printed in Great Britain
by Amazon